BlackBerry for Work

Productivity for Professionals

**Kunal Mittal and
Shikha Gupta**

Apress®

BlackBerry for Work: Productivity for Professionals

ISBN-13 (pbk): 978-1-4302-2626-0

ISBN-13 (electronic): 978-1-4302-2627-7

Distributed to the book trade worldwide by Springer-Verlag New York, Inc., 233 Spring Street, 6th Floor, New York, NY 10013. Phone 1-800-SPRINGER, fax 201-348-4505, e-mail orders-ny@springer-sbm.com, or visit www.springeronline.com.

For information on translations, please e-mail rights@apress.com, or visit www.apress.com.

Apress and friends of ED books may be purchased in bulk for academic, corporate, or promotional use. eBook versions and licenses are also available for most titles. For more information, reference our Special Bulk Sales–eBook Licensing web page at www.apress.com/info/bulksales.

The source code for this book is available to readers at www.apress.com. You will need to answer questions pertaining to this book in order to successfully download the code.

Contents at a Glance

Contents

About the Authors

 **Kunal Mittal** is an entrepreneur who guides startups in defining their business models, technology strategies, product roadmaps, and development plans. Kunal is currently serving on the Board of Advisors for several technology startups.

Kunal's core strengths are in architecting solutions for Web 2.0, SOA, SAAS, and cloud computing using various leading open source technology stacks. He has also done a lot of work on mobile platforms such as iPhones and BlackBerrys.

 With a B.Sc. in Electronic Media, **Shikha Gupta** works with Learnsmart India Private Limited as a content developer for online education. Her background includes script writing for some of the leading channels and production houses in Mumbai, India. A student of the Arts, her other interests are theatre and literature.

About the Technical Reviewer

 **Jeffrey Sambells** is a designer and developer of all things on the Internet. He is currently having fun with mobile and location based technologies as Director of Research and Development for We-Create Inc. The title "Director of R&D" may sound flashy but really that just means he's in charge of learning and cramming as much goodness into the products as possible so they're just awesome. Along the way he's also managed to graduate university, write a few books (www.advanceddomscripting.com), develop some fun iPhone Apps (www.tropicalpixels.com), maintain a blog (www.jeffreysambells.com), and raise a wonderful family.

Acknowledgments

I would like to thank the numerous people at Apress, starting with Clay Andres, Matt Moodie, Mary Tobin, Jeffrey Sambells, and the countless others who have all played an instrumental role in taking this book from concept to publication.

I would also like to thank Shikha, my co-author, who has done all the heavy lifting and sacrificed countless nights and weekends to complete this book. Last and by no means least, I would like to thank my family, wife and pooches for their patience and understanding through this process.

Kunal Mittal

As I set out to write my Thank You note, I realized that the number of people were far too many and space to do so, too small. So keeping it simple, I'd like to thank my family for their undying conviction in me, and Apress, my publishers, and the editorial team, for their continuing patience and support.

But most of all I'd like to thank my co-author, Kunal Mittal…for the encouragement and faith that he displayed in me has made this first-time effort a reality.

Thank you all!

Shikha Gupta

Preface

Tremendous are the pressures of the professional world,
Aggressive are the deadlines.
'Only the fittest shall survive,' has been told,
Within corporate confines…

Setting out to write my first technical book, I was skeptical of my ability to reach out to you in the simplest manner possible. With the backing of experienced editors and a co-author like I have had, I feel I have achieved that and more. We have tackled the subject to give you a basic understanding and clarity, thus reducing the factors that leave a novice lost. In this book, you will find many tips that will help enhance the BlackBerry experience considerably, and that is something which is always welcome now, isn't it?

My approach to the book has been simple. If I enjoy writing it, you will enjoy reading it. The language and style has been kept casual, conversational, and fiercely honest; these are also the factors that set this book apart from other user manuals available. From the contents of the book, you will notice that the matter covered spreads across a wide spectrum. From synchronization and configuration to downloading and usage, this book has a little something to offer to all professionals.

At this point, I would also like to mention a by-product of the book that has now come to mean as much as the book itself. We, Shikha Gupta and Kunal Mittal, the co-authors have decided to direct all proceeds to a charity in India. The Mitr Foundation is a trust founded in the city of Hyderabad, with the objective of contributing its might towards the empowerment of the girl child through education. Thus, we have pledged to undertake the responsibility of educating three children. Somewhere between the elite and the underprivileged lies the core essence of our endeavor…for what is a life that is lived selfishly?

I cannot promise that this book will be your best buy. But I can assure you that it will <u>not</u> disappoint either—neither in its content, nor in its philosophy. With hope that lives and dreams to share…

Chapter 1

BlackBerry Models and Purchasing

A Journal Entry...

I meet someone at the airport—a potential client. With earnest intentions we exchange numbers. A promise to explore is followed by obvious hope. I shoot out an e-mail to my colleagues… Watching one's back is obviously acceptable. I Google the company and what I see pleases me.

My colleagues respond with mutual excitement. Am I at the brink of clinching a fat deal? Hold your horses, I warn myself. Since I'm not one to jump to conclusions, I message my mates to dig a little deeper into the company's background. In a few seconds, I've got the buzz around them. What I hear, I decidedly like.

I calculate a quick ROI and juggle numbers on Excel. By this time, I have received a copy of company policies from my assistant. I review it on my Word doc. Oh, I almost forgot. I check up on their stocks position. In these times of recession, good numbers impress instantly. Relying on memory is too dicey. Voice notes made, memos jotted, I head for my flight.

On my way to the hotel, I check the route for my driver using Google maps. With direction confirmed, I can get back to making my PPT. "Hmm, this opportunity does look lucrative," I realize elatedly. My alarm rings reminding me of my medicines; I am diabetic, you see.

Moving on, I send out the first proposal draft to my boss, PPT and all. Fingers crossed, I settle down to a good game. A pounding heart, an adrenaline rush with optimistic anticipation… Nervous fingers open a just received e-mail. A thumbs-up it is.

I almost forgot I could make calls, too. I dial my husband and scream about an exciting deal; my driver almost dies!

So is a regular day in the life of a BlackBerry user. One handset and you are good to go, and this is just the beginning.

BlackBerry Rocks

If you are still unconvinced about the innumerable advantages of using a BlackBerry, I will illustrate some of them for you (after reading this section, don't forget you can make calls with it, too):

- Calendaring that is synced with your desktop so that you never miss an appointment or a birthday.

- Task management made effortless.

- Address book that syncs with your desktop and corporate data access.

- Instant messaging with colleagues through Google Talk, MSN, and Yahoo! Messenger.

- Free messaging between any two BlackBerrys across the globe.

- Professional aid with Microsoft Word and Excel.

- Advanced multimedia features, which can put any MP3 player to shame.

- Voice and video recorders.

- Simplified navigation with GPS and built-in BlackBerry maps.

- News alerts and web browsing on the run.

- Push technology for your vigorous e-mailing needs.

- Compatibility with social networking sites to keep you in touch with everyone.

- Sophisticated cameras for that perfect picture with geo-tagging ability.

- Reading books using e-book reader, without the hassle of carrying heavy dead trees.

- Discovering new places, activities, and restaurants using the local search.

- Applications for stock alerts and confirmation.

- Great battery life so that your handset doesn't die on you.

- Bluetooth compatible, so forget tangled wires.

- Incredible accessories that are easily available.

The list can truly go on and on. And, you haven't even got to the business applications yet, which I will cover in detail in Chapter 15.

Which BlackBerry Is for You?

Each person has their own unique requirement of a gadget, especially if the gadget is as versatile as the BlackBerry. Some might use the camera and media options to the hilt, while some might abuse messaging using it for informal and formal communication alike, whether or not it is required. For some, the business apps like Word and Excel might be optimum whereas others might prize their e-mail-on-the-go. This brings us to a very important section—choosing your handset wisely.

Contrary to popular belief, BlackBerry models and purchasing isn't as complicated a process as some would like to believe. With basic understanding, you will be able to make a well-informed decision in no time. You need to be sure that your model covers all the features you require while keeping to your budget. This section will help you identify just that.

Picking the Right BlackBerry

BlackBerry has a hoard of permutation combinations for you to choose from. You might want to quickly overview some of the following points which will help you understand your needs better. Ask yourself the following:

- Which feature is most important to me? Do I or will I use the phone option most or will the e-mail and calendaring features play as crucial a role?

- Does the size of the handset matter greatly? If yes, do larger rectangular phones bother me?

- How comfortable am I with the QWERTY keypad? Am I someone already accustomed to the SureType model (more on this in the "SureType" section)? How difficult is it for me to make that switch? (QWERTY keypad is one where each letter is allotted its own key—as in a computer—and the SureType model is one where multiple letters are allotted to the same key.)

- Am I happy with my present service provider? If yes, then which BlackBerry models does my service provider deal in? (All service providers do not offer all of the BlackBerry models. So unless you want to make a switch, I suggest you cross-check with your present provider first.)

- How particular am I about being connected at all times? How significant is internet browsing to me and my professional needs?

I recommend that you borrow different BlackBerry models from your friends and associates in order to get a feel of the phone. It is very important that you are comfortable using the phone, so as to ensure maximum satisfaction from your handset. Let's now look at some common BlackBerry terms as well as the features available on BlackBerry so you can draw up a wish list.

Some Important BlackBerry Features

Constantly looking up the meaning of terms while reading about BlackBerry models can get annoying, but some terminology cannot be avoided. A smart thing to do is to familiarize yourself with some of the most commonly used terms in the world of BlackBerry, such as those that follow.

PIN

PIN is essentially a Personal Identification Number. Each BlackBerry phone has its own unique number called the PIN. This serves as an identity of the handset and can be used for instant messaging between BlackBerry users across the globe, free of cost. For more details on PIN, refer to Chapter 5.

SMS

SMS is Short Message Service, which makes it possible for two mobile users to exchange information through text messages. This is a paid-for service and rates depend on the service plans opted for by the user.

MMS

MMS is short for Multimedia Messaging Service, which like SMS, is used as a means of communication between two mobile phone users. However, the difference here is that an MMS can include multimedia files as well. Through MMS, one can send and receive audio, video, and image files comfortably.

USB Cable

USB is short for Universal Serial Bus, which helps connect your computer to other peripheral devices such as the keypad, mouse, flash drives, mobile phones, printers, hard drives, and digital cameras aiding in data transfer. Thus, a USB cable is a wire that is used to make this connection between the USB port of the computer with the other devices.

MicroSD Card

MicroSD card is the smallest flash memory card available today. It is used extensively in mobile phones due to its small size (about the size of a fingernail) as well as digital cameras and audio players. Different microSD cards have varied memory capacities ranging from 128 MB (megabytes) to 2 GB (gigabyte).

Trackball

Think of a general trackball as an upside-down computer mouse, with the underbelly—the ball—exposed. Therefore, it allows users to navigate the pointer without moving their hands too much. In the BlackBerry, too, the trackball is a means for the user to move the cursor on the screen in any desired direction, with the use of thumb or finger.

Trackpad

A trackpad, like the trackball, is a means to navigate and control the position of the cursor on the screen. The most common use of a trackpad is in laptops. Here, it translates movement and pressure of the finger to the pointer on the screen. Similarly, the BlackBerry Curve 8520 also uses this technology to control the cursor.

SurePress

SurePress is RIM's version of touch screen technology. The BlackBerry Storm uses this, where the screen itself is pressable. This means that this model does not require a trackball or a trackpad to navigate the cursor on the screen. To select something, one merely has to press down on the button (which is on the screen) and the application opens.

SureType

SureType overlays a traditional phone keypad with a QWERTY keypad, which saves space on the phone without losing the convenience of QWERTY input. The SureType software identifies your typing and word patterns, and remembers your style and commonly used words.

QWERTY

QWERTY, pronounced as "kwer-tee," is the order in which the first six letter-keys appear on the keyboard of the computer. It was coined when it first became popular with the typewriter in the 1870s. Most smartphones today use this keypad layout instead of the traditional arrangement used by previous phones, where multiple characters shared keys.

Bluetooth

Bluetooth is a technology that eliminates the use of wires to connect devices that are placed at short distances from each other. As it uses radio technology to communicate between devices, it does not require the gadgets to be in line-of-sight from each other in order to be able to transfer data. It creates Personal Area Networks (PANs) so that this data transfer can be carried out.

Wi-Fi

Wi-Fi is a wireless networking technology that allows the user to access the internet without being physically connected though a cable. Gadgets with a Wi-Fi network card connect wirelessly to a router which is connected to a modem. Typically, gadgets that are enabled and within the range of 200 meters can access the internet. Wi-Fi networks can be open or closed. If open, anyone within the range can use it, but if closed then a password is required to do so.

Geo-tagging

Geo-tagging is the ability to add GPS information to any media. Smartphones with internet connections, such as the BlackBerry, have incorporated this feature, which tags the media (videos or pictures) based on its geographical location.

GPS

Global Positioning System (GPS) uses satellites and computers to provide positioning and navigational services. It determines the latitude and longitude of the receiver on the Earth, thus pinpointing their exact location. Apart from smartphones like the BlackBerry, many cars also use this technology to aid in navigation.

Megapixel

A pixel is a picture element, which is the smallest part of an image. Pixels are tile-shaped particles that come together to make up a picture and define the resolution of the image. The resolution can be measured based on the clarity of an image when viewed at 100% on the computer monitor. The more the number of pixels, the clearer the image is. Megapixel is one million such pixels. The picture quality in digital cameras is measured in megapixels. Therefore, a three megapixel camera takes images that are made up of three million such pixels, providing good image clarity.

Video Conferencing

Video conferencing is an integration of video and audio technologies so that people sitting in different geographical locations can communicate in real time, allowing for natural conversations as though present in the same room. It uses microphones and webcams along with the Internet to make this possible.

Corporate Data Access

Corporate Data Access is a system which allows employees to access the company data when out of the office using their BlackBerry. Checking on customer updates, rescheduling and organizing information, and receiving important business information becomes possible through this solution.

Choose Your Series

Most BlackBerry handsets come with enhanced features such as wireless e-mails, cameras, video recording, corporate data access, browsers, and organizers. Though the basic functioning and usage of all BlackBerry phones remains quite similar, there are distinct features that are offered in particular models setting them apart. I'll give a general flavor of each phone and then present a table of features, so you can compare each one.

There are basically nine series you can choose from. They are the following:

- BlackBerry Tour
- BlackBerry Storm
- BlackBerry Bold
- BlackBerry Curve 8900
- BlackBerry Curve 8520
- BlackBerry Curve 8300
- BlackBerry Pearl
- BlackBerry Pearl Flip
- BlackBerry 8800 Series

BlackBerry Tour

This smartphone has a 3.2 megapixel camera and enhanced multimedia features.

- You can stay in touch through video conferencing, voice dialing, and speaker phone features, no matter which 3G network you are in.
- Location-based-software works closely with your built-in GPS system so that you get accurate details on maps and routes.
- Built-in media player and 256 MB of on board memory.
- Wireless e-mail and advanced calendaring.
- A 35-key backlit QWERTY keyboard.
- Geo-tagging functionality and password protection.

BlackBerry Storm

With equally strong credentials to the Tour, the BlackBerry Storm is the only BlackBerry model that comes in a touch screen format which aids in quick navigation and accurate typing.

- Its SurePress touch screen allows for both SureType and multistep in portrait view and QWERTY in landscape view.

- It has a 3.2 megapixel camera with auto focus and auto flash, a media player, and video recorder.

- It has commendable battery life (approximately five and a half hours of talk time) along with expandable memory support and 1 GB onboard memory.

- GPS technology and preloaded BlackBerry maps.

This phone has so much to offer that even a listing of all these features cannot do it justice.

BlackBerry Bold

A premium smartphone and the finest aid to the business-minded, the Bold balances great looks and functionality:

- With applications like Word To Go, Sheet To Go, and Slideshow To Go, you can not only view but also edit Microsoft Excel sheets, Microsoft Word documents, and Microsoft PowerPoint presentations all on your handset.

- You can sync it to your desktop iTunes and Windows Media Player so that your playlist and videos always stay with you.

- In-built mobile streaming allows you to access information from the web without using up your memory space.

- It uses a QWERTY keypad and is Wi-Fi enabled.

- Built-in GPS with BlackBerry Maps and password protection.

BlackBerry Curve 8900

The BlackBerry Curve 8900 is an elegant phone and is the slimmest and lightest of all the BlackBerry smartphones, in the QWERTY category.

- Wi-Fi support allows you to check e-mails, stream music, and watch videos.

- GPS and BlackBerry maps guarantee that you will never find yourself lost, no matter which part of the world you might be in.

- A 3.2 megapixel camera takes crisp pictures.

- Video recording captures video and audio.

- Includes organizer and corporate data access.

- High resolution 480x360 pixel color display.

BlackBerry Curve 8520

Dedicated media keys simplify controlling music and multimedia along with an easy access mute call button.

- This model offers track pad navigation which can be mastered by gliding ones finger on it, similar to that of a laptop.

- Its compatibility with your Mac, using the BlackBerry Desktop Software, will definitely make syncing calendars and notes a breeze.

- It is Wi-Fi enabled and has strong support for the BlackBerry App World (more on App World in Chapter 15).

- Clear, high-resolution display and media manager.

BlackBerry Curve 8300

This series gives you an option between five different handsets, namely: BlackBerry Curve 8300, BlackBerry Curve 8310, BlackBerry Curve 8320, BlackBerry Curve 8330, and BlackBerry Curve 8350i.

- These are the smallest QWERTY keyboard model of all the BlackBerry handsets.

- Its media player supports the playback of most widely used file formats.

- Though all models come with wireless e-mail, organizer, browser, and camera features, the BlackBerry Curve 8300, BlackBerry Curve 8310, and BlackBerry Curve 8320 do not have video recording facilities.

The BlackBerry Curve 8300 and BlackBerry Curve 8320 also lack GPS technology.

BlackBerry Pearl

The BlackBerry Pearl 8100 series comes in the most vivacious and versatile colors of all BlackBerry models. This series includes four models: BlackBerry Pearl 8100, BlackBerry Pearl 8110, BlackBerry Pearl 8120, and BlackBerry Pearl 8130.

- These models follow the SureType format, making the handset compact and comparatively lighter than the others.

- Syncing your Windows Media Player and desktop iTunes is a simple process so that you derive the most out of your multimedia experience.

- Wi-Fi Support and mobile streaming add to the pleasures this series has to offer.

However, the BlackBerry Pearl 8100 does not support video recording or GPS.

BlackBerry Pearl Flip

This series is decidedly the most compact of all BlackBerry models because of its flip design. It comes in two model types: BlackBerry Pearl Flip 8220 and BlackBerry Pearl Flip 8230.

- The external display screen helps for quick view of the clock as well as call screening and message viewing without flipping at all.

- The BlackBerry Pearl Flip 8220 comes with attractive features like Wi-Fi support, video recording, and mobile streaming but does not include GPS technology.

- The BlackBerry Pearl Flip 8230 incorporates mobile streaming and video recording features.

- Both come with wireless e-mail compatibility.

BlackBerry 8800 Series

The BlackBerry 8800, BlackBerry 8820, and BlackBerry 8830 are part of this series.

▨ All come packed with wireless e-mail, media players, and GPS capabilities.

▨ The GPS and BlackBerry maps can prove to be lifesavers.

This is a series that has been around, and I can assure you will stay around for a long time.

Grids and More

Now that you might have a general idea of the functioning of each phone, it is time for some specifics. Check out Table 1-1 for general features and Table 1-2 for e-mail features. BES will be described in Chapter 4.

> **NOTE:** For detailed comparative charts on features offered by the various BlackBerry models, such as weight and battery life, please log onto the BlackBerry official site.

Table 1-1. *General Features: All Phones Come with Organizer, Browser, Camera, BlackBerry Maps, a Media Player and Corporate Data Access*

Model	GPS	Trackball	Keyboard	Trackpad	SurePress Touch screen	Color Display	Wi-Fi: 802. 11b/g	Wi-Fi: 802. 11a	EDGE
Tour	Yes	Yes	QWERTY-style keyboard			Yes			Yes
Storm	Yes		On screen keyboard: portrait SureType® and Multi-tap, QWERTY landscape		Yes				Yes
Bold	Yes	Yes	QWERTY-style keyboard			Yes	Yes	Yes	Yes
Curve 8900	Yes	Yes	QWERTY-style keyboard			Yes	Yes		Yes
Curve 8520			QWERTY-style keyboard	Yes			Yes		Yes
Curve 8300		Yes	QWERTY-style keyboard			Yes			Yes
Pearl 8100		Yes	SureType QWERTY-style keyboard						Yes
Pearl Flip 8220		Yes	SureType QWERTY-style keyboard				Yes		Yes
Pearl Flip 8230	Yes	Yes	SureType QWERTY-style keyboard			Yes			
8800 Series	Yes	Yes	QWERTY-style keyboard			Yes			Yes

Table 1-2. *E-mail Features*

Model	BES for Microsoft Exchange	BES for IBM, Lotus, and Domino	BES for Novell and GroupWise	Integration with Setup Enterprise E-mail Account	Integration with Personal E-mail Account	Integration with a New Device Account
Tour	Yes	Yes	Yes	Yes	Yes	Yes
Storm	Yes	Yes	Yes	Yes	Yes	Yes
Bold	Yes	Yes	Yes	Yes	Yes	Yes
Curve 8900	Yes	Yes	Yes	Yes	Yes	Yes
Curve 8520	Yes	Yes	Yes	Yes	Yes	Yes
Curve 8300	Yes	Yes	Yes	Yes	Yes	Yes
Pearl 8100	Yes	Yes	Yes	Yes	Yes	Yes
Pearl Flip 8220	Yes	Yes	Yes	Yes		
Pearl Flip 8230	Yes	Yes	Yes	Yes	Yes	Yes
8800 Series	Yes	Yes	Yes	Yes		

BlackBerry for Business

Whether you are associated with an enterprise, public sector, large or small business; whether you belong to the financial services, government, healthcare, education, or the pharmaceutical industry, BlackBerry has an exclusive business solution for you. It takes care of your business intelligence, field service, and sales force automation needs with as much ease as giving you access to critical information instantly and providing at-a-glance performance monitoring.

This is the reason BlackBerry indomitably remains the most preferred handset of the professional world. Therefore, it is a common practice for companies to favor a particular service provider dealing in certain handsets. Corporate plans and subsidized rates that the wireless providers offer only make the proposal more attractive. Hence, if you are going to get an official BlackBerry, then your choice of handset is narrowed down considerably. But let's not discredit your company. The fact that they have these arrangements also goes to prove that your handset will come with all the applications essential for your business needs.

Who is Your Service Provider?

A company that provides constant and stable mobile connectivity, using its own infrastructure is a service provider. Selecting a service provider with a plan that is most suited to your needs is primary. You could either already hold an account with a service provider such as AT&T, Verizon, or Sprint if you are in the United States of America or might need to create a new account based on your requirement.

What You Need to Know About Plans

As illustrated earlier in this chapter, not all service providers deal in all BlackBerry models. Therefore, if you have already identified the BlackBerry model you would like to buy, then you need to find the wireless carrier who deals in that model. Buying the gadget from a retail store is also an option, but in order to activate your data (which is nothing but getting your number and services activated according to the plan you have opted for) you would need a wireless carrier. As most of these providers have predecided purchasing plans and offers that are lighter on the pocket, getting your handset from them does seem to be a feasible option.

Typically, the service provider and the customer enter into a two-year contract, during the course of which the cost of the handset and services is paid out in installments. This setup proves beneficial for both parties involved, as the customer gets to pay the amount comfortably at regular intervals with a greatly subsidized initial pay-up, and the service provider has his confirmation of the person remaining a customer for that period. This arrangement can be terminated prematurely; however, the customer would be expected to pay a certain fee as per the norms. If the person is already a customer with the service provider, then specifications are worked out between the two, based on usage of the account and past history.

Mail-in rebate is also another way for you to save some of that money. It is a process in which, on filling out a coupon or form (which is provided at the time of your purchase) and mailing it to the preprinted address, a considerable amount of money is refunded to the customer. Essentially, this is a process that communicates your data to the manufacturer, for their records or database. In return, an attractive sum of money is refunded to the customer further reducing the price of the handset.

> **NOTE:** Most service providers have special plans for families, business, and individual customers. Make sure you get the right plan so as to make use of the best offers.

Some of the Service Providers who Carry BlackBerry

AT&T

www.wireless.att.com

Sprint

www.sprint.com

T-Mobile

www.t-mobile.com
www.t-mobile.co.uk

Verizon Wireless

www.verizonwireless.com

What's Next?

The BlackBerry is such a powerful tool that failing to optimize its usage seems sinful. If you agree with this school of thought, then for you the next chapter will be one of the most essential of this book. Setting up your BlackBerry correctly is half the work. Beyond that, is what you make of it, be it downloading applications or surfing the net. Don't reduce this marvelous gadget to a mere calling device...

Chapter 2

Setting Up Your BlackBerry

On Your Marks… Get Set… Blah… Blah…

What is an investment? It's the act of providing or putting in something, in anticipation of gaining. If you agree with this, then treat this chapter as a jolly good investment. Taking out a little time to set up your BlackBerry properly can save you a lot of energy in the future. Make that little effort today and reap its benefits tomorrow. (I've started sounding like a self-help preacher. Think I'll stop here.)

What's amazing about the BlackBerry is that it is very intuitive. It's this technology that has given it the reputation of being extremely user friendly and easy to operate. It goes without saying that the setup process also should be a piece of cake… or in this case, a slice of the berry.

You could get a BlackBerry handset either from your company or buy it for yourself. The installation process differs in each case. I will be covering both, so that no matter how or why you get it, getting started will be a simple task.

Getting Started

Assuming you have been convinced and are a new BlackBerry user, you need to get your hands on that device you've been waiting to use. This is one of my favorite parts— opening the box and peeking in at all the exciting components. You should make sure you get the following:

- The Starter Guide
- The BlackBerry handset
- The battery
- The BlackBerry Desktop Manager installation CD
- The charger

- The hands-free/stereo set
- A USB cable (for data transfer)
- A pouch or holster for your device

Once you are done admiring, you can get on with the setup process.

Inserting the SIM Card and Battery

In Chapter 1, you saw how important it was to choose your handset and service provider wisely. For both our sakes, I'm going to assume you have done so, and have your activated your SIM card (if you are using the GSM network) in your hand. A SIM card is an acronym for Subscriber Identity Module. This is a miniature smart card that is used to associate a mobile subscriber with a network. The user's numbers along with their specific encryption details are stored in this. It also stores data such as contact lists and messages sent and received among others. It is in fact the SIM card that gives the user a specific identity and not the handset in itself.

Insert the SIM card in the SIM card holder in the device which is usually below the battery holder. Different models will have specific insertion processes, but it is basically very simple. All you need to do is line up the shape of the SIM along with the outline provided in the holder (in the device). In some devices, you might have a trapdoor that slides to unlock after which the SIM card is fitted in, while in some you might need to slide the SIM card in directly.

Once the SIM card is inserted, place the battery and secure it. Make sure you align the pins or connectors of the battery and the device. Once that is done, close the lid and switch on the device. The battery always comes slightly charged so that you can complete the installation process. However, to continue charge it for a couple of hours for it to reach complete charge status, the level of optimal utilization. BlackBerry batteries are very effective and quick on the recharge. Some commonly believe that overcharging the battery causes it damage in the long run. Though there might not be suitable proof of the same, make sure you don't overcharge it, though you'll never really need to.

Charging Status

Want to know how much battery life you have left? You could check your charge status in one quick glance. The following helpful indicators are at the top left-hand corner of your screen.

This status indicates that you are out of charge.

This status indicates a full battery.

This status means that thebattery is charging at the moment.

Is Your BlackBerry an Official Phone?

If you have received a BlackBerry for official use by your company, then the setup process will vary considerably. This is because, in that case, the probability of you using BlackBerry Enterprise Server (BES) is far greater than your use of BlackBerry Internet Service (BIS). For those who have received the device from their company, the installation—in most cases—will be taken care of by your employers. To check on whether you will use the BlackBerry Enterprise Server or not, contact your employer for details.

The difference between BIS and BES is that BIS uses the Internet to deliver data, like e-mail and webpage access to your device, while BES uses the corporate Intranet to do the same.

The essential difference between the two is the location of the server which is used by the BlackBerry user. In BES, the server typically is in control of your organization or company, while most often the BIS server is the responsibility of your service provider. If you are an individual user and own your device, you would be using BIS.

BES is used by large corporate companies that have a server installed within their organization. This not only gives them much higher levels of security, but also allows them to publish applications at a mass level without having to individually alter specifications on each device. Though it uses the Intranet, the user's access to the Internet is possible, but with layers of security features made mandatory.

Initial Startup

After switching on your BlackBerry, it will start its boot up process. On launching the Setup Wizard, you will need to specify details such as setting the time and choosing your language options. If the Setup Wizard does not launch automatically, press the Menu button on your home screen. In Setup, choose Setup Wizard and proceed.

If the time that is set is wrong, you can change it by clicking on Edit. Confirm your time zone field which is in Date/Time in the Options. Set the date and time in the Date/Time Source field and Update. Click on Save. Follow the rest of the setup process. Taking the few minutes to do this will simplify your use of the device tremendously.

> **NOTE:** BIS users have two options. They can either set up their e-mail account from here or they can set up their online account at the service provider's web site. You could choose either, depending on your convenience. I will go through both processes.

To synchronize your e-mail account from the Setup Wizard, you will need to specify which of the following options are applicable:

- BlackBerry Internet Service
- BlackBerry Enterprise Server
- BlackBerry Desktop Redirector

BlackBerry Desktop Redirector is software that works with Microsoft Outlook. It gathers messages from the Outlook mailbox and forwards them to the handheld device. To work with this, the BlackBerry Desktop Manager and your handheld need to be synced. However, for it to function properly, the main computer and Outlook must be on at all times. Therefore, this option is not the most recommended.

After this, select the "I want to create or add an e-mail account" option and click on Next.

If you are creating a new account with BlackBerry, click on Create New Account and if you are updating an existing account, choose the Update Account option accordingly. If you choose to create a new account, then be informed that this will be a BlackBerry account, so your address would be yourusername@blackberry.com.

When you update an already existing account, the e-mails that you receive will get forwarded to your handset. For this, you will need to type in the e-mail address along with your password. You can add up to ten e-mail accounts which you will be able to access from your handheld individually.

If you agree to the terms and conditions, check the box next to it and click on Next. Complete the steps.

> **NOTE:** If you would like to set up your e-mail account through the service provider's BIS web site, then select the Skip option when the e-mail setup comes on.

Online Account and E-mail Setup

The sections that follow are for BIS users who in all probability would be setting up their account on their own. If you are a BES user, your company will handle this setup process for you. For BIS users on the GSM network, your wireless supplier will provide you with an activated number (SIM card). Contact your service provider for further details on this process.

Once your number is activated, you can proceed towards creating your online account and setting up your e-mail. You can configure up to ten e-mail accounts with your BlackBerry handheld device. The account setup is necessary for your service provider to connect you and your handheld to the Internet and related data, as per the plan you have selected.

To get an online account, follow these steps:

1. Log onto your service provider's BIS web site.

2. Click on New User / Create New Account to register.

3. If you agree with the terms and conditions, select the check box next to I Agree.

4. Now you will be asked for your PIN and IMEI codes. Check on the box in which you received the gadget for these details. If you do not have access to it, don't worry. You can also get the required information from the sticker on your BlackBerry device under the battery.

Complete the process as per the instructions to create your account. You will need to confirm fields such as E-mail Accounts, Send From address, Auto BCC, and Signature. This is where you could also switch the BlackBerry device which is currently associated with your e-mail service.

Once you have specified all these particulars, click on Save. Congratulations, you have successfully set up your BlackBerry device with your e-mail account and server.

A confirmation mail from the activation server will soon follow on your handheld device, confirming this for you.

NOTE: If you are using Edge, look for it to be written in capitals on the top right-hand corner of your BlackBerry screen. This indicates that you are logged onto the net.

Installing Desktop Manager

The Desktop Manager CD comes with your BlackBerry device and is required to be set up so that it can synchronize your information and data between your laptop and desktop and your handheld device. If you do not have the CD, it can also be downloaded from the BlackBerry web site at www.blackberry.com. Once the page has opened, go to Software. Here, select BlackBerry Desktop Software (which is in the left list options). From here, you can download the software required for PC as well as Mac users.

The following steps will guide you through this process:

1. Insert the CD in your CD-ROM drive. The application should launch automatically. If this does not happen, you can select the CD from your CD-ROM drive.

2. Choose your desired language and click on OK.

3. Select Next to proceed.

4. Accept the license agreement.

5. Fill in your details such as your name and the company's for which you work and click on Next.

6. Since you are a BIS user, select the BlackBerry Web Client option and click on Next.

7. Identify the default location to be in your Program Files. Here the usual path should be C:\Program Files\Research In Motion\BlackBerry on a PC. This location can be changed according to your convenience. Once you note this location, choose Next.

8. According to your need, either select the "Anyone who uses this computer" or "Only for me" option. If you want a shortcut to your Desktop Manager to appear on your desktop, select that field and click on Next.

9. Click on Finish after selecting the "Yes I want to start the Desktop Manager Software."

Now to start synchronizing the data between your handheld and the Desktop Manager, you need to follow this procedure:

1. Connect your handheld device and your computer with the help of the USB cable.

2. Click on OK to use your connection settings dialog under the options menu.

3. With Application Loader selected, go to Connection Settings in Options.

4. Select USB-PIN in Connection's drop down and select OK.

5. Select Intellisync by double-clicking on it.

6. Select Synchronize PIM and then click on Configure PIM.

7. You will get options of the handheld applications you would want to sync. Select them individually to sync. Make sure you choose your Available Translator (GroupWise or MS Outlook) appropriately with the Synchronize field selected.

8. Once you have done that, click on OK.

9. Now select Auto Start.

10. Choose Synchronize PIM and Synchronize Now.

11. Confirm the edits of your handheld applications and click on Accept.

12. Close the box, go to file, and select Exit.

13. Restart the computer to find Desktop Manager on your desktop.

You have successfully completed setting up the Desktop Manager. With the help of this, you can transfer data from your handheld to your computer at any given time. Also, because you selected the sync options, all your contacts, calendar entries, tasks, and memos have been transferred to your BlackBerry from your MS Outlook, GroupWise, Lotus or any other translator or platform of your choice.

Let's Explore

From The Famous Five to X-Box, the excitement of new has always lured. When it comes to mystery stories or detective video games, there is little difference between children and adults. The satisfaction one gets from figuring it out is unparalleled. That's why I believe that guiding you through this process is going to take all the fun out of discovering. Select the different icons and see what they've got.

To get options of a particular application, click on the Menu button while the icon is selected. I'll give you one tip here, if you want the full menu (the Application List) on your screen, click on the Menu button when at your home page (see Figure 2–1). It will give you all the applications you could need.

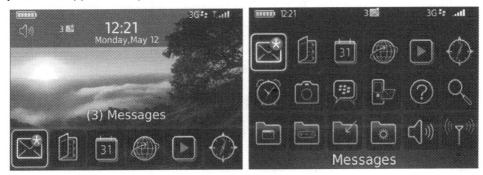

Figure 2–1. *Images showing the home screen and the applications screen*

Identifying the Keys and Buttons

What is the trackball? What is the Menu button? Where do I mute the call from? How do I increase the speaker volume? How do I go back to the previous menu?

If questions like this bother you, stress no more. I'll give you a list of buttons, their functions and most typical location (see Figures 2–2 and 2–3) so that when you do not want to take a call, you will not accept it by mistake.

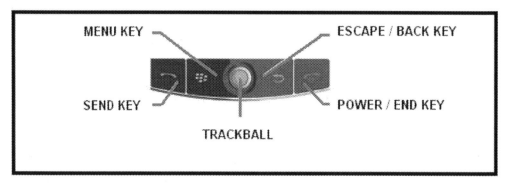

Figure 2–2. *Demonstration of the main keys of most BlackBerry devices*

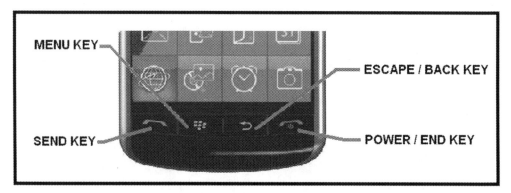

Figure 2–3. *Demonstration of the main keys of the BlackBerry Storm*

Some of the keys you should be acquainted with are the following:

- *Menu key*: Use this key to open the menu in any application.

- *Send key*: Use this key to call the highlighted contact number.

- *Power/End key*: Use this key to end a call. You can also use this key to turn off the device (by keeping it pressed for a while) and to return to the Home screen.

- *Escape/Back key*: Use this key to close a menu as well as return to the previous screen.

This key is Shift. It also is the key that capitalizes a letter.

This is the Number Lock mode.

This is the Alt key. When pressed with another key, it activates the alternate character of that key.

It's Personal

Not liking the order of the icons? Do you want your SMS first and contacts application to follow? You can easily change the order to suit your requirements, so that you do not have to unnecessarily scroll over lesser used ones. The process is extremely simple. While in the applications page (see Figure 2–1) select the icon you want to move. While the icon is selected, press the Menu button. You will get a list of options including Move, Hide, and Move To Folder. Choose the Move option. This will make the icon moveable. You can also identify it by the arrow marks that appear around the icon (see Figure 2–4). Use the trackball to shift it wherever you want. Once you have established the desired spot, press the trackball again. That's it. Your icon has been moved effectively.

> **NOTE:** The first six icons on your applications page are the six that appear on your home screen as well.

Figure 2–4. *Example of moving Calendar icon. Notice the arrows.*

You Got it? Flaunt it

You will likely want your details on your screen—something that reflects your personality—which is displayed in the middle of the home screen. Now some might want important information like emergency numbers displayed while some might just want something fun. You can display your thoughts easily by feeding it in the

Owner section that is part of your Options menu (see Figure 2–5). Do Save once you finish typing.

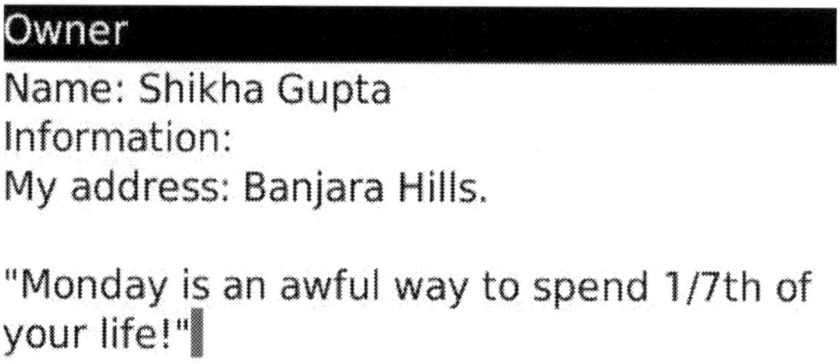

Owner

Name: Shikha Gupta
Information:
My address: Banjara Hills.

"Monday is an awful way to spend 1/7th of your life!"

Figure 2–5. *Example of a screen where the owner's information can be typed and saved*

Themes and More

Your BlackBerry comes with some very interesting themes as presets. A theme is what defines the look and feel of your phone. The background color and design along with fonts and structure all come under a common theme. The appearance of the application list as well as banners and dialogue boxes follow the same theme. You could download some amazing ones which are easily available over the Internet. To use one that comes with your phone (depending on your service provider), go to Theme, which is part of your Options menu. Here select the one you desire and it will appear on your home screen. Another great option is to build your own theme. That's right, using Plazmic Theme Builder, you can actually flaunt your own custom-made theme with stylized indicators and banners included. For more details on that, please go through Plazmic Theme Builder for BlackBerry Smartphones User Guide.

To set an image or picture as your home page background, just go to your picture gallery which is in your Media options and highlight the image. Click on the Menu button and select Set As Home Screen Image.

THEME COMPATIBILITY

Before you go downloading images and themes from the Internet, remember to check whether the theme you are selecting is compatible with the version of the operating system on your BlackBerry.

To check the version of the operating system (OS), go to the Options application from the Application List. Here, select About. After doing this, you will get a list of details about your BlackBerry device, along with model name and wireless connections. In this list, you will find the OS version (see Figure 2–6). For instance, in the mentioned image, the OS is v4.5. You can also upgrade your present operating system. However, the availability depends on your service provider. Please contact them for further details on the process.

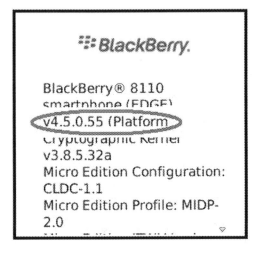

Figure 2–6. *Locating the current operating system version*

Who Called?

Nothing is more annoying than receiving or making an unintentional call because some keys have gotten pressed on the phone. You can easily avoid such embarrassing situations by using the auto lock feature on your phone. To do this, go to Options and select Security. Choose General Options from the menu and further narrow it out to Security Timeout. Here you can set the time after which the keypad will lock itself automatically. Some handsets also have this feature listed under Password in the Options menu.

If you use the BlackBerry Bold, you can do this by keeping the A / * key on your keypad pressed for a little while. To unlock, press the A / * key and then the call button.

Is Your Wi-Fi On?

Checking this is child's play. Just select Manage Connections (see Figure 2–7), which is in your Applications list. Here you will see a list confirming your status on mobile network in use, Wi-Fi and Bluetooth. Select the applicable fields.

You could also set up your Wi-Fi and Bluetooth connections from here.

NOTE: To utilize this feature, you need to make sure you are in a Wi-Fi coverage area and that your plan with the service provider includes use of this feature. Also, if your device is associated with the BlackBerry Enterprise Server, your company or organization might prevent you from using this feature for security purposes.

Figure 2–7. *Manage Connections Icon in the applications page*

Options for All

Part of your application list is a feature called Options. This is by far the most important application on your handset. It is nothing but your settings. To check or edit any preset, this app is your best option. Settings ranging from Bluetooth and Wi-Fi to Date, Time, and Language, from Memory status to Profiles and ringtones, and Owner details to Password setups. Voice Dialing, Spell Check, SMS and MMS details can be edited here as well. For everything you want, anything you might want, and that something that you do not want in your handset—Options is your answer. In fact, you will notice that Options is one of the handiest tools, which will be touched on through the course of the book.

Status Indicators You Will Need to Recognize

Status indicators, well, indicate your status. These will give you vital information based on how many messages you have in your inbox; whether a particular call is one that was received, dialed, or perhaps missed; if you have an alarm set or if a particular e-mail message was sent, received, or just a draft. Get the drift?

Home Screen Status Indicators

If you have the following on your home screen, it indicates:

That you have an alarm set.

That you have missed calls along with the number.

That you have unopened messages along with the number.

That you are in the middle of sending some data.

The number of missed calendar reminders. (Ouch, you don't want too many of that indicator.)

That you are receiving data.

That you have voice mail messages.

Whether you are on roaming or not.

That your Bluetooth is turned on.

That your device has been paired with a Blutooth enabled one.

Message Status Indicators

These symbols in your inbox represent the following:

E-mail—an unopened message

E-mail—an opened message

E-mail—a message with an attachment

E-mail—a message of high importance / priority

SMS—new message

MMS—new message

A sent message

Sending message in progress

Message is not sent

A draft in your inbox

Phone Status Indicators

These are the indicators you will encounter in your call log.

Incoming call—the call was received

Outgoing call—the call was made

Missed call—the call was missed

What's Next?

What does one call a device which e-mails, surfs the web, doubles as an MP3 player, is an alarm clock, is your personal assistant reminding you of your appointments and almost as good as a pocket pc? Is it still just a phone? The dictionary defines a phone as a process of transmitting sound or speech to a distant point using an electronic device. Very well then, let's remind ourselves that the BlackBerry can also make and receive calls. After all, it *is* a smartphone...

Chapter 3

BlackBerry as a Phone

A Phone's Gotta Do What a Phone's Gotta Do…

From the Princess phone to smartphones, telecommunication has certainly come a long way! The past century has witnessed growth at a laudable rate, and why shouldn't that be the case? Communication has and will remain one of the most important aspects of human and social existence. And what can be a better medium than a compact, mobile, and flexible gadget—the smartphone! In addition, the multitude of bells and whistles only contributes to its appeal, making it a winner all around. As means of communication take on newer avatars, you can be assured that the smartphone promises to keep up.

Verbal communication is not only direct in nature, but is also one of the fastest mediums of communication. Barring the advantage of visuals and nonverbal communication offered by video conferencing, telephone delivered messages do prove to be one of the most effective means of sending and receiving instant responses without the requirement of close proximity while adding personalization. Let's delve into the wide spectrum of options that the BlackBerry's Phone application offers.

It's a Phone Alright

Who said the job of a phone is only to make and receive calls? What if I told you that the BlackBerry's conference calling facilities; voice attachment playback in MP3 format; Bluetooth enabled technology that allows hands-free usage built-in speaker phones; and voice activated dialing is only the tip of the iceberg? Without further adieu, let's get cracking and have a look at some of the basic functions of the Phone application along with guidelines to using them.

Receiving a Call

When you get a call, if you want to answer it, just press the green button or Answer key to activate the call. There are other options that are made available to you as well. Depending on convenience, you can set your BlackBerry device to automatically answer the call on removal from the holster. To do this, set the Auto Answer Calls to Out of Holster, which is part of your General Options in the Phone application. There is another feature that is offered to the flip-phone users (BlackBerry Pearl) which allows for answering calls upon flipping open the phone.

To end a call, just press thered key or Power button. If you have assigned a picture to a contact, then the picture along with the name and number of the person flashes on your screen. For details on how to assign pictures to contacts, check out Chapter 7.

Muting an Incoming Call

If you want to switch the ringer off without disconnecting the call, press the mute button, which for most BlackBerrys is at the top of the screen. However, in the BlackBerry Pearl 8230, this button is situated on the upper-left side of the device. The symbol for the mute button is a speaker with a strike across it.

Rejecting a Call

Many times, one does not or cannot answer an incoming call. If you do not wish to do so, just press the Ignore button on your screen. This is usually the red or end call button on your BlackBerry screen.

Making a Call

Similar to receiving a call, if you are calling someone from your contacts list with a picture attached to it, their name, number, and picture will flash on the screen (as shown in Figure 3–1).

To make an outgoing call, you can do one of the following:

- Activate it from the Call Log application.
- Activate it from the Contacts application.
- Activate it directly.

Figure 3–1. *An example of an outgoing call from Shikha*

Activate Calls from the Call Log Application

This is a feature usually used when one has recently received, made, or missed a call and knows of its presence in the call log. If this is the case, then calling the person can be carried out by pressing the Answer key (green button). On doing so, a list of all the calls (up to a maximum storage time of 30 days) appear on the screen. You can select the desired number from here with the help of your trackball. Once this is done, press the Answer key again to call. You can also add the person to your list of contacts from here. For further details on this process, please refer to Chapter 7.

Activate Calls from the Contacts Application

You can also choose whom you would like to call from your Contacts application. If this icon is not on your Home screen (which happens if it isn't one of your first six icons on your application page), then go to the application page and select Contacts. Here you will get a list of your contacts in alphabetical order, along with specific details such as company name, if you entered this at the time of saving the contact's details. Select the desired person using the trackball and press the Answer key.

Activate Calls Directly

This actually is an extension of your Contacts application, and allows you to make calls using your keypad directly. Once you start typing the contact's name, you will get a list of names that are applicable to the keys you have typed on the screen. Select one using your trackball or track pad and press the Answer key. Your call will be activated. You can also simply dial a number from the keypad. How easy it is to forget the simplest processes!

Call in Progress

With phones as advanced as they are today, you can have multiple calls activated at the same time. No more do you hear the engaged tone when the person being called is busy. Instead, you are greeted with a computerized voice asking you to hold and your call will be answered shortly. Thus, while you are in the middle of a conversation on your BlackBerry, there are various features available to you. To access these features, during the course of the call press the Menu button. Let's have a look at some of them now.

Notes

That's right, no more scrambling for paper or pencil to take down notes. You can take notes while you are in the middle of a call. Just select this feature from your menu list. Type out your note and end the call normally. You do not need to save it either. It's been saved already in your call history. To view the note(s), go to your call log and highlight the person with whom you had the conversation and press on the Menu key. One of your options here is View History. Upon selecting that, you will get a list of calls made to and received from that person. If there is a note attached with a particular call's log entry, you will see a draft icon next to it (see Figure 3–2). After clicking on the call entry, select Edit Notes to get all the notes you made during that particular call. Here, not only can you view the note, but can edit it also. To delete the note, press the Menu key again and select Clear Field. The note will be removed.

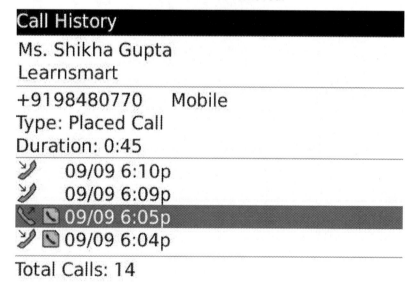

Figure 3–2. *History of calls made to and received from Shikha along with drafts saved*

Mute

Do you have an embarrassing or noisy situation in the middle of the conversation? Or get into a crisis that requires your attention while talking to a potential client? Well, tackling it won't be difficult. Just politely excuse yourself for a short period and mute the call. Select this option from your menu list and no one will hear what's going on at your end (see Figure 3–3). To resume the conversation, just click on the Mute key again. Remember, even though you mute the call blocking out the possibility of being heard, you will still be able to listen to what is being said on the other side of the line.

Figure 3–3. *A call on Mute. Notice the circle around the symbol.*

Hold

This is a feature that may or may not be available to you depending on your service provider and the plan that you opt for. This is used when one is already part of a three-way conversation (involving two other numbers). As Figure 3–4 shows, to invite a fourth person to the conference, the existing call must first be put on hold before the third number can be dialed.

Figure 3–4. *A call on Hold. Notice the circle.*

Transfer

This is your ticket to get out of a conference call without disturbing the existing setup. Just click on this option and you will exit the call alone.

Activate Speaker Phone

You could activate the speaker phone, either by choosing Activate Speaker Phone from the menu, or by simply pressing the speaker phone key on your keypad. To turn it off, do the same. Remember, when you activate this feature, the volume is increased considerably. Holding the phone next to your ear can cause serious damage to your hearing. Hold the phone at a slight distance from your face and continue conversing (see Figure 3–5).

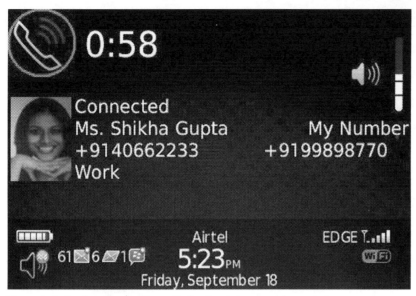

Figure 3–5. *A call on Speaker Phone. Notice the circle around the symbol.*

Enhance Call Audio

You could adjust the bass or treble of the audio as per your preference by selecting this option. However, if you are using a Bluetooth enabled device or hands-free, this feature might not be available to you (see Figure 3–6).

Figure 3–6. *A call with enhanced Audio. That is the symbol for enhanced Bass.*

View Contacts

This will take you to your Contact list. You can check numbers and details directly from here.

View Calendar

Need to check your schedule in the middle of a conversation? Simple. Click on this option and it will take you to your Calendar. Work on your Calendar from here while the call remains undisturbed. You can also save entries.

View Messages

If you want to confirm something but need to check your mailbox first, choose this option. It will take you to your messages inbox where you can work on it even while the call is on. Check your e-mails, text messages, and PIN messages through this application.

Switch Application

If you wish to switch to another application that is not one of the above, you could choose this feature. This allows you to stay in the call and check out other applications simultaneously. End the call normally. Another option is to press the Escape key. Here the device confirms your request by asking if you would like to exit to the Home screen. When you select Ok, it takes you back without disconnecting the call. To return to the call, just press the Call key (green button).

This is particularly useful for professionals using the device. Cross referencing a document that is in the Word To Go application or forwarding an e-mail can be done while the call is on. One could edit a calendar entry or compose e-mails with attachments without having to hang up. The advantages of such a feature are tremendous. Even though the handset needs to be physically moved from the ear to accomplish such tasks, that can be easily altered by using hands-free devices and through Bluetooth.

Accepting a Second Call

Accepting a second call while in the middle of one is also possible. By pressing the Menu key, you could either:

1. Put the previous call on hold by selecting Answer–Hold Current. This will activate the incoming call. To return to the previous call, press on the Menu button and select Swap.

2. Drop the current call and answer the incoming one by selecting Answer–Drop Current. This ends the previous conversation and makes the second call the only one activated.

Some Minor Adjustments

Everybody has their own likes and dislikes. That's what makes everyone an individual, right? While some might like a flashy ringtone; some might prefer more sober ones; some might like high speaker volume and some might not.

You can make adjustments to the ringer volume, ringtone, and vibration options, when in and out of the holster as well as whether you would want a repeat notification, in just one quick step.

In your call log, without highlighting any one particular contact click on the Menu button. Here select Set Ring Tones. On doing this, you can adjust all of the above parameters to your liking (refer to Figure 3–7). Once you are done, Save it from the menu list.

Phone in Normal

Out of Holster:	Tone
Ring Tone:	AirtelJingle
Volume:	Medium
Repeat Notification:	LED Flashing
Number of Vibrations:	2
In Holster:	Vibrate+Tone
Ring Tone:	AirtelJingle
Volume:	Medium
Repeat Notification:	LED Flashing
Number of Vibrations:	2
Do Not Disturb:	No

Figure 3–7. Settings to alter ringtone, volume, and notification

Downloading Ringtones

Choose the ringtone of your choice from the innumerable sites available online and select the option that allows you to e-mail it to yourself. Make sure you mail it to an e-mail id that is associated with your BlackBerry device. On receiving the e-mail, highlight the link and click on the Menu button. Next, select the Get Link option. When it opens in your browser, choose the Save option. Make sure you save it in your ringtones folder. You'll find this in Media Application. You could also find the list of ringtones and save it in your Media Card Memory. The path is as follows: Media Card/BlackBerry/ringtones. Once it is downloaded, close the Browser screen. Congratulations, you have successfully downloaded the ringtone. Now, you can set it up as your default ringtone. Please see Chapter 9 for more details on Downloading Ringtones.

Setting the Default Ringtone

To set your default ringtone, go to your Profiles application and select Advanced. Highlight the profile you want to set it for (Loud or Normal), press the Menu button and select Edit. From the list that appears, choose Phone. Now you are just one tiny option away from setting up your downloaded ringtone: go to the Ring Tone option (see Figure 3–7) and hit the trackball. Here in the list, you will find the ringtone you had downloaded. Select it and voilà, it's set.

Call Logs

Relying on memory is one thing, having it stored is quite another. The information provided in the call logs is simple to digest as the indicators next to the number give a clear understanding as to whether a call was received, made, or missed (see Figure 3–8). To learn about the different indicators, check out Chapter 2.

You will find your call log if you press the Answer key from the home page.

Figure 3–8. *Call log list in the Phone application*

> **NOTE:** Sending a call log entry, its history, and the notes attached with it is also possible. To do so, highlight an entry and click on View History. Once that is opened, click on the Menu button again and select Forward.

You could also send the selected person an SMS, MMS, and e-mail from here directly.

The Call Log feature is very crucial as it gives vital information on who, what, when, why, and how. Let's take one at a time.

Who

This tells you who called. If the person is already a saved contact, then the number is displayed along with picture (if any). Another *who* that it illustrates is who called whom—without any ambiguity on the latest received, dialed, or missed call lists. These can be easily identified with the help of the indicators next to the call.

What

This tells you what time the call was made along with the date.

When

This tells you when you called and when a call was received. Without taking up extra space, it records the history of the conversations. When highlighting a contact, pressing the Menu button and selecting View History gives you details of the calls made and their durations along with notes (if made) on each.

Why

This tells you why the call was made in the form of *notes*, which can be saved during the course of a conversation (as was illustrated earlier in the "Call in Progress" section).

How Long

This tells you how long the call lasted, accurate to the second.

Speed Dialing

We all have our set favorites—people we call most often—so it makes sense to assign them a speed dial number so that you do not have to select their names from call logs or contact lists repeatedly. But what is speed dial? It is nothing but the ability to call someone without having to select their contact details. If you assign a number to that contact, then, upon pressing that number for a couple of seconds, the contact is called automatically. You can do so from any application or screen, be it your message list, Home screen, or Phone application.

Assign a speed dial number to a person from your Phone application, by choosing the Add Speed Dial option from the menu list. After confirming the name and number of the person you wish to assign the speed dial number or letter to, you will be taken to a page from where you can select the character (see Figure 3–9). If at a later stage, you wish to alter this, it can be done by selecting Remove Speed Dial instead.

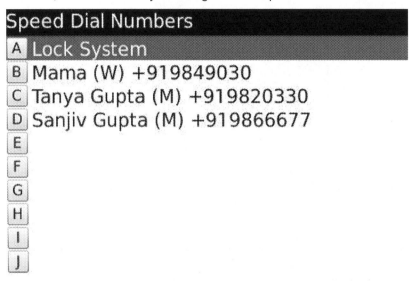

Figure 3–9. *Page showing speed dial numbers and the characters assigned to each*

View Speed Dial List will take you to a page listing out all the assigned keys to the contacts. It is from here that the contact assigned to a speed dial can be edited. When you highlight the contact in the list and press the Menu button, the contact can be moved to another speed dial key, can be replaced by another contact, or can be deleted altogether from the speed dial list.

Conference Calls

The flexibility of more than two people using individual handsets communicating simultaneously is offered by a conference call. Thus, through this feature three or more people can engage in a conversation together. The reason why this becomes special in the case of the BlackBerry as opposed to using any other conference line is the portability and easy accessibility that the device offers. Also, all the callers involved do not have to have the same gadget and can join the call from any telephone device that they use. Calling multiple people on the go has its own set of advantages—suddenly, I do not dread traffic jams or waiting rooms any longer. Another great example of the BlackBerry's "keeping you connected" advantage!

Make a Conference Call

While you are in conversation with one person, if you wish to turn it into a three-way conference, click on the Answer key. Select the person you wish to invite and click on the Answer or Call key again. All the while, the person you were originally having the conversation with is on hold. Thus, once contact is established with the new caller, click on the Menu key and select Join. Your three-way conference is activated.

Leave a Conference Call

To leave a conference call—irrespective of whether you initiated it or not—without disturbing the setup, press the Menu button and select Transfer. In this manner, you will have disconnected yourself from the call while the other participants carry on.

Have a Private Conversation During the Conference Call

If during a call you wish to discuss something with your associate on the side, click on your Menu button. From the list select Split Call and choose the person you wish to speak to separately. Now you have been muted from the conference call and can hold your own conversation without fearing that you will be overheard. To return to the conference call, select Join from the menu list.

Disconnect Someone from the Conference Call

In order to drop a particular participant from the conference call, you need to select the Drop Call option from the menu list. On selecting the person's name, she will be disconnected from the conference call.

> **NOTE:** Leaving a conference without disturbing it, having a private conversation while the conference continues, and disconnecting someone from the call are features that are dependent on your service provider and the wireless connection your BlackBerry device is connected to. For further details, please contact your wireless provider.

Your Voice Is My Command

Voice dialing is a feature in which the handset identifies the command by your voice. It is almost like talking to your phone or dictating to it. Though the obvious limitations that come with accent are understandable, the features are responsive enough to deal with them. So get ready to start talking to your phone.

You can activate the voice dialing application by pressing the key on the left side of the phone—the Left Convenience key. After doing this, a computerized voice will ask you to "say a command." If you wish to call someone, say, "Call." After this, the phone will ask who you wish to call. Here, you can either take a name or can spell out a number then after a confirmation, the call is connected. To end the call, press the End button.

When using this feature, specific needs require specific instructions. You might not want unnecessary confirmations or prompts, or you may choose to alter something as basic as the language of communication. Some of these settings can be changed as discussed in the following sections.

Altering Language

If you would like to communicate with your device in another language, you can do so by changing the Language settings in your Device options. In the Voice Dialing Language (see Figure 3–10), you will find multiple languages to choose from. Change it accordingly and Save.

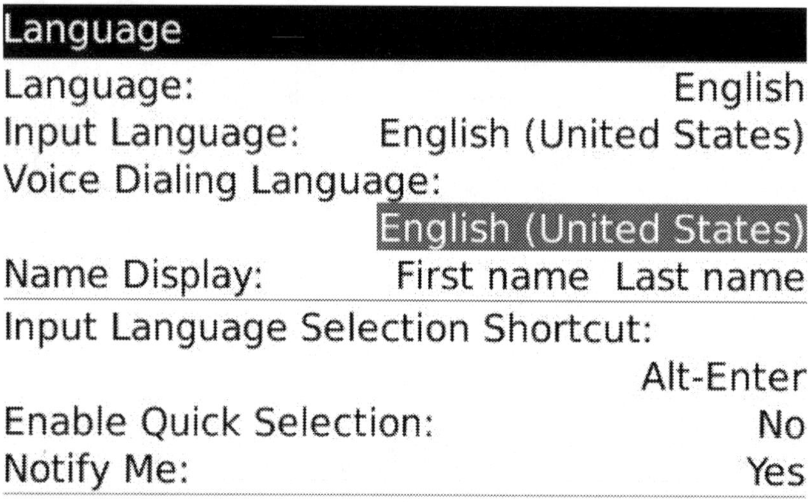

Language	
Language:	English
Input Language:	English (United States)
Voice Dialing Language:	
	English (United States)
Name Display:	First name Last name
Input Language Selection Shortcut:	
	Alt-Enter
Enable Quick Selection:	No
Notify Me:	Yes

Figure 3–10. *Voice Dialing settings where language can be altered*

Altering Sensitivity Levels

According to your settings, you could end up with too many matches or too few. Neither of them is desirable and that's why they can be altered so easily. Just go to Voice Dialing in the Device options and change the settings accordingly. For fewer matches, set the Sensitivity level towards Reject More. For more matches, set it towards Reject Less. Save and exit.

Altering Voice Prompting

Much like a talking parrot repeating your every word can be frustrating, so can excessive prompting. A prompt is a display screen or suggestion that the device is waiting for further specific instructions in order to carry out a task. This instruction could be the confirmation of an action, a password, or a file name.

So if this double-checking or prompting gets on your nerves, you might want to consider turning it off. Prompting is necessary when one does not know what to do. If you have been a regular user of the voice dial feature and are aware of the process, turning off the prompts might be a good option for you. To do so just command, "turn prompts off" when you are in the Voice Dialing application. If you wish for the prompts to resume, say "turn prompts on."

> **NOTE:** The voice recognition feature does not limit itself just to making calls. You can carry out various jobs using the voice command. For instance, you could check your battery life, check your own number, and check your coverage level by simply saying so to the device.

Blocked Road Ahead

What's the best part about holidaying? Leaving all your woes behind, the pressures at work, the drudgery of domesticity, the struggle to stay on top of your game—the list is never ending. Do you know the worst part about a vacation? It's being reminded of all that you left behind. So, a feature like call blocking is going to be a boon for all of you who believe in working hard, playing harder, and want to keep those two as far from one another as possible. The BlackBerry gives you many options on call blocking. You decide when you want to block calls and who is it you do not want reaching you. You can:

- Block all incoming calls
- Block incoming calls on roaming
- Block all outgoing calls
- Block outgoing international calls

How to Block

You can make use of the call blocking feature only if it is supported by your service provider. If it is, then your wireless network provider needs to set up your SIM card for this, providing you with a special call blocking password. For further details, contact them about how to proceed through setup.

Assuming you have this feature setup, you can block the calls by selecting Call Barring which is listed in the Options section of your Phone Application's Menu list (see Figure 3–11). Here highlight which barring option is most applicable to you and then choose Enable from the menu list. After this, the phone will ask for your password which your service provider already gave to you. Punch it in to activate the feature. To undo, simply choose Disable.

You can also choose to change your password from the same list.

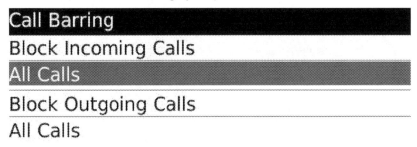

Call Barring

Block Incoming Calls

All Calls

Block Outgoing Calls

All Calls

Figure 3–11. *Example screen of the Call Barring option. A lot more call barring options can be made available, depending on the service provider.*

In an Emergency

First, I want to remind you of the Emergency Calls feature. Should you find yourself in a situation that requires immediate assistance, you can depend on your BlackBerry to get you connected to your rescuers. To use this feature you do not need any network coverage or an active SIM card. In fact, this feature will even work without a SIM inserted, which is designed especially to help people who might find themselves in locations and circumstances that demand official intervention. Only emergency numbers like 911 for North America, 000 for Australia, and 112 for the European Union are included.

Call the emergency number directly and press the green button, if the keypad is unlocked. If the keypad of the handset is locked then press the Menu button, select Emergency Call, and click on Yes. Your BlackBerry is designed to connect to emergency numbers at all times, whether or not you are in your network area. This is because if you find yourself in a place that does not have your network coverage, the BlackBerry connects to the next available network and activates the Emergency and SOS call feature for you.

Tips and Tricks

Time is money, as we all know, which is why I've listed a few convenient shortcuts that you can take.

- Hold the Answer key in the Phone application to get to your Contacts.

- Add an extension to a number by typing X (Alt + X) between the two.

- Hold 1 to hear your voice mail.

- Hold a key in the Home screen to assign a speed dial to it.

I got my mom a BlackBerry recently and she just couldn't remember her own number. If you have a similar problem and are unsure of your number, you can check it in the Phone application. It appears at the top of your screen. If, instead of the number, the display says "Unknown Phone number" then the phone hasn't been set up yet. To do so, you need to go to Advanced Options in your Device Options Application and click on SIM Card. Highlight the phone number and press on the Menu button. Choose Edit SIM Phone Number, type it out, and click on the trackball. Your number will appear in your Phone application.

What's Next?

Storing, forwarding, and delivering data is an imperative part of any organization or business. However, relying on the spoken word can often lead to misinterpretation and misrepresentation, hence the value of a reliable tool that categorizes and structures this communication transparently. No wonder all industries today bank so heavily on e-mails. Chapter 4 will focus on accessing and use of e-mail on your BlackBerry.

BlackBerry for E-mail

My Mantra—Polite Yet Firm

Whoever said that "The spoken word is like an arrow—once it leaves it cannot be taken back" could well apply the same sentiment to electronic mails, with even more emphasis. The accountability that the written word bears is far greater, due to its permanent documented nature. Thus, electronic mailing with its innumerable advantages—as against traditional mailing—also bears great responsibility. That's why it becomes extremely vital for us to tread cautiously—once the e-mail is sent there is no way of getting it back. E-mail is one of the most crucial inventions in communication of the 20th century. That's why I will introduce this chapter focusing on general concepts about e-mail first, before elaborating on e-mail for BlackBerry.

Introduction to E-mailing

The father of modern e-mail is widely regarded to be the American, Ray Tomlinson. He was the person who introduced the use of the symbol @. This brought with it the advantage of being able to direct a communication to a particular user. Until then, messages could be transferred, but only to people using the same computer. In fact, e-mail played a pivotal role in the creation of the Internet.

What is an e-mail? It is a method of sending, receiving, and storing data or communication. It broadly consists of two sections—the header and the body. The header includes the sender and the recipient, and recipients' addresses while the body contains the main communication matter. As part of the header, a subject line is included which ideally should reflect the purpose of the mail giving a brief overview of the content and intended reason for the communication. E-mail is essentially text based. However, a whole lot of files ranging from text and spreadsheets to multimedia such as music, images, and videos can be added to the mail in the form of attachments.

Most web mail services today such as Gmail, Hotmail, Yahoo! among others are designed keeping the World Wide Web as its primary interface, which are not only offered free of cost, but also allow for anytime-anywhere access. The e-mail's popularity as a means of communication—both formal and informal—is incomparable and thus it has earned the respect of the personal and professional world of communication.

Advantages of E-mail

It is true that the world is getting smaller by the day. Traditionally, communication was primarily face-to-face and did not require any other medium. Today, conferences between people in different time zones situated hundreds of miles apart is as common as taking your dog for a walk. With this shrinking, fast-paced world has come the requirement to document quickly and correctly while offering easy accessibility to all parties, irrespective of their geographical location. Some of the obvious advantages of e-mail are discussed in the following sections.

It's Quick

E-mailing is one of the fastest ways of transferring the written word between people while providing formality. No sooner does the correspondent send the e-mail than it is received by the addressee.

It Can Be Organized

E-mail allows for storage of information and communication in a categorized manner. Systematic folders simplify understanding and referencing. However, their proper utilization depends on the end user.

It's Simple

E-mail does not require complicated and lengthy postal addresses nor does it ask for phone numbers or reference contact details, thus minimizing the miscommunication risks often involved in cross-cultural negotiations. All that is needed is the e-mail address of the recipient.

It's Environmentally Friendly

With our growing awareness toward our environment has come the realization of how fragile it really is. In these circumstances, preserving our natural resources becomes a prime concern. E-mail eliminates the need for paper, thus salvaging hundreds of forests along with their flora and fauna.

It's Inexpensive

Most web-based mail services are offered free of cost. Therefore, the only expense borne by the individual is the charge they pay for the Internet. Compared to telephones, faxes, and postal communication, e-mail is far easier on the pocket.

It's Conversational

Because of its ability to deliver quick responses, e-mail can aid in speedy communication, making a whole series of content-exchange possible.

It's Contextual

E-mail users have an added advantage over traditional written or verbal communication users as there is also the option of attaching or recording the history of the conversation, which helps put the exchange in context. This in turn aids in avoiding any confusion or wasted time.

It's Personal

E-mail can be a very personal medium of communication as only the intended recipient can access the information, eliminating the need for a third person's intervention.

Disadvantages of E-mail

There are a few drawbacks that come with the whole e-mail package. E-mail attachments can cause a lot of damage to your system if they bring a virus along with them. This is why one should be very cautious while opening an attachment from an unknown source. There are other sources of viruses affecting your system which include browsing through unknown sites and downloading content from the Internet. These can be tackled by making sure you have an updated firewall installed so as to minimize your vulnerability.

Because of the ease with which e-mails can be sent, many times they are forwarded to people who are not directly related to the subject at hand. Therefore, another disadvantage of the e-mail is that it can cause an overload of information sent to you that you might not be concerned with. Other dreadful possibilities include accidentally viewing confidential material by unrelated sources if the mailbox is left open or the hazards of hacking. Along with that, care should be taken to make sure entire mailing lists are not included in the To field, if unintended. Another hurdle includes the difficulty in understanding the tone of a particular e-mail. For instance, sarcasm or humor are often misconstrued and could lead to complications.

Due to their wide usage, e-mails have earned the reputation of being casual. If not structured properly, e-mails can lead to considerable problems in the professional sphere. Therefore, it becomes essential to understand the basic difference between personal and work e-mails.

Personal vs. Work E-mail

E-mailing for professional use and personal need are two very different things. Apart from the format, the e-mail's manner, tone, content, and the language can differ. Using your work e-mail for personal use or sending formal e-mails in a casual format are equivalent to going to a board meeting in your PJs. In fact, even that is better in comparison—at least there aren't company laws and regulations involved.

People often misuse their official e-mail accounts to carry out their personal business. The jobs could range from receiving newsletters and shopping online to forwarding private jokes and comments. Company internet connectivity is usually faster in speed, more convenient to use, and available at all times, thus tempting employees to misuse it. However, as a practice this is greatly frowned upon and could land the employee in some serious trouble. I strongly suggest knowing your company's policies regarding e-mailing before taking them for granted.

Why You Shouldn't Use Your Work E-mail for Personal Errands

Accessing your personal e-mail accounts in the office or receiving personal e-mails at your work account can have affects on the quality and output of your work. This is because these e-mails cause the following problems.

Distractions

The temptation of opening an interesting mail or forwarding it to your friends is common. Whether you are in the middle of drafting a formal proposal or are researching, one ping from your inbox with an exciting forward and you can kiss goodbye to a good few minutes. Needless to say, your work suffers.

Informality of Style

By separating your personal and work e-mail accounts, one does not have to fear about slipping into a casual mode of communication in a professional situation. This can save you a lot of awkwardness if your company demands formal conduct. The following are other points to ponder regarding privacy and misuse:

- Did you know that your company e-mails can be (and are) monitored? This could be a random check or could be instigated by specific occurrences. So, if you have anything to say to someone that you might not want everyone in the office to know about, I suggest you do not use your work e-mail account for that conversation.

- Most companies have regulations in place to avoid misuse. Make sure you review this policy well.

- Lots of personal e-mails have movie and music attachments which can easily be carrying viruses. This can pose a threat to your and your colleagues systems, as most work e-mail accounts are accessed thought a network. Although it can be argued that work e-mails could pose a similar threat, the frequency of such attachments received from unknown sources are far more prevalent in personal e-mails as apposed to ones at work.

That said, some companies also allow personal e-mail access either at all times or during break hours. This primarily depends on your company policy and subject. Please check with your company before assuming its validity.

E-mail Etiquette

With the explosive popularity of the Internet, new terms were coined such as "netiquette," which is nothing but net + etiquette. So put the use of "dude" aside for a while, will you?

Now that we have established that etiquette is important, let's go over a few things you should keep in mind.

Subject

Always clearly state the purpose of the mail in the subject box. This is the best way to avoid any ambiguity. It also simplifies later searches and makes for easy referencing.

Respect

Address the person you are writing to with respect. In the case of formal mails, appropriate titles are always appreciated. For instance, the use of titles such as Mr., Mrs., and Dr. are fitting and proper. Use Ms. if you are not sure of the marital status of a woman. Use the first name of the person only if you are on first name basis or in case of informal communication. It's best to address strangers as Sir or Madam if you do not know their name. Signing off also follows similar rules. Some examples of formal sign offs could be "Yours sincerely" or "Yours faithfully." A semiformal sign off could include "Thanks and regards." "With love" is an example of a casual sign off.

Brief is Best

Being brief does not mean you should be rude and terse. Get to the point politely, but there is no need to beat around the bush.

Beware of Abbreviations

"I wuld luv 2 go der 2day." While it's OK to use common abbreviations such as Pvt., Ltd., or FYI, common SMS language is not appreciated in formal communication.

Checked

Please use the spell check. But do not blindly follow it either. Instead, use it to identify mistakes and rely only on a good dictionary in case of any confusion.

Don't Shout

This is a very common mistake people make. Using capital letters in an e-mail conveys aggressiveness. IT LOOKS LIKE YOU ARE SHOUTING! If highlighting is what you are aiming at, make the desired text bold or underlined, but not all caps. The following are some other standards to keep in mind:

- *Good grammar is very important*: Correctly framed sentences with correct usage of words are key.

- *Be polite*: Maintain a well-mannered and polite stance.

- *Keep gender neutral*: Assuming you do not know the person, it is best to keep the gender neutral. This communicates that you are not taking the gender of the person for granted or jumping the gun.

- *Review the e-mail before you send it*: It may save you a lot of embarrassment.

- *Once sent, it cannot be taken back*: So be sure of what you send.

- *Avoid attachments, especially if it is a first time interaction*: People are wary of attachments as they breed viruses. It's preferable to send the information in the body of the mail.

- *Keep it short and simple in language and presentation*: Short and to-the-point sentences are always a pleasure to read.

- *Don't assume the other person has fancy formats*: Use basic effective formatting. Sticking to HTML e-mails is always appreciated. However, use of basic fonts that are widely available is also common. Colors also play an important role and the use of a neutral black or grey for text is proper.

- *Formal communication does not appreciate over-familiarity*: However, appropriate use of smiley's can add "body language" to the e-mail. But remember not to go overboard.

- *A prompt reply is always appreciated*: If the recipient is going to have to wait for it, they might as well have sent it via post. Setting deadlines for yourself (usually 24 hours or less) will help you achieve the same.

- *It's no place for secrets*: Remember an e-mail is a written document. So if it is a secret, don't send it via e-mail.

- *Maintain threads of conversations*: This could include responding inline with the previous message or by including it in the message body. They help understand the context as well as the chronology of events for ready reference.

Uses of E-mail in Different Industries

E-mail is used widely across various platforms. It could be used for surveys and research; as a marketing tool (which is now being explored by smaller businesses as well); for releasing papers in the field of medicine and science to increase awareness among people regarding pressing issues; to carry out group communication effectively; to raise money for charity through forwards; or for online shopping—the list is endless. Whether you are involved with pediatrics, education, marketing, or finance or whether your focus is on art, culture, environmental issues, social service, or aerodynamics—you can be assured that you will use e-mail extensively.

BlackBerry and E-mail

We have already established the importance of e-mailing and how it plays a vital role in any business, so let us begin exploring how BlackBerry makes this feature more accessible to you. Using a Blackberry gives you access to your mail at all times. The push technology that the BlackBerry adopts delivers your mail to your handset inbox immediately. Once you do not have to go to your mail, it comes to you. This means that no matter where you are—stuck in a traffic jam, out of town, or in some small village in the countryside, you have a hundred percent access to your inbox.

To get details on setting up your e-mail and synchronizing it with your device, refer to Chapter 2.

Receiving Messages

Once your e-mail has been set up on your handset you will start receiving your e-mail and messages on it. The appearance of a star on the message icon in the homepage or the application page means that you have new unopened mail in your inbox. After highlighting, your phone will display the number of unopened mails in brackets along with the e-mail account associated with that icon (see Figure 4–1).

Figure 4–1. *Application screen highlighting the e-mail address associated with the icon along with the number of unopened messages*

Press the trackball to open the application. Here by default, the messages are listed in chronological order with the latest ones at the top. Along with the date, the inbox also tells you at what time the e-mail was received. You can differentiate between new and old messages with the help of the icons next to the messages (see Figure 4–2).

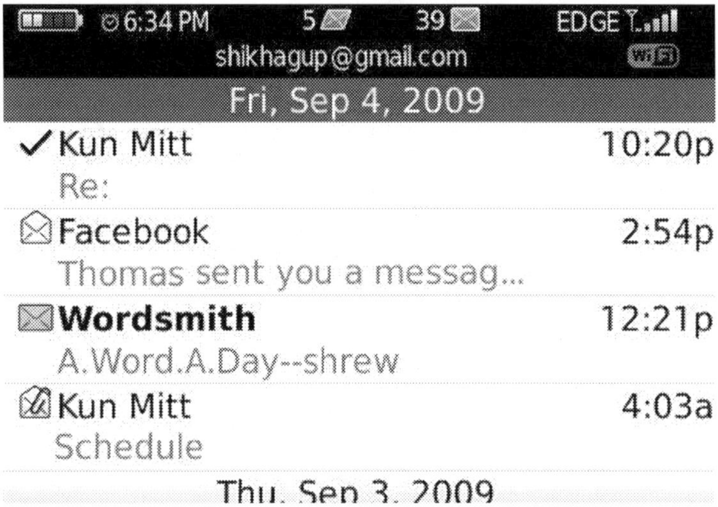

Figure 4–2. *The Message Application inbox*

For details on message indicators and their meanings, please refer to Chapter 2.

To view a particular mail, just click on the highlighted message with the trackball. After opening the message, it will list details like the receiver's e-mail address (To), the sender's e-mail address (From), the subject line of the mail (Subject), and the date and the time when it was received along with a link to open the attachment (if any). As you scroll down with the help of the trackball, the body of the message is revealed.

Communication is a two way process requiring responses. Thus, if you want to reply to a particular mail, you can do so right from the message. Blackberry's intuitiveness is best illustrated with the number of options it provides you, reducing your need to navigate from one page or application to another. On pressing the Menu button while a message is opened, you will be offered a number of choices for your next move, as described in the sections below.

Find

This is a feature similar to search. You can search for a word or phrase in the message. Just type out the word and press enter. The find feature is case sensitive.

Select

As shown in Figure 4–3, by choosing this, you can select a paragraph or chunk of data that can be copied and pasted elsewhere.

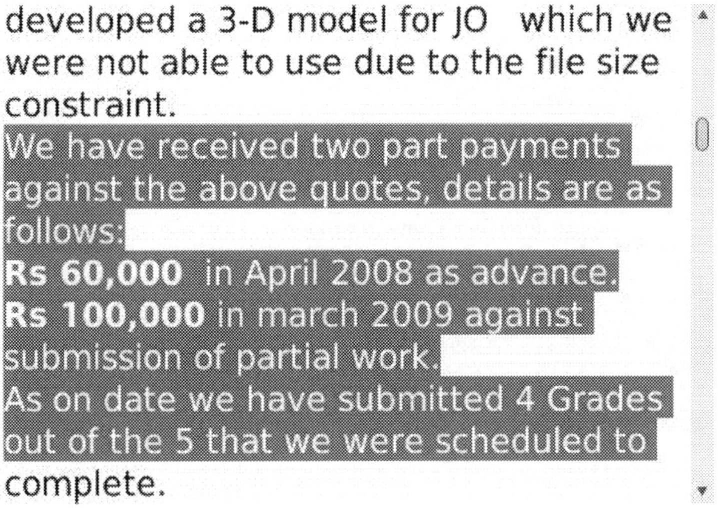

developed a 3-D model for JO   which we
were not able to use due to the file size
constraint.
We have received two part payments
against the above quotes, details are as
follows:
Rs 60,000 in April 2008 as advance.
Rs 100,000 in march 2009 against
submission of partial work.
As on date we have submitted 4 Grades
out of the 5 that we were scheduled to
complete.

Figure 4–3. *Example of a selected section from a message*

Mark Unopened

This feature allows you to mark the present message as unopened. By choosing this, the icon next to the message in your inbox changes back to unopened.

File

You can file the message away, according to the desired location. After choosing this, your handset will list probable places where you could file the message. As shown in Figure 4–4, choose accordingly and proceed.

Figure 4–4. *Select the desired folder from this page*

Save

You could save the particular message if you choose this option. According to your settings (covered later in the section "E-mail Settings"), your message inbox stores data only for a fixed period of time. By saving, you can be assured the message will not get deleted until you do so physically. If you would like to delete a message, press the Menu button and select Delete. After deleting a message, your BlackBerry will ask you whether it should delete it from the mailbox and handheld, from the handheld only, or cancel to return to the previous page.

Reply

To reply to the sender, click on this option. By doing so, you will be maintaining the history of the communication as the previous interaction will get attached to the present message with the new messages on the top of the page (see Figure 4–5).

To: SanGupta
To:
Cc:

Subject: Re: It's all possible

―――――――Original Message―――――――

From: SanGupta
To: SanGupta
FW: It's all possible
Sep 22, 2009 1:39 PM

Figure 4–5. *A Reply screenshot, maintaining the thread of conversation*

Reply To All

If the message has been sent to multiple people and you wish for all them to receive your reply, choose this option. As shown in Figure 4–6, their addresses and communication history will already be established. Notice the cursor appears at the top of the history for your reply.

To: SanGupta
To: TanGupta
To:
Cc:

Subject: Re: For my

―――――――Original Message―――――――

To: SanGupta
To: TanGupta
For my
Sep 19, 2009 4:44 PM

Figure 4–6. *A Reply To All option screenshot, maintaining the conversation history*

Forward

This is an option which allows you to send the same message to other recipients.

Forward As

This gives you the option of forwarding the same message that you got as an e-mail, as an SMS, MMS, PIN message, or as an instant message directly. This is one great example of the BlackBerry's intuitiveness. Here you eliminate the need to copy and paste in another application. You can immediately navigate to another application without losing your data.

Delete

Choose this if you want to erase the message from your inbox. On pressing this, the application will ask you if you would like to delete it from your handheld only or from both your mailbox and handheld. You could also cancel to return. The following are your three options to delete:

- *On mailbox and handheld*: Choosing this will delete the message from the phone's inbox as well as from the server.

- *On handheld*: This will only delete the message from your handheld mailbox, but not from the server.

- *Cancel*: This will abort the action and return you to the previous page.

Send E-mail

By choosing this, you get to send a new e-mail to the person who mailed you. The difference between this and Reply is that Reply maintains the thread of conversations whereas this opens a new window altogether with the e-mail address of the recipient already established as shown in Figure 4–7.

To: Ridh Jai
To:
Cc:

Subject: |

Figure 4–7. *The name and address of the recipient pre-established*

Send MMS

You could use this if you want to send an MMS to your sender. This is another great example of inter-application compatibility.

Call

If the sender's phone number has been recorded in your address book, you can call them directly from here.

Send SMS

Even this option requires the phone number of the intended recipient to be included in their contact information. For further details on Contact Management, please refer to Chapter 7.

Show Address

If you cannot see the e-mail address of the person who has sent you the mail, click on this and the address will become highlighted. After doing so, the same field Show Address will be replaced by Show Name. As the name suggests, on selecting this, the name of your sender will become highlighted.

View Folder

This allows you to view another application in the message format. Right from this point, you could view folders like Missed Calls, MMS Outbox, MMS Inbox, SMS Outbox, SMS Inbox, SMS SIM Card Inbox, Phone Call Logs, Missed Calls, Wap Push Messages, and Browser Messages.

Previous Item

Again, you do not even need to navigate out of the present page to view your other messages. Choose this to go to the previous mail.

Next Item

Skip going back to the inbox if you want to read your next message. Select this option to go to the next mail.

Next Unopened Item

If you only want to check your unopened or new messages without having to go through the already read ones, choose this. It will directly jump to the next message that hasn't been opened yet.

Add To Contacts

Add the sender to your contacts directly from here. After you choose this, the phone will take you to the Contacts page where you can fill in the details. If the person is already a contact, then this field is replaced by View Contact.

Switch Input Language

You could change the language for your reply from here. However, this does not mean that the application will translate the text for you. To be able to make use of this feature, you will need to upgrade your software to a higher version. After this, you also need to make sure your alternate languages have not been disabled in your Language section. You will also need to install the multilingual software after which, this feature will be made available. You can do this by downloading it from: http://na.blackberry.com/eng/support.downloads/download_sites.jsp. Here, choose your service provider to proceed.

Switch Application

Change to another application by choosing this option.

Attachments

If the message has an attachment along with it, then you have the following two options.

Open Attachment

If there are multiple attachments in the same mail, open a particular one by highlighting it after choosing this option. It will retrieve the attachment's contents for you.

Download Attachment

You could choose to download the attachment also. You could save it in a desired folder or location.

Composing Messages

To send out a message to someone, use this feature. It is exactly like composing a message from your e-mail account. When in your inbox, press the Menu button then choose Compose E-mail. The next screen is a blank page with fields like To, CC, Subject, and Body.

Sending out a message is very simple. In the To field, you can identify the contact by typing out either their name, e-mail address, or just a part of their name. On doing this, the phone lists out a directory of people whose name (part of the name) is applicable to the characters you have typed. Pick the appropriate one by highlighting it using the trackball. Select by pressing the trackball. As soon as you select a contact in the To field, another To space opens up for you to feed in another recipient. However, it is not mandatory for that field to be filled out. Utilizing this is completely your choice. Once the recipients have been established, type out the Subject and then the body of the message. Once done, click on the trackball or Menu button and select Send.

Before sending out the message, there is another whole list of options that is made available to you based on your preference. It goes without saying that these options show up when you press the Menu button. The following choices are available to you from here.

Paste

Assuming you have selected or copied certain data from another application, you can choose this option to paste it in the desired field.

Select

If you have typed out some data in either of the fields, then this option appears, allowing you to select a certain amount of content for later use.

Check Spelling

Like Select, assuming you have typed some content in either the Subject or the Body field, and that is the space that is highlighted, this option is made available. By choosing this, the misspelled words become apparent along with a list of probable words. Pick the correct one to replace.

Clear Field

Choosing this option will clear whichever space or field the cursor is in at that point.

Save Draft

You could save a draft of the message through this option. The draft gets saved toward the beginning of your inbox based on when you save it, because the latest interactions or activity is showcased first. Identify the draft icon as a green note, as shown in Figure 4–8.

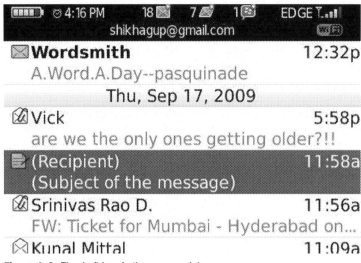

Figure 4–8. *The draft icon in the message inbox*

Add To

You can also choose to include more recipients from this space.

Add Cc

Cc is a short form of carbon copy. This means that a copy of the message will be sent to the e-mail address of the person identified here. It is a means of addressing the same interaction to multiple people without them being the directly intended recipients.

Add Bcc

Bcc is short for blind carbon copy. This means that the receiver established here will receive a copy, but will not be known to the other recipients. Their name and details will not be displayed to the others.

Attach Contact

You could attach a contact's details through this feature. This means that all the contact details of the person get attached to the mail in the form of an attachment.

Attach File

You can attach absolutely any saved file to the message. After you choose this, the handset will ask you the location of the desired attachment. Depending on whether it is in your Media card, Device Memory, or System you could add files such as documents, music, pictures, ringtones, videos, voice notes, mms tunes, or folder icons.

Edit Auto Text

Auto text is a very useful feature that comes preloaded with your handset. This is the feature that recognizes common typo's (typing errors) and rectifies them immediately. So if you type "feild" for "field" or "didnt" instead of "didn't," you needn't worry. The software will replace and correct it for you automatically and instantly. However, if you want to edit these settings to your customized requirements, you can do so by choosing the Edit Auto Text option. On selecting this feature, a list of words will appear. Select the one you would like to edit by clicking on the trackball and proceed.

Options

Two options are made available to you from here (see Figure 4–9).

Importance

You can set the importance of the message to either: Low, Normal, or High.

Encoding

You can alter the encoding from Automatic to Japanese, Korean, Simplified Chinese, or Traditional Chinese from here (see Figure 3-9).

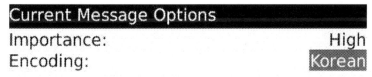

Figure 4–9. *Set the importance and encoding from here.*

Show Symbols

This takes you to a screen with all the signs and symbols listed out for you to choose from. This includes punctuation marks and numbers.

Switch Input Language

You can change the language from English to Dutch, Spanish, French, Italian, Traditional Chinese, or simplified Cantonese from here.

Switch Application

Select this to change over to another application.

Signed

A custom signature designed by you for your requirement is a sure-shot winner. Whether a casual "Cheers" or "Ciao" is your style (and acceptable in your professional and personal circles) or a formal "Thanks and regards" is needed, you can set it up very easily.

The process, however, differs based on whether you are a BIS user or a BES customer. To understand the difference between the two, and to understand your arrangement, refer to Chapter 2.

If you have a BES (BlackBerry Enterprise Server) connection, then you can add your signature by choosing Options from the Menu list of your Message application. Select E-mail Settings and tweak the Message Services field accordingly. Make sure the Use Auto Signature field is enabled and type out your signature in the text box. Once that's done, choose Save.

If you are a BIS (BlackBerry Internet Service) user, then this process is slightly altered for you. In your case, setting the signature is not carried out using your handset but through the official web site of your service provider. You might remember that while setting up your e-mail account (Chapter 2), we had also mentioned the setup process involved in creating an online account with your service provider. In order to create an automatic personalized signature, go to the official web site of your service provider and log into your account by typing your username and password. Once logged in, you can Edit the settings of the e-mail address. Since the exact process might vary slightly depending on your service provider, I suggest you get in touch with them directly for further details.

To Save or Not to Save

Saving important messages is a good option, for they then aren't susceptible to getting deleted. This usually happens when the time period for keeping the messages has been reached. Your handset by default has a preset that keeps messages in the handheld inbox for a period of 30 days. This setting can be changed by going to Options from the Menu list of the Message Application. Here, in General Options, you could configure the mailbox to keep the messages for a period ranging from 15 days to forever.

Saving a Message

If a message proves important enough for you to save it for later use or reference, then I suggest you save it ASAP. To do so, choose Save from the menu options, as previously discussed.

Deleting a Message

Sadly, some forwards or irrelevant messages that fail to prove their importance do get discarded. No point cluttering your mailbox now, is there? Just select Delete from the options instead.

Deleting individual messages can be quite a pain. To erase messages in bulk, highlight a message and press the alt button. With this button pressed roll the trackball to select multiple messages. This will highlight the messages. Click on the Menu button and choose Delete.

BlackBerry also offers you another option. In one quick step, you can delete *all* messages prior to a particular date. When a date is highlighted, click on the menu button. Choose the option Delete Prior, and watch all messages recorded previously disappear.

Messages Through the Strainer

One filters tea leaves out before drinking tea; one filters a crowd to choose a select few who matter; one even filters information and retains what one relates to. We are constantly in a state of sieving through hoards of options, so that what we are left with is what is most important to us, right?

Similarly, BlackBerry gives you a wonderful tool that allows you to filter out your messages, giving you control of which messages reach you on your handset and which are retained in the mailbox. This involves creating the filters which get activated almost immediately. The process varies for BES and BIS users. In either case, you needn't worry, the method is very simple.

> **NOTE:** The BlackBerry basically uses push technology so that the messages you receive on your server are parallely received on your handset as well. However, maintaining the two inboxes can be kept individual and changes made in one may or may not reflect in the other. You can also filter the messages that you receive on your handset, which means that you decide which messages reach you on your phone. But remember, your BlackBerry filters will have no effect on your server mailbox.

For BES Users

For BES users, activating and controlling the message filters is a process that is carried out directly from the handset. There are a number of options that are provided to you based on which you can filter your messages. This means that based on the specifications that you give here, the filter will sort through all your messages. The filter could work based on the following requirements:

- *Importance*: According to the importance of the e-mail message, the filter either is applied to it or not. This means that the filter will be applied to a message only if it falls under the specified requirement of importance.

- *From*: Here you need to set whether the filter should be applied if an e-mail message contains the specified addresses or characters in the From field.

- *Sent To*: Set whether the filter should be applied if the specified address or character appears in the Send To field.

- *Send Directly To Me*: Confirm if the filter should be applied to any message that includes your e-mail address in the To Field.

- *CC To Me:* Confirm if the filter should be applied to any message that includes your e-mail address in the CC To Me Field.

- *BCC To Me:* Confirm if the filter should be applied to any message that includes your e-mail address in the BCC To Me Field.

- *Sensitivity:* The sensitivity level of the e-mail message that the filter applies to is set here.

- *Action:* Here you need to set whether on filtering if these messages should or should not be forwarded to your BlackBerry. The filter could work both ways. You could either set it up so that you *do not* get certain mails, or so that you *only* get certain mails.

NOTE: Separate multiple specifications with a semicolon (;). Use an asterisk (*) along with certain characters, to signify that any word or address with part of the specification becomes applicable to the filter.

Set Up a Filter

To create a message filter, press the Menu button while in the Message application. Choose E-mail Filters, which is part of the Options list. Press the Menu button and click on New. Give the filter a name. Now set the filter based on the above options. Click on the Menu button and Save. There, now you just set up your first filter.

Are Your Settings Right?

There could be two reasons for the filter to not work properly.

1. *The filter is not turned on*: To cross-check whether it has been turned on or not, in the Message application click on the Menu button and select Options. In E-mail Filters, make sure the box next to the filter is checked.

2. *The filter is low on priority*: If you set up multiple filters there are bound to be messages that are applicable to more than one. In that case, the filter on top gets priority. That's why you need to make sure that the most important filters come first. To shift the order of your set filters, go to Options from your Message application. Select E-mail Filters and highlight the one you want to move. Press the Menu button again and click on Move. Use your trackball to move it up or down (the higher, the more the priority it gets). Click the trackball again to release. The filter is moved.

BIS Users

If you are a BIS user, then you can control your filters through the account you have setup with your service provider. Remember, if you have more than one e-mail account synchronized with your device, the filters that you set up for one will not affect the other.

Type your username and password, to log in to your account. Here, with the e-mail account highlighted, click on Filter (see Figure 4–10).

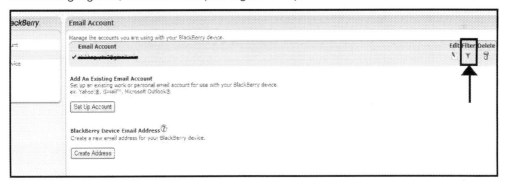

Figure 4–10. *The location of the Filter next to the e-mail account*

From here, choose the Add Filter option. On doing this, you will reach the page where you can make all the changes you want, in order to set up your filters (see Figure 4–11).

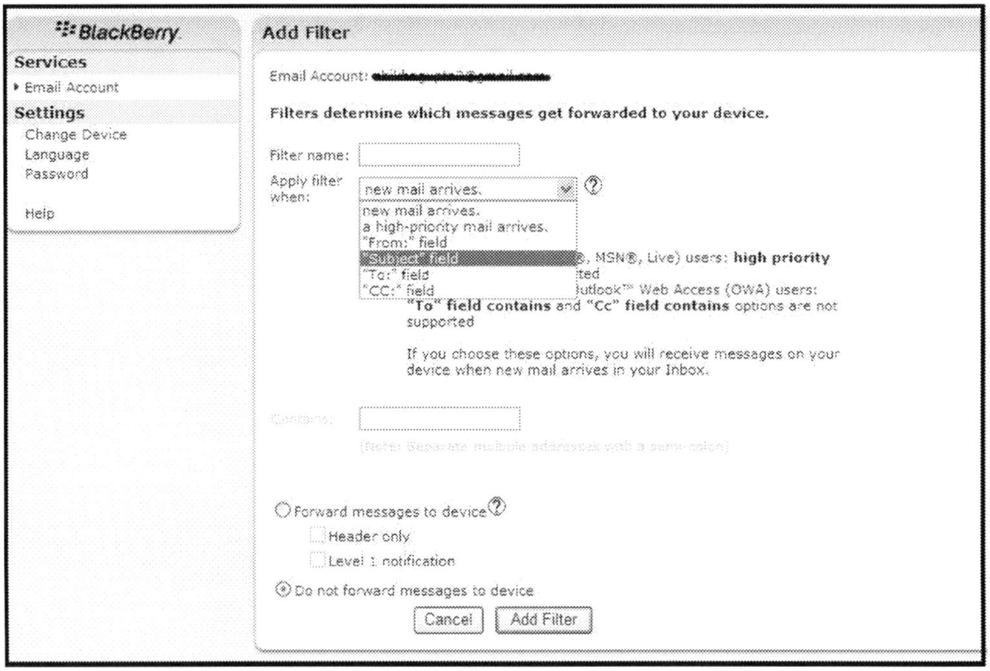

Figure 4–11. *Set the filter options accordingly*

You will need to:

1. Give your filter a name (as per its function).

2. Set when the filter should be applied. For instance, whether you want the filter to be applied when a New Mail Arrives (this means for all mails), when a High Priority Mail Arrives (this means only for mails that are marked as important), when the From field, To field, or Cc Field include one or more e-mail addresses in particular or when the Subject Field includes certain words or characters.

3. If your filter is related to identifying according to the From, To, Cc, or Subject Fields; then you need to specify what they need to contain for the filter to be applied to them. Separate between multiple ids or words with a semicolon.

4. Finally, you need to establish whether upon meeting the above requirements the mail should or shouldn't be forwarded.

5. Complete the process by clicking on Add Filter.

NOTE: If you have multiple filters, make sure you prioritize sensibly. For example, if two or more filters are applicable to the same message, then the filter on top will get preference over the other(s).

Attachments

An attachment is a computer file that is *attached* to the e-mail. This means that apart from the main body of the message, another file (video, audio, document, or excel sheet) is also sent along. It is very easy for an attachment to carry viruses. That is why most people are wary of them. Unless the sender is a reliable and trusted source, I suggest you treat them with caution.

Your device is equipped to receive and view most attachment types. These include: .zip, .htm, .html, .doc, .dot, .ppt, .pdf, .wpd, .txt, .vcf, .xls, .bmp, .gif, .jpg, .png, .tif, and .wmf files. It also can play .wav and .mp3 files. Downloading and saving these attachments is also possible. If you save them in your device memory, and delete the message from your mailbox, the attachment is not deleted until you physically do so from the storage location. To edit these attachments, applications like Word To Go, Slideshow To Go, and Sheet To Go have been preset in your device (on several BlackBerry models).

Opening an Attachment

To open an attachment from a message, highlight it using your trackball and press the Menu button or click on the trackball. Choose Open Attachment. If there are multiple attachments from the list, highlight the one you want to open and click on it. If the attachment has already been retrieved, then a tick mark appears next to it. If it is in the process, you will see a clock icon (see Figure 4–12).

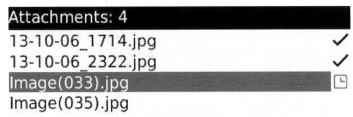

Figure 4–12. *Mulitple attachments and their downloading status*

Downloading an Attachment

Similar to opening an attachment, if you want to download it, highlight it in the message and click on the Menu button or the trackball. From here, select Download Attachment. Choose Download and then select the folder in which you would like to save it in. Press the Menu button and Select Folder. To stop downloading an attachment, choose Cancel Download after pressing the Menu button.

Opening a Link from an Attachment

If the attachment has a link to a web page that needs to be opened, then highlight the link and press the Menu button. Here select Retrieve or Get Link. By doing this, the application with the help of the located URL, takes you back to the original web page. To go back to the attachment, press the Esc or Back key.

Document Attachments

Let's see some of the advanced capabilities when working with document attachments.

- If the .pdf file attachment that you receive is password protected, then press the Esc or Back key when the "Password Protected Document" statement appears. Now select Password from the Menu options. Type the password and press Enter. Select Retrieve.

- If you would want to view the track changes in a document, press the Menu button and press Show Changes.

- To view a table, press the Menu button and select Table of Contents.

Excel Attachments

Working with Excel is quiet easy. Let's look at a few of them.

- If you want to check the contents of a particular cell, highlight it and press the trackball.

- To view a list of worksheets, select Table of Contents from the Menu options.

- Click on Next Sheet or Previous Sheet from the Menu options to move between sheets.

PPT Attachments

Working with PowerPoint on your BlackBerry is quite similar to working with it on your PC or Mac.

- Select Next Slide or Previous Slide to move between screens in a PPT.

- To rotate slides, choose Rotate while a slide is highlighted.

▓ Zoom into a slide by selecting Zoom from the Menu options. Use the trackball to zoom in or out by rolling it up or down (up for zoom in and down for zoom out). To get back to the original screen, choose Fit to Screen from the Menu options.

▓ You can switch between views (only text or text + slides) by pressing the Menu button. Here, either select View Text or select View Both.

NOTE: Word documents, Excel sheets, and PPTs are not supported by all BlackBerry devices and thus opening them also depends on the model. For more details on models and features, please refer to Chapter 1.

Quick and Slick

Here are a few attachment shortcuts that will help you navigate and access the attachments faster.

▓ Press F in an attachment to look for particular text.

▓ After reopening any attachment, press G to go to the last cursor position.

▓ Press Space to view the contents of a particular cell in a spreadsheet.

▓ Press G to move a particular cell to another position in a spreadsheet attachment alone.

▓ Press H to view or hide columns or rows in a spreadsheet.

▓ Press M to switch views in a presentation.

▓ Press N (next) to move to the next slide in a presentation.

▓ Press P (previous) to move to the earlier slide in a presentation.

Documents To Go

Included as a preset in the BlackBerry Bold 9000, Documents To Go allows for document creation, viewing, and editing all on your handset. Documents To Go supports Microsoft Word, Excel, and PowerPoint giving the user as authentic an experience as possible.

It supports attachments received via mail, Bluetooth, or media card, which can be edited directly using this feature while retaining original document formatting. You can view track changes in word processing files and use spell check features. Editing bullets, numbering, and tables in Word are simple processes which are listed in the Menu options.

French, Italian, German, and Spanish versions are also available. For more details on the functionality and uses of this feature, please refer to Chapter 15.

Options and More

This section is for you if you want your messages to be stored for a longer period than the default preset of 30 days; if you want delivery confirmations; if you do not want to load pictures in the HTML messages or desire the presentation in plain text format; if you want to hide filed messages; if you want to change the display order of the names; or if you require an automatic spell check. All of these options are customizable on your BlackBerry.

E-mail Settings

You will find that most of these settings are made available in the E-mail Settings Option that is part of your Message Options (see Figure 4–13).

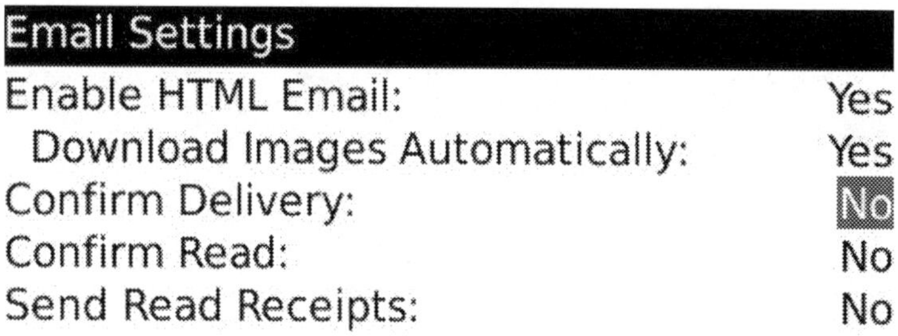

Email Settings	
Enable HTML Email:	Yes
Download Images Automatically:	Yes
Confirm Delivery:	No
Confirm Read:	No
Send Read Receipts:	No

Figure 4–13. *Page for e-mail settings*

Is It There Yet?

If you are one who needs to be in control, who needs to know exactly what is going on and where, if you feel the need to stay on top of your game at all times, I'm guessing you would want your delivery reports. If you want a confirmation on Delivery or on Read, then set the field to Yes.

I'll Take Plain Text to Go...

If you do not want your messages to appear in the HTML format and want plain text instead, set the field next to Enable HTML E-mail to No. If you do choose to do so, remember that no pictures will be downloadable.

Who Wants Pictures?

If you want to retain the HTML format but do not want pictures to download automatically, set the Download Images Automatically to No. However, if you want to download a particular picture that has come as an attachment, you can do so by clicking on the Attachments in the message and downloading them individually.

General Options

General Options is in the same list as E-mail Settings, which is part of the Options menu in the Message Application (see Figure 4–14).

General Options	
Display	
Display Time:	Yes
Display Name:	Yes
Display Order:	Name, Subject
Display Message Header On:	2 lines
Display Message Count:	Unread
Display New Message Indicator:	Yes
Hide Filed Messages:	No
Hide Sent Messages:	No
SMS and Email Inboxes:	Theme Controlled

General Options	
Hide Filed Messages:	No
Hide Sent Messages:	No
SMS and Email Inboxes:	Theme Controlled
Separators:	Lines
Actions	
Make PIN Messages Level 1:	Yes
Auto More:	Yes
Confirm Delete:	Yes
Confirm Mark Prior Opened:	Yes
Keep Messages:	30 Days

Figure 4–14. *Setup pages for General Options*

It's On Display

You can alter and change the display order of name and subject, display the time, name, or message count, along with the display of new message indicator from here. Set the field according to your choice.

Hide and Seek

You can hide filed messages or sent messages from the General Options, too. Set the field to Yes or No for that reason.

Thirty Days Old

Decide for how long you want the device to store your e-mail messages. By default, it comes preset to 30 days. You can change it ranging from 15 days to forever, based on your requirement. But remember, as was mentioned earlier, even though the messages get deleted after the completion of the time period on your handheld, they will not be affected on the server.

Spell Check

Needless to say, this also is an option made available in your Options menu. Here, you can set your spell check requirements based on:

- Whether the case should be ignored or not (capital and small letters)
- Whether the acronyms should be ignored or not (short forms of words)
- Whether the words with numbers should be ignored or not
- Whether the application should spell check automatically before sending
- Whether it should check spellings as they are typed

You also have an option of creating your own Custom Dictionary, so that your specific lingo is incorporated (see Figure 4–15).

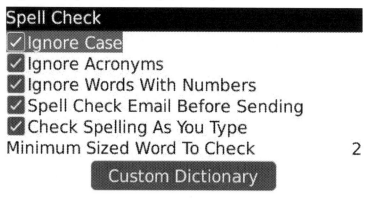

Figure 4–15. *Page where spell check options can be edited*

What's Next?

From notes tied around pigeons' necks to electronic mailing, messaging has come a long way. Today with the flexibility that the BlackBerry provides, any form of messaging apart from the e-mail might seem obsolete. However, let's not jump to conclusions. Some of BlackBerry's unique features might help restore the value of traditional messaging, which has primarily been reduced to a form of casual communication. Throw in the PIN messages, and you have got one exciting chapter ahead!

Chapter 5

BlackBerry for Text and Multimedia Messaging

The Shorter, the Better

"Sup? R u gonna do dinner tonight? Meet me @ 5G in 20."

As ridiculous as the above statement may seem, in reality it is a confirmation of dinner plans between two people. This kind of language usage—typical to SMS and text messaging—is probably one of the reasons texting has been reduced to more of an informal medium of communication. What is interesting though is the reason for the development of such a language. Notice the short forms that have been used through the message. Most words were abridged in such a manner because of the tedious methods of typing that were demanded by traditional handsets. To add to that, the common option of "dictionary" wasn't available either. Thus came into prominence this edited version of language.

But now, with your BlackBerry, messaging has been made simpler, more effortless, and quicker than ever before. The QWERTY keypad of the BlackBerry conveniences typing to a great extent, luring us to believe that text messaging probably stands a chance to be restored to its former importance.

So, what is an SMS? It is a means of communication. If the correspondence has been carried out successfully, the SMS has done its job. Is SMSing for work too much of an illusion? Let's explore.

Your BlackBerry and Messaging

Messaging as a feature had gained enormous popularity in the recent past. The growth, however, has not been restricted to text messages alone. Various forms of communication have been built in to your BlackBerry that provide a flexible platform for your communication needs. Whether your preference lies in instant messaging (through

Google Talk, Windows Live Messenger, Yahoo! Messenger, or BlackBerry Messenger), e-mails, SMS, or MMS; the BlackBerry has a solution for all that and more.

BlackBerry, in addition to other messaging options offered by other smart phones, has a special texting feature, unique to it alone. This allows free messaging between two BlackBerry users irrespective of their geographical location, absolutely free of charge. All that is required is the PIN number of the other user, which can be saved along with the contact details of the person.

SMS and MMS

Short Message Service or SMS is a service offered by the GSM digital cellular telephone system which allows the user to send and receive short messages (160 alphanumeric characters) which are displayed on the mobile screen. The popularity of SMS as an application is not only apparent but also convenient. For instance, statistics claim that in the 2008 US elections, mobile campaigning proved to be an attractive and effective alternative to traditional campaigning methods (according to a study carried out by researchers from Princeton and Michigan Universities, along with the US Student Public Interest Research Group (PIRG) New Voter Project Mobile Voter, and Working Assets). This very fact has also been illustrated by Airwide Solutions' Vice President of Product Marketing, Chris Lennartz. You can refer to his article through this URL: http://www.mobilemarketingmagazine.co.uk/2008/11/mobiles-big-mom.html.

The fact that text messaging is one of the most-used applications, among all cell phone users, has been common knowledge for a while now. But with the simplicity that the BlackBerry has brought to sending and receiving e-mails, this could easily be argued.

An MMS (short for Multimedia Messaging Service) is very similar to the SMS, with the added advantage of attaching a video clip, sound file, or image along with the text.

These are charged applications and the rates depend on the service provider or the plan that has been opted for by the user. Typically service providers offer bulk plans where you can buy 100, 500, or unlimited SMS and MMS messages for a fixed price. It is also important to note that there are usually different plans for domestic versus international messages.

BlackBerry's SMS Application

Your BlackBerry device comes with all the presets or elements required to send and receive an SMS along with a notification (through an assigned tone) at the receipt of a message. However, make sure the message is restricted to 160 characters or less, for longer messages are likely to get broken down into multiple messages. You can send a message to up to ten recipients at the same time by specifying the required contact details in the "To" column of your message box.

Sending an SMS

The exact process involved in sending an SMS differs according to your BlackBerry Model, but the design and thought remain constant. You can send a message in two ways:

- By going through the Text Messaging feature on your home screen (please refer to Figure 5–1).

- By going through your address book and choosing the desired recipient first.

Figure 5–1. *Message application in the menu for the operating system v4.6*

In the first case, after you open the Message application, your Message Inbox will list the received and sent messages in chronological order, showing the most recent communications at the top (see Figure 5–2).

Here, you can either reply to a message already in your Inbox, or you can select the Compose message option by clicking on the Menu button. After doing so, select the recipient of the message by either:

- Typing the name of the person in the "To" column. After you do this, your BlackBerry will list the names of the people from your address book to choose from.

- If the person is not a contact in your address book, then you may need to add the number to your contact list. Make sure you include the country or area code for later convenience (though country code isn't a requirement for local SMSs).

- You can also just type in the number of the recipient, and then add her as a contact afterward.

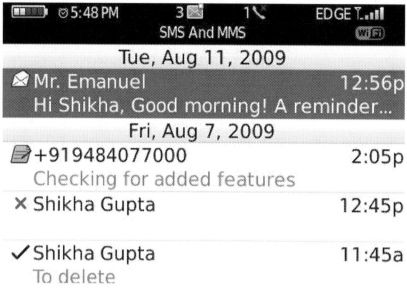

Figure 5–2. *Screen illustrating different icons in the inbox*

Once your receiver has been established, enter your message in the text box and press the Menu button. If you are using a device with a trackpad or a trackball, then you may press on this too for the desired option.

When you do this, the BlackBerry will list out a number of options for you including saving a draft of the message and checking spelling. Now choose the Send option. The sent messages will appear along with your received messages, and can be differentiated by specific icons next to the message.

If you want to use your address book to find a recipient before starting the messaging application, you need to open the Contacts application first, after which you can select the preferred person from your list using your trackball. Once you have chosen the contact, press the menu button for a list of options including sending an SMS. After choosing this option, you will land on the text page, and the process of typing the message and sending it remains the same as above.

Delivery Notifications for Sent Messages

Sometimes, you're not sure if your message was received properly. A late or no reply could either mean that the message had not been sent properly, was lost in transaction, or improperly received. Though these are rare instances while using a BlackBerry, they aren't unheard of. This kind of confusion could lead to miscommunications and affect business relationships gravely. You could counter that by requesting a Delivery Notification of messages to be sent. For this, you need to click on SMS in the Device Options. Set the Delivery Reports field to On and save it through the Menu key.

Receiving an SMS

When you receive an SMS, along with the tone notification, an icon appears on your home page that suggests the presence of unread messages in the Inbox. To access these messages, simply select the SMS and MMS option from your Menu. Unread and read messages can be differentiated by the icons next to the message. See Figure 5–3.

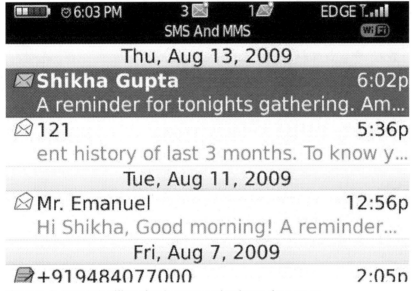

Figure 5–3. *Icons help differentiate between read and unread messages*

Deleting an SMS

Deleting an SMS (sent or received) is very simple. All you need to do is select the particular message from your Inbox and press the Menu button. After doing this, select Delete and after confirming your wish, the phone will delete the message.

NOTE: The SMS application may aggregate conversations to provide a better picture of the flow of the dialog. This is called the history. Just the history of an SMS can also be deleted by pressing on the Menu key while replying to a message and selectingRemove History.

BlackBerry's MMS Application

Media messages are very similar to text messages with the added advantage of attaching a video, image, or sound clip. You can send and receive messages that are in any of the file formats shown in Table 5–1.

Table 5-1. *Accepted Media File Formats*

Format	Description
.avi	Audio Visual File Format
.mpg	Sound File Format
.jpg	Image File Format
.gif	Animated/Image File Format
.wbmp	Image File Format
.midi	Sound File Format
.vcf (vCard)	Contact Card/Business Card Format
.ics (iCalendar)	Calendar Format
.mov	Movie Clip

Sending an MMS

Like the SMS, you could choose to send an MMS either through the MMS option on the Main Menu or by going through Contacts.

After establishing the recipient of the MMS and feeding in the text (if any), a click on the Menu button or the trackball lists various attachment options. Select the desired attachment (video, picture, audio, or voice note) depending on where the file is saved on your device, and then choose send. There is a possibility that the desired image is not already part of your library. You could also take a picture (by selecting the Camera option) at this point which then becomes your attachment.

> **NOTE:** You should always view the size of the MMS before sending it out. This is because some service providers have an upper limit to the size of the image sent and a very heavy file might not be received. However, the BlackBerry does downsize the image to an extent. You can check the size by choosing Options from the Menu key of the MMS. The Estimated Size field shall display its size.

MMS Attachments—Contacts or Appointments

You could attach a contact or an appointment to your MMS too. While composing the MMS message, through the Menu key, select either Attach Contact or Attach Appointment (with the desired details selected from your Address Book or Calendar) and click on continue. Refer to Figure 5–4 for an example of an attached contact's details in the message box.

To: Meenal Ahuja
Subject: Shikha's number

Shikha Gupta

Figure 5–4. *An MMS with a contact's details attached*

This feature also allows you to save a contact or an appointment from an MMS received. In the MMS message, highlight the iCalendar attachment for an appointment or the vCard attachment for a contact. Click on the Menu key and follow instructions to save the details successfully.

BlackBerry's PIN-to-PIN Application

BlackBerry handsets and BlackBerry enabled devices are identified on the wireless network using the PIN. A PIN is nothing but a Personal Identification Number. Every BlackBerry handset has its own unique PIN which can be used for communication between BlackBerry users.

Sending a PIN message involves selecting the contact from your Address Book and choosing the PIN option before proceeding. The rest of the process is very similar to sending an e-mail.

On delivery of a PIN message, a D with a check mark will appear in the message list beside the PIN message.

> **NOTE:** You could also include voice messages and picture files to your conversations. To do so, just press the Menu button on your handset during the conversation and select the desired function.

Finding Your PIN Number

Your PIN number is clearly written on the box of your handset. If for some reason, you have misplaced your box or do not have access to it, you could also get your PIN by typing 'mypin' and a space in the subject box of an e-mail message. As soon as you do this, your PIN number will appear on the screen (see Figure 5–5).

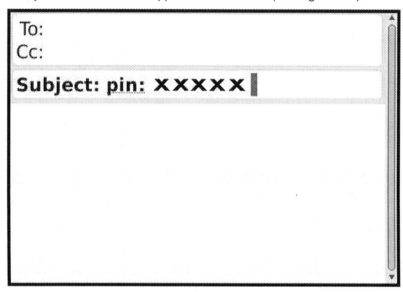

Figure 5–5. *Sample screen of PIN display*

Messaging for Work, Not Just an Illusion

In this section, you will find listed a number of industries and uses of the text message in a professional setup that have become so common that they have stopped registering.

The professional world has been wary of text messaging, and rightly so. It is often considered too informal a means of communication. However, its effectiveness and efficiency cannot be argued and have played a pivotal role in promoting it to the professional realm.

- Even if text messaging as a means of communication with clients might still be frowned upon, its competence in delivery within the organizational structure and communication between coworkers remains commendable. Quick updates about rescheduling meetings or sudden changes can be completed successfully. This is especially effective while communicating with teammates and employees who use traditional devices without push technology or instant e-mail options. Similarly, communicating while in a noisy environment can get quite difficult. Text messaging can be a simple and highly valuable substitute to talking.

- Text messaging is also a great alternative to providing and receiving instant information, in the unlikely event of server or phone line breakdown. It could be used to direct people to your mobile number temporarily so that you always stay connected with your client and customer.

- Tracking packages and shipments has been made very easy through messaging, as they keep you clued in at all times along with important information.

- Flight details and changes in schedule are another big advantage of text messaging. Though the BlackBerry also makes this possible through other notifications such as e-mail, an instant text message with crucial information for traditional device owners proves to be an invaluable boon.

- Mobile marketing and product updates are other areas where text messaging has proved beneficial. Customers can sign up for regular information on new products, discounts, and offers which could be seasonal or singular.

Convenient Shortcuts for Messaging

BlackBerry has devised many shortcuts for messaging that are time saving and delightfully handy. Here are some of them:

- When a message is opened, you could either:

  - Press R to reply

  - Press F to forward

- When in a message list, you could do the following:

  - Press Enter to open the highlighted message

  - Press C to compose and e-mail from the message list

  - Press Alt + U to mark a message as opened or unopened

  - Press Alt + O to view sent messages

  - Press Alt + I to view received messages

  - Press Alt + S to view all messages

  - Press Alt + P to view call logs

- To navigate within the message list, you could do the following:

  - Press T to get to the top of the list

  - Press B to get to the bottom of the list

  - Press Shift + space to move to the top of the page

- Press space to move to the bottom of the page
- Press N to move to the next date
- Press P to move to the previous date
- Press U to open unopened items

Other Features Offered

Some of these clever elements included in your messaging application could prove greatly advantageous. These appear in a list for you when you click on the Menu button while typing a message in the text box.

- *Spell Check*: A quick spell check never hurt anyone, did it? Especially if your SMS is official, a spell check could save you much embarrassment. So after typing out your message, be sure to do one by selecting it from the list.

- *Switch Input Language*: Some of the language options include Spanish, French, German, Italian, and Cantonese, to name a few.

- *Save Draft*: You could save a draft of the message being sent.

- *Show Symbols:* Can't find the desired symbol on your keypad? A simple alternative is to view all the symbols through this option.

- Clear Field: Instead of tediously deleting a typed message, a simple Clear Field option provides the perfect solution. This will require a confirmation on which the entire text will be deleted.

PLEASE NOTE

If you have more than one number assigned to your BlackBerry, the phone sends messages from the first number that appears in the drop down which is at the top of the screen in your phone application.

Also, if you own a corporate owned BlackBerry, you might not be able to use the PIN-to-PIN application as it does not document the messaging on paper, which could reflect as a liability for the company.

You can forward SMS messages as PIN or e-mail messages too.

What's Next?

Birthdays, anniversaries, meetings, rescheduling appointments, parties, concerts, bookings—the list is endless. With busy lives come busy schedules. And busy schedules bring with them the need to plan and program. Who could do that better for you than BlackBerry's Calendar Application? It's time to indulge, for the BlackBerry Calendar will certainly pamper.

Chapter 6

Calendaring on Your BlackBerry

A Grid, a Date, and a Few Numbers…

Who doesn't like customization? From a tailor-made suit to kitchen cabinets specially designed for your needs, customization has always pleased. Well, that's exactly what the BlackBerry Calendar does for you. Its flexibility and ability to adapt to your requirements plays a pivotal role in making it one of a BlackBerry's most valued features.

Setting Up Your Calendar

The obvious question here is: "What is there to set up in a calendar?" I agree that a calendar is a display table of the days, weeks, or months in a year (like the week view that you see in Figure 6–1), but your BlackBerry has many functions over and above this, such as a personal scheduler, an alarm clock, and a reminder.

You could format your calendar to the extent of establishing the first day of the week (as per your convenience), the start time, and the end time of your day (see Figure 6–2). This can be altered by going to Options which appears on clicking the Menu button on your Calendar. Select General Options to set up.

Figure 6–1. *Typical monthly view of the calendar*

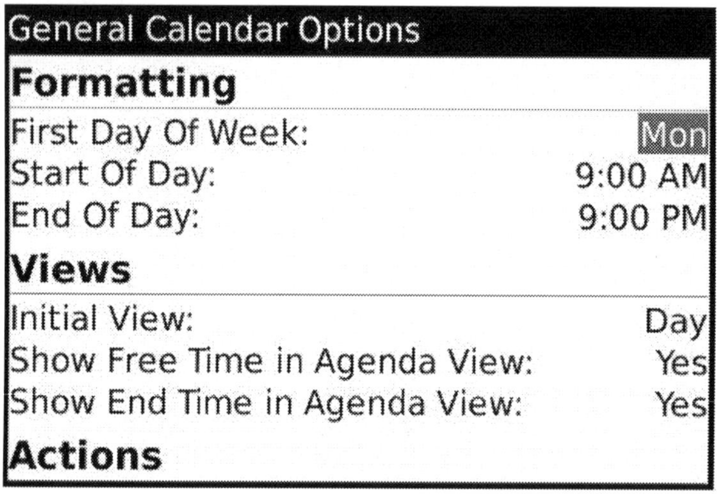

Figure 6–2. *Alter your calendar details according to your convenience*

Making Each Day Count

Among others, the BlackBerry offers four basic views. These are: Day, Week, Month, and Agenda, which display your schedules and appointments accordingly. You can switch from one to the other by simply choosing the most appropriate one from the Menu list or by using some special shortcuts which are listed later in the "BlackBerry Calendar Tricks" section. Apart from the basic views, you also have the option of Last View. This view maintains the last format in which you had exited the Calendar Application, so that you return to the same page on reopening.

Schedules, Memos, and Tasks

Making entries and scheduling appointments is very easy. All you have to do is highlight the date of the meeting with the help of your trackball. Once the date is established, click on the Menu button which will list various choices for you. Here select the New option and set up your appointment. You can enter details like the location of the meeting, the duration of the meeting, whether it is confirmed or tentative, as well as its recurrence (see Figure 6–3).

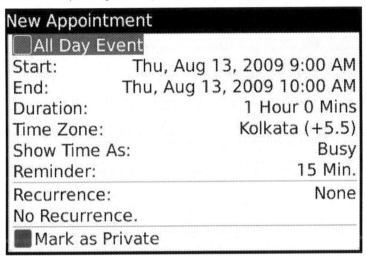

Figure 6–3. *Sample screen with filled in appointment details*

There Goes My Alarm

You could set yourself an alarm either by going through the calendar option or by selecting your clock.

- In the Calendar, highlight the particular date (if you are in the Month view) or the desired hour (if you are in the Day view) and press the Menu button. Here, select New Alarm and fill in details such as Subject and Time. Don't forget to confirm its recurrence too.

- On selecting the Clock option from the menu bar, you will see a display of the time and the date (see Figure 6–4). Here, press the Menu button and select Set Alarm. Once the alarm is set, make sure you select Save. The nature and sound of the alarm can also be altered. To customize this, you need to go to your Profiles Application. Here, go to the Advanced option. On doing that, select the Normal profile. When you do this, a list of applications will appear which require notification specifications. Choose Calendar from this list and alter the Out of Holster and In Holster fields according to your requirements. You can set the number of times it vibrates, number of beeps, volume levels, and repeat notifications among others.

Figure 6–4. *Display of time, date, and preset alarm*

Clear the Clutter

Deleting is as important a task as scheduling. It not only simplifies understanding but also makes space in your memory for crucial future entries. To do so, just highlight the appointment, meeting, or alarm and select Delete from the Menu options.

Desktop Synchronization

Let's assume a scenario. You have meetings and appointments set up on your e-mail calendar which is on your desktop. You are out at a business lunch and accidently bump into a group of old friends at the restaurant. They force you to join them in celebrating one of their promotions. You do not have access to your schedule and your handheld devices' calendar shows a free slot. You give in and miss a very important appointment with a client which could very easily have been rescheduled. Ouch! Not so pleasant, is it? What purpose did your handheld calendar serve? Neither did it remind you of your prior commitment, nor did it help you reschedule it. The point being, multiple calendars that do not synchronize information between each other are far more dangerous than no calendars at all.

The BlackBerry offers the option of synchronizing your desktop calendar with your handheld scheduler, so that you always stay on top of things. For more details on synchronization, refer to Chapter 2.

Yet, a quick review never hurt anyone. Let's quickly go over the main synchronization steps discussed in Chapter 2 with special attention to Calendaring.

1. Launch BlackBerry Desktop software in your computer.

2. Connect your device with it using the USB cable.

3. Select Synchronize from the options on the screen.

4. The Synchronize Organizer Data box should be checkmarked.

5. Open the Configuration tab (on the top of the page) and choose Configure Synch.

6. Now the program that is used to store the data on your computer will be the one highlighted here (for instance Microsoft Outlook, Groupwise, and so on). However, you can also change this option to another one from this point so that your calendar syncs with another program.

7. Make sure the Calendar is checked and select OK.

8. Go to the Synchronization tab and select Synchronize Now.

That's it. Your synchronization should commence.

> **NOTE:** Check out Chapter 11 for details on Google Calendar and syncing options.

Wireless Calendar

Often due to changing schedules, calendar entries change rapidly causing discrepancies between handheld devices and desktop calendars which require a USB cable or cord to synchronize data. With the wireless feature of the BlackBerry, your desktop calendar and your handheld scheduler automatically synchronize data so that any entry or change made anywhere shall be accessible from everywhere. To synchronize your desktop calendar with your BlackBerry, all you need to do is set the Wireless Synchronization field to Yes, which is part of your Calendar Options.

Some added advantages being:

- Flexibility to accept or decline meetings from your BlackBerry directly.

- Initiating meeting requests from your handheld device.

- Inviting attendees using your address book.

- Uniformity of changes made across desktop, e-mail, and handheld calendars.

- Confirmed security with end-to-end encryption.

Added Features

When a certain task, meeting, or schedule is opened, by clicking on the Menu button, you get a list of choices which enhance your calendaring experience greatly. They are as follows:

- *Spell Check*: This feature can really save you from a spelling disaster. You could accept the suggested spelling by selecting the highlighted word, ignore it by pressing on the Escape key, ignore all instances by selecting Ignore All, or add the word to the custom dictionary. To stop the spell check, simply choose Cancel Spell Check. Make sure you use this, for you could be saved of many a faux pas in front of your subbordiantes… ooops, subordinates?!

- *Invite Attendee*: The BlackBerry also offers the ability to invite people to the meeting as you set it up on your own calendar. However, to avail yourself of this feature, your BlackBerry must be associated with an e-mail account that uses BlackBerry Internet Service or the BlackBerry Enterprise Server (as was illustrated in Chapters 2 and 4). After typing the meeting details, click on the Menu button and select Invite Attendee. This will take you to your contact list. Select the attendee/attendees and click on Save. Voila, you just scheduled a meeting and announced it too.

- *E-mail All Attendees*: After establishing the attendees, you could also simply send them an e-mail illustrating the details of the meeting. This option will take you to your e-mail application where the attendees' addresses will be set, with a blank subject box for you to update them on any processes involved regarding the scheduled meeting. Apart from this e-mail, the attendees will also receive an invite in their mail inboxes displaying the details of the appointment.

NOTE: As this application sends out invites to the e-mail addresses of the invitees, make sure you have correct/appropriate e-mail addresses stored along with their details in your Contacts.

Confirming Your Presence

Nothing makes a better impression than a quick response to a meeting invitation. It displays your commitment and efficiency. Responding is probably one of the simplest processes. When you receive an invite in your e-mail inbox from the sender, press the Menu key and select one of the three options: Accept, Tentative, or Decline. You could also add your comments to go along with your RSVP.

If you are unsure of your availability, you could also check your own calendar simultaneously. In the Menu options, click on View Calendar. Once you have scanned your schedule, press the Escape key to return to the invite.

Change List of Invitees

Remember, you must be the meeting organizer to carry out this task. Here, you need to highlight a contact in the Accepted or Declined field. When you press the Menu key here, you can either Invite Attendee (on doing this, a new attendee is added to the list); Change Attendee (this replaces the currently highlighted invitee); or Remove Attendee (this option removes them from the list). Select Save in the Menu options to complete the process.

Multiple Calendars

If you are someone who likes to keep business and pleasure separate, and if your BlackBerry is synchronized with multiple e-mail accounts (work and home) that have different calendar entries, this section is for you.

You could switch between calendars by selecting the desired calendar under the Select Calendar option which will appear when you press the Menu key. Differentiating between different calendar entries is as simple as color coding them. To assign a color to entries from a calendar, do the following:

1. Press the Menu key in a calendar and click on Options.

2. Choose a calendar and change its Appointment Color.

3. Press the Menu key and select Save.

BlackBerry Calendar Tricks

To use these shortcuts, you need to set the Enable Quick Entry field to Yes. This can be altered from the General Options. Select the Calendar application and click on the Menu key then Select Options. After this, select General Options and set the required fields accordingly.

- **Adding Appointment**

    1. Use your trackball to highlight the desired hour in the Day view.

    2. Type in your details and click on Enter.

- **Modifying Appointment**

    1. Use the trackball to select an existing appointment and select Enter.

    2. Now you can edit the name, location, time and date of the appointment and press Enter.

- **Modifying time of Appointment**

    1. To add a specific appointment time that ends in x:15, x:30 or x:45, select the slot closest to the desired time.

2. Type in the entry.

3. Press Alt and scroll the trackball. Select the desired time and press Enter.

▦ **Deleting an Appointment**

Highlight an entry with the help of the trackball and hit backspace.

If you set the Enable Quick Entry field to No, then:

a. Press D to get to the Day View

b. Press M for the Month View

c. Press W for the Week View

d. Press A for the Agenda View

e. Press T to go to today's date

f. Press G to go to a specific date

What's Next?

Gone are the days when one knew a handful of people and you owned one number alone. Multiple addresses, multiple numbers, and multiple ids seem to be the need of the hour. This is networking at its best. With this comes the added requirement of contact management. Read on to see how the BlackBerry simplifies this for you.

Chapter 7

Contact Management on Your BlackBerry

Friends, Family and Business Associates...

According to a survey carried out by UPI, nearly 65% of Americans lost their cell phones in the year 2005 (http://www.textually.org/textually/archives/2006/07/012936.htm)! Now a number like that screams for attention. Most people who lose their phones, apart from the cost of purchasing another, dread the loss of contacts and important information. The tediousness of jotting down contacts is far from practical thus making you solely reliant on your phone's address book.

No more! Your BlackBerry synchronizes your contacts and addresses so that no matter what may happen to your phone, you will still have all your client details intact.

Synchronize Your Contacts

Synchronization is the process of syncing data between the source and the targeted storage location while maintaining consistency in both. So synchronizing your contacts would be maintaining uniformity between your address book on your computer and your smartphone. If the data in the mobile device is different from that on your computer, either one can overwrite the other, depending on your settings and preference. The synchronization tool also warns you when there is a disparity in content, so that you can decide how to proceed. How is all this done? Well, the answer my friend is not blowing in the wind, but lies in the BlackBerry Desktop Manager. Your smartphone comes with the software, which needs to be installed on your computer or laptop. (For further details on synchronization, refer to Chapter 2.)

Once you have this in place, all you need to do is connect your handset with your desktop through a USB cord and the Desktop Manager should launch automatically. If it fails to do so, just click on the Desktop Manager icon. If it has been saved as a desktop shortcut, just click on that or from any other location where you saved it. Once opened, select Backup and Restore in the software and choose Advanced Options. After which, click on your contact list and select your backup option. Your contacts will copy onto your hard drive, which can then be transferred to another BlackBerry device at your convenience.

Adding a Contact

This is probably the simplest process ever. You could do this in various ways:

- By going through the Contacts application. Select Contacts in your main menu and highlight Add Contact, then click on the trackball or the Menu button. Clicking on the trackball will directly take you to the screen where you can feed in the details (see Figure 7–1). If you press on the Menu button, select New Contact to proceed.

- By directly punching in the number. Simply type out the number and then press the Menu button. Along with other options, you will see an Add to Contacts option. Select this and continue.

- By saving it from a message or your call log. In a message, call log application, or in a web page highlight a contact. Press the Menu button and choose Add to Contacts. Feed in the information as desired, and Save.

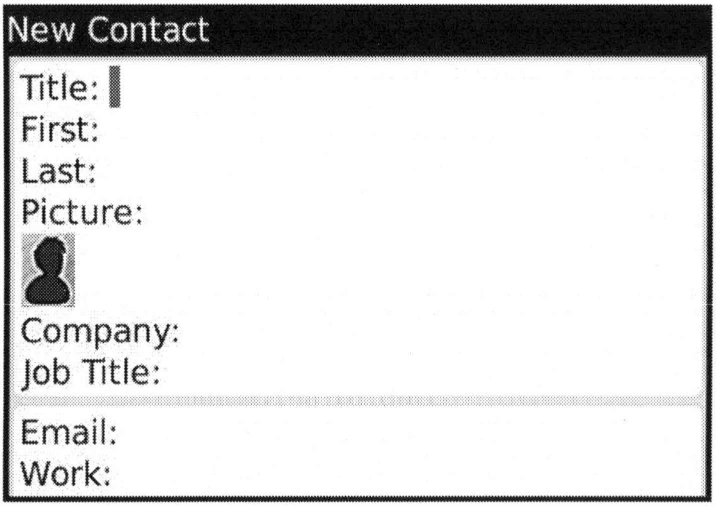

Figure 7–1. *Contact information screen*

NOTE: With the name and number of the person, you could also record other details such as addresses (work and home), e-mail addresses, web page links, birthdays, anniversaries, company names, and job titles along with special notes, to name just a few.

Deleting a Contact

Highlight the contact in your contacts list and press the Menu button. On choosing Delete, your prompter will ask you to confirm the command. On doing so, the contact will be deleted from your device. However, this does not erase the contact from your desktop, if the person's details have been synchronized already. Remember, if you choose to delete a particular contact, all of his her details (such as addresses, birthdays, and so on) will be erased from your device.

Then, when you launch the Desktop Manager next (with the device connected) it will start synchronizing your contacts so as to update any changes. At this point, upon detecting a change, it will prompt you, asking whether you would like to accept or reject the change. It will also allow you to go through the details before making a choice. If you do not want any changes to be made in your desktop address book, you could choose to cancel as well.

Editing a Contact

If you wish to make changes in any entry, you can edit the information too. Choose the Edit option from the menu and make your changes, after which you can select Save.

Customize Your Contacts

Customization is nothing but convenience. If you take a couple of minutes out to do this in the beginning, it will reap great benefits later.

Ringtones

You could assign specific ringtones to your contacts so that no matter where your phone is, you know your caller even before you get to it. This can work for you both ways—to decide when you want to or do not wish to take a particular call. Personalization is not only convenient but can also prove as a great stress buster. So whether your boss's ringtone is a screeching owl or your partner's is a cheesy love song, your customized ringtones will definitely be appreciated. However, on a more serious note, personalization of ringtones could prove tremendously advantageous in a professional context. Quick identification of your caller by the tune assigned to them could be quite a savior. Missing the call of your client or boss cannot go down well in any situation now, can it?

To do this, select Add Custom Ring Tone directly from the menu list that appears when you press the Menu button while a contact is highlighted. Change the ringtone as desired and Save.

Pictures

The problem of knowing too many people with common names is very possible. Your address book is sure to have duplication in this manner. So if you find yourself confused as to how you should tackle this problem, fear no more. Just assign their pictures to their names. You will always know exactly which Tom, Dick, or Harry is calling.

Adding pictures is very similar to assigning specific ringtones. For this, just as above, select Add Picture from the menu list while a contact is highlighted. Now you can either choose an existing picture from your Media library or take a new photograph through the Camera option. To use an existing picture Select the desired one. Here, you can center the picture according to your requirement. Press the Menu button and select Crop and Save. The picture has now been assigned to the contact (see Figure 7–2).

Figure 7–2. *Screen sample with contact image included*

> **NOTE:** You can delete or edit a picture at any time. All you need to do is highlight the picture and press the Menu button or the trackball for options.

Grouping Contacts

Grouping your contacts is a great idea as it reduces extra work and is a real time saver. By making these groups, you could send out SMSs, MMSs, e-mails, and PIN messages to everyone in that list without having to specify each contact individually.

To set up a mailing list press the Menu button in your contacts list and select New Group. Now type out the name by which you would like to call the group (for example, Administration team). After this, click on the Menu button and select Add Member.

Choose the contact(s) from your address book and choose Save Group. You could add as many members to a group as you desire before and after creating it.

You can change your list of members (add, delete, edit) at any given point. Just select Edit Group from the menu options when a mailing list is highlighted and Save Group once you are done.

Organization Address Book

Lost your phone and need to update all your numbers? Here is an effective and simple process, which in minutes will have most of your official contacts with you. This is a feature that uses your organization's address book as your reference point. In your menu list, choose the Lookup option. Type part of the contact's name and press Enter. You'll get a list of contacts as the result. Highlight a contact and press the Menu button. Here you could either add a particular contact, add all the contacts from that search result, view information about one particular entry, or delete a contact from the search results. It couldn't get simpler than this now, could it?

> **NOTE:** To make use of this feature, your BlackBerry device needs to be associated with an e-mail account that uses a BlackBerry Enterprise Server.

BlackBerry Contacts Tricks

Here are some useful tips and tricks when dealing with contacts on your BlackBerry:

- Many times, there are additional numbers like extensions that need to be remembered. For this reason, the BlackBerry gives you the Pause and Wait feature. You could include these extensions to the main number while feeding in the contact details by selecting it from the menu.

- If you want to change the way in which the names are displayed (last name-first name order) in all your applications, change the Name Display field which will appear when you choose Language from the Device application (see Figure 7–3).

- To check the number of contacts on your device, choose Options from the Contacts Menu list. Here select the contact list (Default) and the number of entries will appear (see Figure 7–4).

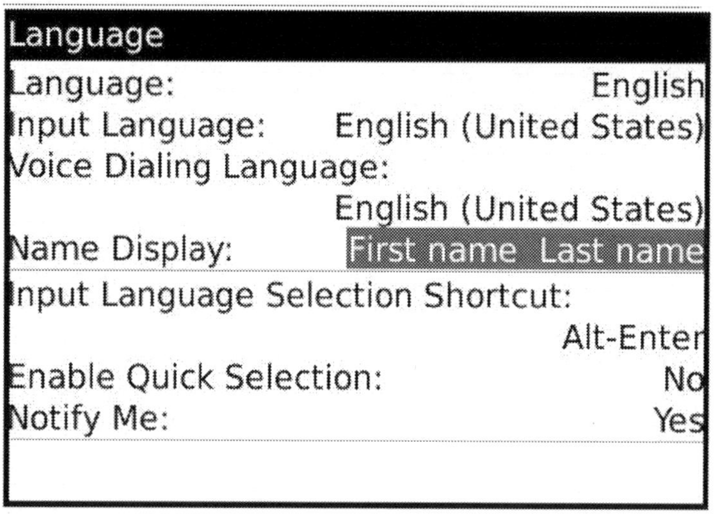

```
Language

Language:                            English
Input Language:      English (United States)
Voice Dialing Language:
                     English (United States)
Name Display:        First name  Last name
Input Language Selection Shortcut:
                                   Alt-Enter
Enable Quick Selection:                   No
Notify Me:                               Yes


```

Figure 7–3. *Screen to alter contact name display*

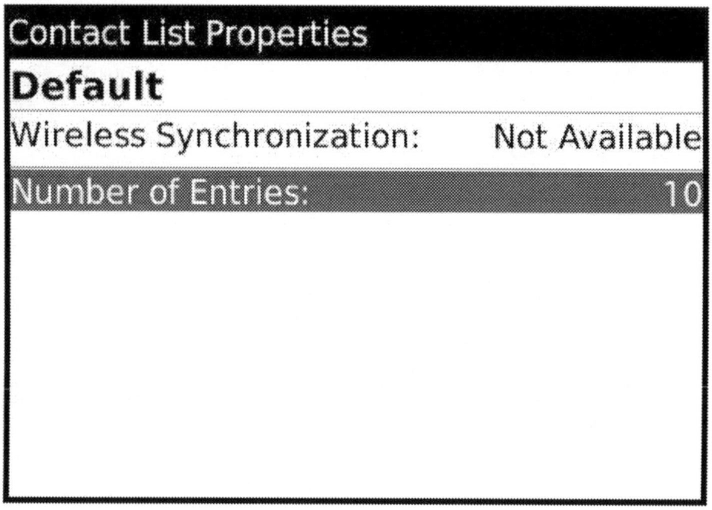

```
Contact List Properties
Default
Wireless Synchronization:    Not Available
Number of Entries:                       10




```

Figure 7–4. *Screen display of number of contacts/entries*

What's Next?

In this age of speed, the value of instant results is unparalleled. From fast food to racy cars, from immediate access to global information to communication, the world today is impatient. It wants it all and it wants it now. No one has the time, patience, or inclination to wait till they get their hands on a laptop or desktop in order to surf out information. Who better to quench that thirst for immediate gratification than the BlackBerry? Browse to your hearts content on this smart phone—super quick!

Chapter 8

Web Browsing

Browsing Experiences Enhanced...

What is a web browser? Is it a computer program used to access sites on the World Wide Web? Is it a program that interprets HTML coding so as to display formatted data? Well, it's all of the above and more; a web browser (or simply browser) is an application/software program that retrieves, interprets, and renders HTML or another language, such as JavaScript, so that the user can view web pages easily. Some of the popular web browsers online are: Internet Explorer, Mozilla Firefox, and Apple's Safari for Macintoshes. The act of locating and looking through these web pages is called web-browsing.

Understanding the BlackBerry Browser

Your handset comes with other pre-installed browsers as well as the BlackBerry browser. However, this choice of browsers depends on your service provider. You might want to check on this aspect so as to make a well-informed decision. You can also download and install browsers, irrespective of your wireless provider.

Along with the regular ones like Internet Explorer and Firefox, there are browsers that are exceptionally compatible with mobile phones like the Opera Mini and Safari for the iPhone. However, the traditional BlackBerry browser (though decently advanced) was one that had not made a real mark. Now, with the launch of the free software BOLT (which has been developed by Bitstream—who is responsible for BlackBerry Fonts), this browsing experience has been greatly enhanced. This offers a full PC-style browsing experience complete with rich media applications available to entry-level mobile phones as well. Along with browsers, most BlackBerry handsets also come with provisions of popular search engines such as Google, Live Search, Wikipedia, and Dictionary.com.

Basics

The browser icon (see Figure 8–1) can be selected from the Applications page or directly from the home page if it happens to be one of the first six applications. To learn more about moving applications, please refer to Chapter 2.

Figure 8–1. *The Browser icon on the Applications page*

The Browser landing page covers a taskbar-like feature allowing for URL feed-ins, a search engine (depending on the one chosen), a list of bookmarks, and recent history (see Figure 8–2). We will go through each of these features in detail through this chapter, as well as giving you vital tips, as always!

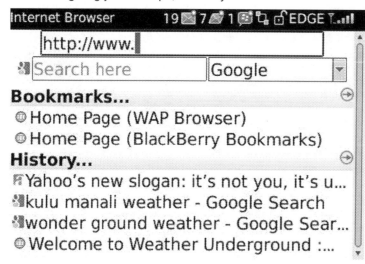

Figure 8–2. *Browser landing page along with fields for web page URL's, search engines, and Bookmarks along with History*

Options

By this point, no doubt you will have realized that this feature holds the key to most of your problems and settings. Therefore, we will touch upon it first. To get to Options, press the Menu button on the browser page. From here, you will be able to establish Browser Configurations, General Properties, and Cache Operations. The details of which are described in the following sections.

Browser Configuration

This is your main settings feature. You can determine whether you want the browser to Support JavaScript or prompt you before you enable it, or Use Background Images and Embedded Media (such as multimedia files). If used, you can choose in which format you want the browser to be displayed, be it HTML/WML or both, as well as an option to first open either the Home Page, the Last Page Loaded, the Bookmarks Page, or the Start Page (see Figure 8–3).

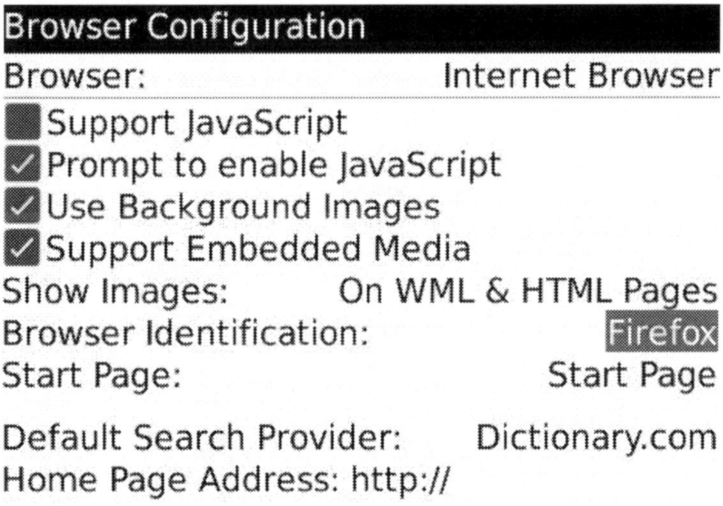

Browser Configuration

Browser: Internet Browser

■ Support JavaScript
☑ Prompt to enable JavaScript
☑ Use Background Images
☑ Support Embedded Media
Show Images: On WML & HTML Pages
Browser Identification: Firefox
Start Page: Start Page

Default Search Provider: Dictionary.com
Home Page Address: http://

Figure 8–3. *Illustration of the Browser Configuration page*

General Properties

This is the feature you need to turn to, in order to set up properties regarding display and quality. Using this option makes it possible for you to ascertain properties such as Font Family, Font Size, and Font Style (Plain, Bold, or Extra Bold). You could set your Default View to either Page (the original page layout with images, and so on) or Column (a listing of the contents of the page without maintaining the original web page design, which is faster to download); the image quality to Low (which is faster to download but of lesser quality), Medium, or High (which is slower to download but better in quality); along with Repeat Animations.

Also, decide when and where you would like Prompts by checking the box next to the option (see Figure 8–4).

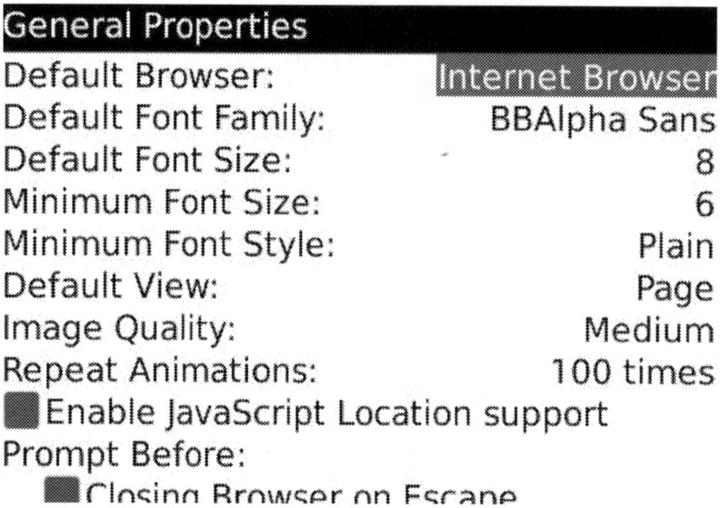

General Properties

Default Browser:	Internet Browser
Default Font Family:	BBAlpha Sans
Default Font Size:	8
Minimum Font Size:	6
Minimum Font Style:	Plain
Default View:	Page
Image Quality:	Medium
Repeat Animations:	100 times

■ Enable JavaScript Location support

Prompt Before:

■ Closing Browser on Escape

Figure 8–4. *Illustration of the General Properties page*

Cache Operations

Cache is a type of high speed memory. In the case of internet accessing, the Cache stores limited browsing memory and history so as to improve speed and reduce downloading time of the same pages over and over again. (In other words, when you access the same page over and over again, the browser displays the local copy instead of requesting the original over the Internet.) While deleting Cache memory is a wise choice when one is accessing the Internet through public computers, this isn't necessary if the system is used by one person or a core group.

Now, in your BlackBerry too, the Cache Operations primarily deal with this. They store content in the Caches, based on the type of data. From here, you could Clear History, i.e., Browsing history as well as clear the memory of the Content Cache, Pushed Content and Cookie Cache (see Figure 8–5).

- The Content Cache stores all the cached data, which happens as a result of regular browsing.

- The Pushed Content Cache stores information that is pushed to your handset, typically subscription services like tickers and updates, along with search engine preferences.

- The Cookie Cache stores information assigned to the browser by the visited web pages.

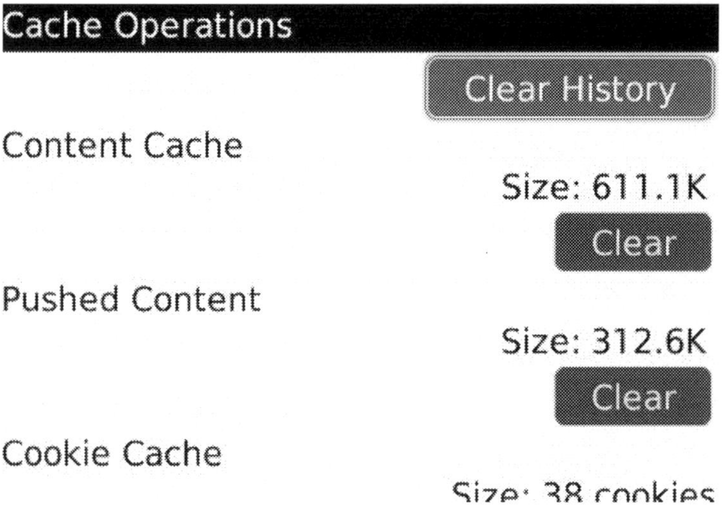

Cache Operations

Clear History

Content Cache

Size: 611.1K

Clear

Pushed Content

Size: 312.6K

Clear

Cookie Cache

Size: 38 cookies

Figure 8–5. *Illustration of the Cache Operations page*

NOTE: Clearing your history and caches clears up disc space and saves on your memory. It makes space for new app downloads too.

Web Pages

This section will concentrate on helping you move around in and between web pages, visit the desired ones, and maneuver through them like a pro. So without further adieu, let's get to some core facts:

- If a web page address field does not appear on the screen, you could also access it by pressing on the Menu button. Here, select the Go To option, type the address and Enter.

- Even if the "search here" feature (search engine) does not appear on the screen, you can search the Internet by going through the Go To option as above. Here, instead type the search details and Enter.

- If the history is not already illustrated in your browser landing page, you can go to it by selecting History from the Menu options.

- Choose Zoom In or Zoom Out from the options provided by pressing the Menu button while any web page is opened.

- Go to the previous or next pages directly by selecting Back or Forward from the Menu options.

- Save a web page by choosing the Save Page option from the Menu list. But remember that the current view of the contents of a page is what will get saved and not the whole page itself. The web page gets saved to the message list for further referencing.

- Choose Home from the Menu list to go back to the home page.

- The Refresh option refreshes the presently opened page.

- Select the highlighted multimedia file in order to play it. Upon doing do, you will be asked if you would like to Open or Save it. You could also just select Cancel if you wish for neither. After you have chosen to open it, the phone automatically launches and opens it in the Media Player so that accessing the content of the file becomes instant. (See Figures 8–6 and 8–7.)

Figure 8–6. *An example of a page with a media file (audio)*

From the Menu list, you can also choose the following:

- Select Page Address to view the address of a web page.

- Select Link Address to view the address of the highlighted link.

- Select Image Address to view the address of the highlighted image.

After you have selected one of these three options, your smartphone, as well as showing you the addresses, will give you Copy and Send options as well. From here, you can send the address to someone, copy it and paste it, or simply choose OK if you just wish to view it. If you choose to send the address to someone, you can also decide which medium you would like to use to do so—E-mail, PIN, SMS, or MMS.

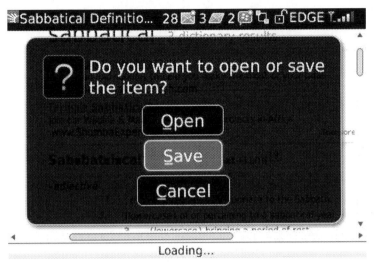

Figure 8–7. *Options given for the media file on selecting*

Bookmarks—More Than Just Folded Page-ends

Who remembers the time when education was on slate, and bookmarks were the bent ears or stripes of quotes on pages? Simple as needs were then, this setup sufficed and did it well. But today's world is all about swiftness and accuracy at your fingertips. So your little bookmarks have also undergone an exemplary transformation. Today it doesn't merely point out where you left off, but helps you capture the link for further use and frequent visits. You can also set it to check for updates periodically so that you always know what the latest developments on your favorite pages are. If a page that has been set is updated, the link to that page will appear in italics (see Figure 8–8).

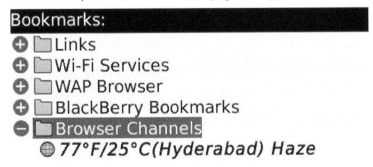

Figure 8–8. *The Bookmarks page with an updated link in italics*

If your bookmarks field does not appear on your browser landing page, you could go to it by selecting Bookmarks from the Menu list.

You can also change, send, or delete a bookmark easily. To do that, select Bookmarks from the Menu list. Highlight the bookmark you wish to edit and press the Menu button again. Here you could either choose Edit Bookmark, Send Bookmark, or Delete Bookmark, as per your requirement. You could also Add Bookmark from the same Menu list, if necessary.

After selecting Add Bookmark, you will be asked to specify the name and address of the web page/web site. Along with that, details of where you would like to save it (the folder in case of multiple options), the frequency of synchronization, the preferred browser details, and so on, will be enlisted. Choose the most appropriate for your requirements. You can also add and create folders from here.

Added Tip—Excuse Me! My Wallet's Ringing!

Now that is a sentence I never thought I would say. But with the BlackBerry, you'll soon get used to such conveniences and luxuries. So what I mean by this section's title is that the BlackBerry offers you an application called Wallet, brought to you by RIM. It helps improve the online shopping experience making it quick, easy, and effortless.

This application retrieves your personal data from the phone, helping you to fill out credit card details, shipping information, retail web site login details, and gift card information with just a few clicks (see Figure 8–9). You can be assured that all this information is as safe as can be… or actually as safe as your password. Even the main user cannot access this application without feeding in the password first, so make sure you have a complicated enough password to ward off unwanted snooping, yet a simple enough one that you wouldn't forget yourself.

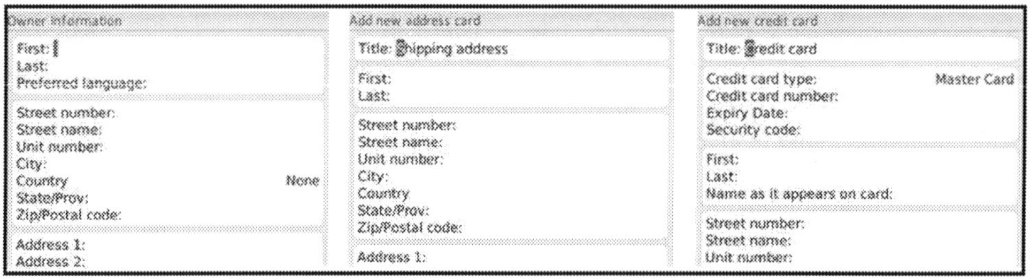

Figure 8–9. *Screenshots illustrating the information feed-in for the BlackBerry Wallet application*

However, it requires mobile Internet access along with an activated data plan. This application is available to the user at no extra charge. You could download it from mobile.blackberry.com from your smartphone or visit the blackberry.com website, using your computer. The app is also available at BlackBerry App World (details of which are covered in Chapter 14).

At the web site home page, go to the Smartphones category and select Smartphone Features. Select Browse, Shop, and Buy from this page and further narrow the search to BlackBerry Wallet. In the Download section, all you need to do is fill in an e-mail address (the one associated with your smartphone) and have a download link sent to your inbox. You can follow the instructions to complete the process.

Like I said earlier, this application is available at no extra charge. However, the charges associated with downloading the software (download time/browsing time) are determined by the data plan you opted for with your service provider. Please contact them for further details on this.

Tips and Tricks

- Press Alt + LGLG to view your event log. From here, after pressing the Menu key, you can copy the day's contents which can be shared with colleagues, as well as deleted, to free some memory space.

- Press Alt + CAP + H to bring up the Help Me screen, which lists details like PIN, IMEI, signal strength, battery life, and so on.

- Press Alt + CAP + Backspace to reboot your handset.

What's Next?

Calculators and memo pads, task trackers and password keepers, stock and weather updates along with a whole storehouse of applications…The BlackBerry's built-in functions are for all of you who want to get more out of your phone—games and media included! Now when BlackBerry does facilitate you for such exploitation, who wouldn't take advantage of it? Why settle for the basics when the premiums are available?

Chapter 9

Exploring Other Built-in BlackBerry Functions

Laurels in Its Kitty—and Still Growing

Though external accessories and third party applications do provide the BlackBerry with that extra personalization and appeal, they cannot compete with its built-in features. Let's just say, if push mail lies at the heart of your 'Berry, its ever dependable functions constitute its soul.

These functions are not only user friendly but also greatly beneficial to the professional user. Along with guidance through the usage of the applications, we also list some of their numerous uses in the world of business.

Media, Gallery, and More...

Your Media application works like a warehouse of your music, pictures, videos, ringtones, and voice notes, all laid out for your perusal and use. You will find it in the Applications page, as shown in Figure 9–1. Once you select it, your landing page displays the various media functions that are available to you, such as voice notes, music, videos, pictures, and ringtones.

Voice Notes

Use this feature to hear and study your recorded voice notes at anytime and anywhere. When you open the Voice Notes feature, it lists all your voice notes in chronological order, with the earliest at the top. Along with the name of the file will be the date and time of recording. The duration of the recording can be seen alongside (see Figure 9–2).

Figure 9–1. *The Media application on the Operating System v4.6*

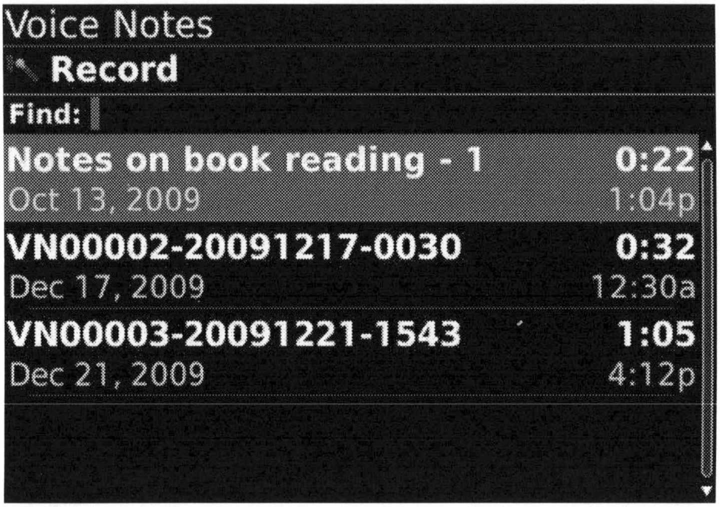

Figure 9–2. *A list of voice notes from the gallery*

You also have the option of recording a new voice note; the Find feature allows you to quickly locate any file that you might have recorded previously using the file name as the search term.

If you press the Menu button with one of the recordings highlighted, you will be given a whole list of options to choose from including:

- *Play*: Plays the recording.
- *Delete*: Erases the recoding after confirming the delete.
- *Record*: Takes you to the recording feature for fresh footage.

- *Rename*: Allows you to rename the file.

- *Properties*: Displays the size, location path and when it was last modified.

- *Send as E-mail*: Facilitates e-mailing of the file.

- *Send as MMS*: Facilitates sending the file as a multi media file.

- *Send to Messenger Contact*: Facilitates forwarding the file to a BlackBerry Messenger contact.

- *Set as Ringtone*: Helps set the chosen file as your ringtone.

- *Send using Bluetooth*: Allows you to send the file to someone via Bluetooth.

- *Options*: Takes you to the Media Options where presets can be altered.

- *Switch Application*: Assists in switching between multiple applications without losing the present screen.

- *Close*: Exits from the feature back to the Media page.

Pictures

Share special moments with friends and colleagues, go back in time to the magic of a vacation to beat the pressure and demands of professional life, rediscover your smile amidst tension or frustration… Ah! Pictures can do wonders for you. Along with the personalization they allow, picture galleries can also play important roles in the professional setup. Let's take a few careers as examples:

- *Real estate agent*: Maintaining a gallery of available properties will take you a long way; you never know where business might knock on that door. Preparation won't do you any harm.

- *Fashion coordinator*: It would be like maintaining a mini portfolio on your handset. It's advisable for you to keep pictures of photo shoots worked on and design elements added, so as to display your talent at the right time.

- *Educator*: Boring lectures seldom teach. Make your classes more interesting by adding projections of pictures from your gallery to help brighten the subject.

- *Social worker*: If you feel strongly about a cause and feel the need to fight for it, a few images in your gallery proving your stand might come in handy at any point.

Gallery Walk-through

Visit your gallery from the Pictures option of your Media application. Listed for you will be the following three options:

- *All Pictures*: Here you'll find all the saved pictures on your handset, irrespective of folders or categorization.

- *Picture Folders*: Here your pictures are sorted on the basis of folders created by you along with the location at which they are saved, i.e., device memory, external memory such as a Micro SD card, or media card.

- *Sample Pictures*: These are the pictures that come preloaded on your handset.

Other Available Options

An option to go to the Camera application directly from here is also available. After opening any section, you will find the pictures that come under that category. If you press the Menu button with any picture highlighted, the following options are presented to you:

- *View List/View Thumbnails*: You can either view the photos in a list format or as thumbnails. Whichever one is chosen and in use, the other option appears in the Menu list, just in case you want to switch.

- *Set As Home Screen Image*: Choose this option if you want to set the selected image as your home screen background image.

- Reset Home Screen Image: This option resets the home screen image to the one that was originally set on the device at the time of purchase.

- *View Slide Show*: If you would like to view the images in a slide show format, this is the option you should choose. By default, the duration each image stays on the screen is set to 2 seconds. You can adjust this to a duration ranging from one to fifteen seconds by altering it from the Media Options.

- *Set As Caller ID*: Assign the highlighted picture to a contact by choosing this option.

Along with the above, you also have the regular Open, Delete, Copy, Move, Rename, Properties, Send as E-mail, Send as MMS, Send to Messenger Contacts, Send Using Bluetooth, Receive Using Bluetooth, Options, Switch Application, and Close options.

Audio

With increasing work pressures comes the requirement to destress, and what better way to do this than listen to your favorite music in order to unwind? Relaxation through soothing music before a big presentation can really help calm those frazzled nerves.

Other than its recreational benefits, you can also use it for some business purposes. The spoken word is also important, so the following are some ideas for using music and the spoken word in your business life:

- You could download (from the Internet) or upload professional training courses which can be heard at your leisure.

- A great place to get some education programming that can be downloaded directly onto your BlackBerry is www.audible.com. Audible for BlackBerry can be downloaded either by registering your e-mail id (the one associated with your phone) at the online site, following which you shall receive downloading instruction on your device. Alternatively, you can also visit audible.com/bb from your handset Browser and download the app directly. Once the process is completed, you will be eligible to download and play audio from over 60,000 titles spanning across various genres.

- If your job requires you to be proficient in a language, you could train yourself through recordings of classes in it. There are a whole bunch of applications that you can choose from, depending on your requirement from the BlackBerry App World. Here, under Translation, you will find various third party applications that can be downloaded onto your handset.

- You could add appropriate music from your phone as the background score of a presentation to enhance the essence of the message.

- Its usage in the classroom by educators cannot be overlooked. Clips of animal sounds for instance, immediately bring life and interest into that 'Food Chain' chapter.

- For the media worker, a good collection of songs will never be wasted. You never know which edit might need inspiration. The BlackBerry App World has some great apps that can be downloaded, one of which is Pandora. This free application personalizes the radio for you so that your favorite songs and artists are explored, playing back music of your choice or requirement.

Podcasts, audio (or video, covered later) media files that are released by episode, cover many of the above items. They can be downloaded and reviewed through media syndication. There are a whole bunch of amazing podcasts that help in business training, concentrating specifically on tips, strategies, insights, leadership, and conceptual sales that can be downloaded from the web. A quick keyword search on any leading search engine yields great results.

There are various ways of listening to a podcast. One of them is to download it onto your computer and then transfer it to your device through Roxio Media Manager (from the Desktop Manager feature). You could also just visit the site directly from your mobile browser and download the audio file onto your handset. However, there might be data download limitations set by your service provider, so this option is not the most feasible.

Another method is to install a podcast aggregator and player that helps you listen to episodes directly on your handset. One such software is the PodTrapper. This by default is designed to download the latest two episodes of your preferred podcasts. PodTrapper Podcast Manager is brought to you by Versatile Monkey and is available for a minimal charge at BAW. A free trial is also available before payment requirements.

However, if you want to concentrate on the music, you will not be disappointed either. The application by default categorizes your music for you in seven sections (see Figure 9–3).

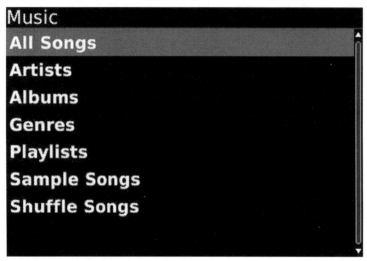

Figure 9–3. *The available music categories*

They are the following:

- *All Songs*: Here you will find all your songs.

- *Artists*: The songs in this section are filtered by artist.

- *Albums*: It is the various albums that provide the distinction in this section.

- *Genres*: Music of different genres is organized separately here.

- *Playlists*: Custom made, programmed music lists can be created from here. These playlists can be of two types—standard and automatic. A standard playlist is created by adding existing music files manually from your BlackBerry device. An automatic playlist is created by specifying an artist/genre/album criterion. Thus when a new song is added to your device, if it fits any of the stated criteria, it automatically gets added to the playlist. For further details on playlist creation and management, please refer to Chapter 13.

- *Sample Songs*: This is the set of songs that comes along with your device, preloaded.

- *Shuffle Songs*: This is a fun feature that shuffles the songs on your device in random order so that what you finally get is a medley of all your favorite songs.

For further options, you need to press on the Menu key with a song selected. Upon doing that, you will get choices such as Play, Add to Playlist, Delete, Properties, Set As Ringtone, Send Using Bluetooth, Receive Using Bluetooth, Options, Switch Application, and Close.

Video

It goes without saying that this feature is your video gallery. All recorded and downloaded videos can be found here. When you open the application, a list of previous videos is seen along with a Find and Video Camera option (see Figure 9–4). The Find feature is nothing but your search and the Video Camera takes you directly to your camera, from where a new video can be recorded.

If you are a marketing person, short video clips of the products you offer would be a wise choice. You could also download videos that help you train in your chosen field to better your skills. You can then study this on the bus ride home, or while waiting at the car wash, the flexibility is yours. The class comes to you on your handset.

Figure 9–4. *The list of Videos in the gallery*

Professional training videos are also available in the form of podcasts on the Internet. We covered podcasts in the audio section, so go back there if you need more information; the principles are the same for video.

Playback and maneuver by highlighting a video and press on the Menu button to see the following options: Play, Delete, Record, Rename, Properties, Send Using Bluetooth, Receive Using Bluetooth, Options, Switch Application, and Close. You also may have an addition option stating Send as E-mail, if the video in question is not one that came preloaded along with your device.

Ringtones

Set and adjust your ringtones from here. You can either set a ringtone that you downloaded or one that came with your device. It's uncomplicated and requires just one step. After launching the feature, you have three folders that help sort your ringtones, as shown in Figure 9–5.

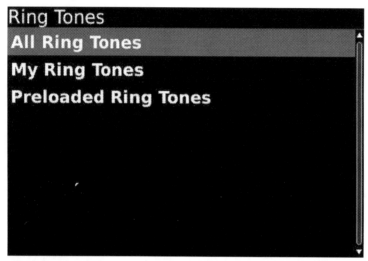

Figure 9–5. *Folders that help categorize your ringtones*

All Ring Tones

This lists all the ringtones, irrespective of whether they came along with the device or you downloaded them.

My Ring Tones

Here you will find the ringtones that you specially picked and downloaded from various sources including the Internet.

Preloaded Ring Tones

The ringtones that came along with the handset can be found here. If you choose to acquire new ringtones, even that can be done right from here. Carry this out in two ways, either by downloading a ringtone from the BlackBerry web site through your phone's browser or by receiving it using Bluetooth.

Download Ring Tones

There are certain download terms and conditions that are laid down by BlackBerry and your acceptance of them is vital for you to proceed. Click on I Accept, if you do so. Once you do this, the application will take you to the Ringtones section of the official BlackBerry site. From here, you can download as many ringtones as you would like to. Apart from Top Ringtones, you also have them listed in various categories including BB Fun, BB Groove, BB Holiday, BB Inspired, BB Intense, BB Pro, BB Tech, BB Relaxed, and BB Premium (see Figure 9–6).

Figure 9–6. *Ringtone downloads available at the BlackBerry site*

Transfer and Import Media

Receive and send media files to your computer and vise versa easily through the Desktop Manager software. You can also transfer files using Bluetooth, provided the device is Bluetooth enabled. The mass storage mode allows for quick transfer of data from your computer. To do so, just connect your device to the desktop/laptop using the USB cable. Once that is done, launch the Desktop Manager and select the Media Manager (Roxio Media Manager) tool. Afterward, all you have to do is drag the media files from one location to another. Thus whether you transfer files from your handset to your computer or the other way around, the process remains constant.

Sending and receiving files using Bluetooth is equally effortless. For this, you need to make sure your device is paired with a Bluetooth enabled device. Once that is done, do one of the following:

- *Receiving a media file*: Go to the appropriate media option and click on the Menu button. Select Receive Using Bluetooth. Select Yes and then Save.

- *Sending a media file*: Highlight the desired media file and click on the Menu button. From the list of options, select Send Using Bluetooth.

NOTE: To make sure you Bluetooth is on, just go to Manage Connections from your Applications page and verify that the box next to Bluetooth is checked.

Media Tips and Tricks

- Press N to play the next song in a category.

- Press P to play the previous song in a category.

- Press the Space key to shift the song controls to the bottom of the screen while you view a list of songs.

- Hold the Volume key Up to play the previous song.

- Hold the Volume key Down to play the next song.

- Press the Mute key to pause a video or song.

- Press L to rotate a picture.

- Press 3 to zoom into a picture.

- Press 9 to zoom out of a picture.

- Press 7 to return to the original size of the picture.

- Press 1 to fit the picture to the screen size.

NOTE: You will even find training courses at the BlackBerry App World (BAW) which is covered in Chapters 14 and 15. From BAW, you can download applications like Dictionary of Business Terms or Finance Glossary, that help you enhance your skills and usage of key terms.

Tick Tock, Tick Tock

It is your clock that warns you against time wastage. It is your clock that reminds you of forgotten tasks. It is your clock that guides you through various processes and it is your clock that takes on responsibilities, allowing for soundless sleep, and it is the clock we will discuss in this section.

Figure 9–7 shows the Clock application.

Figure 9–7. *The Clock application with the Analog clock display and set alarm*

When you open it, you will find a display of time, along with the date as well as the time set for the alarm (if any).

Apart from telling the hour of the day, the Clock also covers some other functions, such as Stopwatch, Timer, and Alarm. After pressing the Menu button while in the Clock application, you will see the following options:

- *Set Alarm*: You can set your alarm for all days as well as just weekdays, depending on your preference. Once you have set the alarm, you will see a clock indicator that appears on your Home screen.

- *Enter Bedside Mode*: This feature facilitates two main functions. First, it sets the clock as the display screen and leaves the backlight on dim, so that the screen doesn't black out. However, for the light to be on, the BlackBerry must be on charge. If it isn't so, the light will go off as after a few seconds, the screen defaults into the Backlight Time Out settings (if set to go out). Second, it blocks incoming calls and messages so that they do not disturb you. To exit this mode, just press the Escape key. After confirming the action, the Bedside Mode will be switched off.

▓ *Stopwatch*: This stopwatch helps you measure the time taken for any activity. This is especially good as it makes recording individual lap timings very easy. A clean design, with start and end carried out by the same button. A reset next to it makes for quick usage (see Figure 9–8).

Figure 9–8. *The Stopwatch feature that is part of the Clock application*

▓ *Timer*: You can set the timer to any duration and watch as the clock ticks backwards completing the time. For instance, the timer in Figure 9–9 is set to thirty seconds. Thus, when you select start, the timer starts calculating backwards (counter-clockwise) till it reaches the 60-second mark. To set the timer, click on the Menu options and select Set Timer. Once set, choose start.

Figure 9–9. *The Timer feature, which is part of the Clock app*

- *Options*: The Clock Options assists in determining the Clock, Alarm, Bedside Mode, Stopwatch, and Timer settings. The Clock settings help you lay down factors such as the clock face or type, be it Analog, Digital, Flip Clock, or LCD Digital; along with Home Time Zone and actions When Charging. The Alarm setting asks you to state the Alarm Type (Tone, Vibrate, Tone + Vibrate), Alarm Tune, the Volume of the alarm, the Snooze time, and the Number of Vibrations. While in the Bedside Mode section, you can affirm whether you would like to disable incoming calls and messages if it is turned on, by changing the Disable Radio field to Yes. Decide whether the Stopwatch and Timer clocks should display as Analog or Digital as well as the Time Tune and Volume from here.

- *Switch Application*: This helps you to toggle between multiple applications simultaneously.

- *Close*: This exits the application, taking you back to the Application List page.

> **NOTE:** Another great feature is that you can have two clocks displayed with two different time zones together. This is especially useful when you are out travelling and need to check your home time frequently. To do this, just go to Options and set your Home Time Zone accordingly.

Clicked

Keeping a camera handy can be one of the smartest things one does. Missing priceless moments sure is a bummer. That's why it has become such an integral part of any mobile handset today. Well, your BlackBerry isn't behind. The business uses of the camera are tremendous. You will notice how this application can be used by many professionals across various vocations. Let's explore some of them:

- *Research and development*: Most kinds of research and development that include involvement in the field have the added requirement to document what they see. For instance, taking pictures of available sites if you are a real estate agent or locations if you are a television producer is vital. If you are a corporate employee who works in administration and has been assigned to rekey available office spaces, a good camera will sure come in handy. Click-click and send, and they'll call it a job well done. If you happen to be the assistant in a fashion house, trying to organize photo shoots, you can be assured that the camera application will be used extensively, for getting approvals of costume, setup, lighting, and makeup will be essential.

▓ *Law and order*: This might digress a little from the "business" point of view but is important enough to be mentioned anyway. Suppose, for instance, that you have been in an accident that was no fault of yours. A few quick pictures of the scene will help you with that insurance claim as well as justify your stand to the law.

▓ *To substantiate an argument or claim*: The camera will also help you prove your innocence and efficiency. Suppose, for instance, that you work for an import and export company, and the latest shipment carried with it a few damaged goods which you refused to accept. Before the matter escalated, you took pictures proving your stand and sent them to the authorities concerned. By doing this, you proved not only your vigilance, but also your loyalty to the organization.

▓ *Advertisement*: A simple example to prove my point—you run a motel or a resort, and, on one occasion, a famous celebrity walks into your property. After serving them, you take a picture of them and include it in your brochures and pamphlets (with their permission, of course). There, you've advertised and with no great costs incurred.

▓ *Health care*: Even in this area the camera has some uses. Let's imagine a scenario where you are an archeologist, miles away from civilization. You hurt yourself very badly and need medical supervision till help comes. At this time a good camera and Wi-Fi connection can be your saviors.

▓ *Marketing*: A good camera can be an important tool used in marketing—like its presence as a selling point for a mobile company… I rest my case.

Third-party Business Applications That Require the Camera

We'll see more business applications in Chapter 15, but the following are a couple to inspire you just now:

▓ *Business cards*: A third party application by SHAPE services is the Business Card Reader that uses phone camera to capture details that are saved in respective fields in the address book. It is a scanning application that uses text recognition technology. The requirement though is a good camera with auto focus.

▓ *Expense tracking*: Oomph (Office on my phone) has launched the Mobile Receipt application. This allows you to take pictures of your bills and receipts and helps turn them into expense reports that can then be submitted, directly from the application itself.

Camera in Action

The BlackBerry Camera application provides some interesting features that help enhance your pictures and share them with everyone. After launching Camera from your Applications list, you will reach a screen with the image that is seen through the lens/viewfinder along with the option to zoom. Please review Figure 9–10. Apart from that, at the bottom left of the screen is displayed the number of pictures that can be taken before you run out of memory space. If you have been saving the pictures to your device memory, you can insert a media card so as to save more images. Also displayed to the right are details such as the amount of zoom and the use of flash.

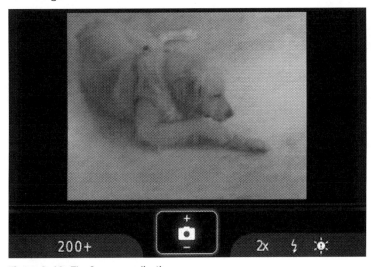

Figure 9–10. *The Camera application*

While in the Camera application, if you press the Menu button, the following options are made available to you:

- *Full Screen*: This increases the size of the screen, spreading the image across it. Press the Menu button and select Full Screen again to exit from it.

- *View Pictures*: This takes you to your photo gallery.

- *Video Camera*: Go to your Video Camera by choosing this option.

Apart from those, the regular Help, Switch Application, and Close are also available.

There also is another Options feature that brings to you a whole load of permutation-combinations that can be set for the desired effect. These settings are the following:

- *Flash Setting*: The flash option could be set to either On, Off, or Automatic. Automatic means that the camera uses the flash only when it is required, as would be the case in dim lighting.

▨ *White Balance*: It is a method to render the image of the subjects to a color as true to reality, thus removing excessive color casts and influences caused by color temperature. Your camera is set to Automatic White Balance by default. However, it also offers you the option to change to manually, thus setting it to suit light that reflects sunny days, cloudy days, night time, incandescent light, and fluorescent light.

▨ *Picture Size*: This is the size of the picture taken, that can vary from Large (1600 × 1200) to Medium (1024 × 786) to Small (640 × 480).

▨ *Picture Quality*: The picture quality is the fineness or clarity of a picture. This could be set at Superfine, Fine, or Normal. However, the better the image quality, the more space it takes up in the memory.

▨ *View Finder Mode*: Set your Viewfinder to Normal or Full Screen.

▨ *Color Effect*: The color effect feature allows you to choose between Normal, Sepia tones, or Black and White image settings.

▨ *Geotagging*: Enable Geotagging if you want the software to add geographical identification data to your pictures. This means that the software uses GPS to add geographical coordinates to your images.

▨ *Store Pictures*: Choose the folder in which you would like to save your images from here.

Video Camera

You can take videos from your mobile and send them to anybody as an e-mail attachment using this feature. To take a video, select the Video Camera feature from your Camera's Menu list. After that, press on the Record button to start your recording. To end it, press the same button again. Once you stop, the application gives you a list of options on the Control bar to choose from, as is illustrated for you in Figure 9–11. They are: Record, Stop, Play, Rename, Delete, and Send. Choose the appropriate one to proceed.

Figure 9-11. *The Video Camera application, with a video paused*

Camera Tips and Tricks

- Press 2 to pan up in a picture.

- Press 8 to pan down in a picture.

- Press 6 to pan right in a picture.

- Press 4 to pan left in a picture.

- Press 5 to return to the center of the picture.

- Press the Right Convenience Key to take a picture or to enter the Camera Application.

- Press the Symbol key to change the view finder setting.

- Press the Space key to change the flash settings of a picture.

- Press the Space key to turn low light mode for a video.

Applications, Anyone?

The Applications feature brings you a plethora of options to choose from, serving the purpose of a calculator, memo pad, and much more. Launch Applications to view all the options that come with your device, as shown in Figure 9-12.

Figure 9–12. *The list of apps available in the Applications folder*

The next few sections will discuss the various applications you can utilize and some of the core features.

Tasks

You can set yourself tasks as well as reminders for them, with occurrences as often or rare as you need them to be. Go to the tasks option from the Application folder and select Add Task. When you do so, you will be given a list of combinations vis-à-vis its repetition and recurrence. Once you have set the task, select Save from the Menu options. The various factors that determine the frequency of reminders are the following:

- *Status*: Set the status of the task, whether it has Not Started, In Progress, Completed, Waiting, or Deferred.

- *Priority*: High, Normal, or Low priority can be set for the task

- *Due*: This is the date from which the task begins. You can either choose None or By Date from its options. If you choose By Date, then you need to set a starting date, from which the task commences.

- *Time Zone*: Specify the time zone that is applicable to you.

- *Reminder*: You could set the reminder to None, By Date, or Relative. Choosing the By Date option opens another factor that is Recurrence. Set it to Daily, Weekly, Monthly, or Yearly as per your requirement. Choosing the Relative option requires specification on how often you would want the reminder. You can choose the appropriate one from a range of one minute to one week.

- *Categories*: Specify whether this is a Personal or Business task.

- *Notes*: Make special notes for better referencing.

Figure 9–13 shows an example task.

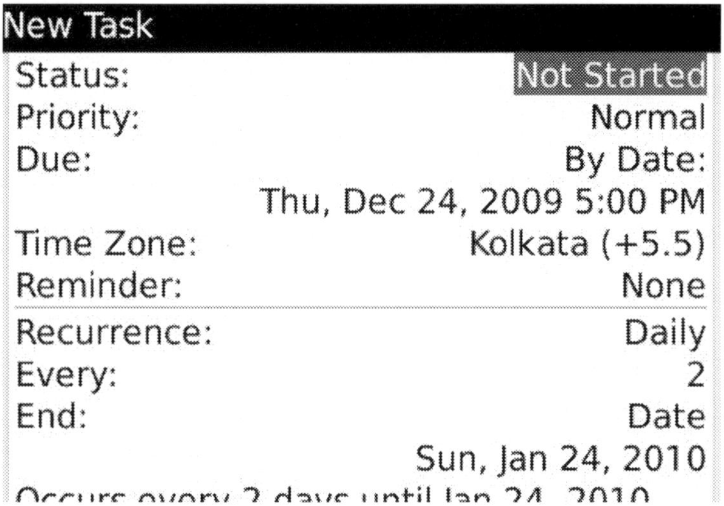

```
New Task
Status:                           Not Started
Priority:                              Normal
Due:                                  By Date:
                  Thu, Dec 24, 2009 5:00 PM
Time Zone:                     Kolkata (+5.5)
Reminder:                                None

Recurrence:                             Daily
Every:                                      2
End:                                     Date
                      Sun, Jan 24, 2010
Occurs every 2 days until Jan 24, 2010
```

Figure 9–13. *The settings for Tasks*

If you press on the Menu key with any one task highlighted from the list, the following options are at your disposal:

- *Filter*: You can filter through the tasks on the basis of Personal and Business segregation.

- *Forward As*: You could forward the task in question either through e-mail, PIN, SMS, MMS, or Messenger.

- *New*: Opens a new task to compose.

- *Open*: Opens the present task.

- *Delete*: Deletes the task at hand.

- *Delete Completed*: Deletes all the tasks already completed.

- *Mark Completed*: Marks the tasks already accomplished.

- *Mark In Progress*: Helps identify tasks that are still applicable.

- *Hide Completed*: Hides the ones that have been concluded. If this option is chosen, then the option is replaced by Show Completed in the Menu list.

- *Options*: Here, you can define factors such as: whether the View should be sorted by Subject, Priority, Due Date, or Status; the Snooze time ranging from None to 30 minutes; whether it should confirm before deleting and the number of entries made.

The Help, Switch Application, and Close options are available as always.

> **NOTE:** To view your tasks in your calendar, go to your Calendar Options and set the View Tasks field to Yes.

MemoPad

Quick notes that need jotting down can best be done in the MemoPad. Open the Memo feature and select the Add Memo option. Fill in the required material in the body section of the memo and give it a title. You can also choose from the Menu list options like: Find, Paste, Check Spelling, Clear Field, Save, Categories (Business or Personal), Delete, Show Symbol, Switch Input Language, Switch Application, and Close.

Calculator

A quick calculation calls for a handy calculator. With a slick layout like the one shown in Figure 9–14, this calculator will make you forget any traditional one.

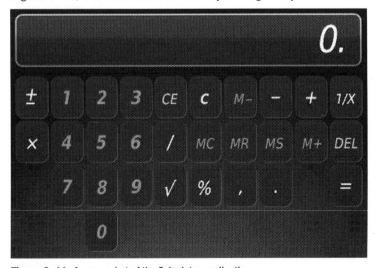

Figure 9–14. *A screenshot of the Calculator application*

You can either use your trackball (if you use a device with one) or you can press the corresponding key on the keypad to carry out the calculations. You can convert numbers between metric and imperial, and choose the conversion type you would like, all by selecting the appropriate one from the Menu options.

Voice Notes Recorder

Take down voice notes on the go with this feature. Just go to it from the Applications folder and you are ready to record. Once you press Stop (which is the same button that you used to start the recording), you get varied options to choose from, which are displayed on the control bar at the bottom of the screen, as shown in Figure 9–15.

Figure 9–15. *An example of a paused voice recording with the control bar*

You can choose to either: Continue Recording, Stop, Play, Rename, Delete, or Send the recording to an associate. Once you have completed your task, the recording will be saved in your Gallery for later reference.

The Voice Notes recorder is also a very powerful business tool. Some of them are illustrated for you in the following list:

- *Brainstorming*: This is a great application to have running while brainstorming for new ideas and concepts. This way you will make sure that you never lose out on vital leads and information.

- *Research*: Giving description of surroundings in scouting a location, e.g., real estate, helps you capture minute details which could easily slip your mind otherwise.

- *To substantiate argument or claim*: If you have this application handy, a quick recording of situations/uncalled-for outbursts could help you prove your innocence and even save your job.

- *Development*: While in the midst of project discussions and meetings, a record of important facts will help formulate a way forward in a much more organized manner.

■   *Media*: Get reviews on television shows or movie releases by collecting bytes from the crowds firsthand.

Voice Dialing

This feature allows you to call people from your contact list, as well as other numbers, by speaking to your phone. To make a voice call, launch the feature and say "Call," followed by the name of the receiver after the beep. You can also spell out the number you wish the app to dial for you. It will list out various options, which you can accept by saying "Yes," "No," or "Cancel."

You can check your number, your coverage status, or battery level by saying, "Check my phone number," "Check coverage," or "Check battery" after the beep.

> **NOTE:** To change the voice dialing language, you will need to alter it from the Device options and further narrow it down to Language.

Password Keeper

You can store all your passwords for various accounts here. This folder is in turn safeguarded by a unique password that you need to establish. Once that is done, you will not have to use the "forgot password?" option from any site again. The trick is, try not to forget the password to this folder though.

Choose New from the Menu options of the Application to enter information about a new account. The app also helps you to generate new passwords. Create completely random passwords by choosing Random Password from the Menu list. If you get a password option that you do not like, you can try again till you find one that is satisfactory.

Password Keeper settings can be customized to your needs by altering them through the Options feature that is part of the Menu list (please refer to Figure 9–16). They are the following:

■   *Random Password Length*: The length of the password generated by the random Password feature. This length could range from four to sixteen.

■   *Random Includes Alpha*: Whether or not the Random Password generator should include alpha characters or not.

■   *Random Includes Numbers*: Whether numbers should be incorporated.

■   *Random Includes Symbols*: The use of symbols in the randomly generated passwords can be controlled from here.

■   *Confirm Delete*: Whether the software should ask for a confirmation before deleting or not.

- *Password Attempts*: Determine the number of allowed password attempts before the application is blocked from here. The range stretches from one to twenty.

- *Allow Clipboard Copy*: Fixes if the Copy Clipboard option should be disabled or not.

- *Show Password*: Whether the password should be visible or hidden is determined from here.

- *Number of Entries*: Establishes the number of entries made thus far.

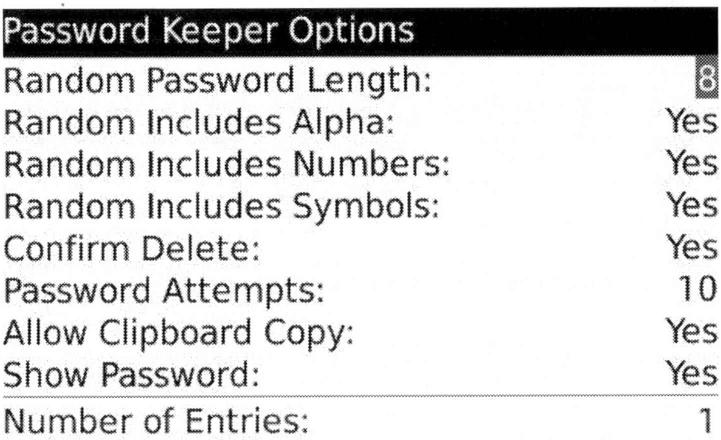

Password Keeper Options	
Random Password Length:	8
Random Includes Alpha:	Yes
Random Includes Numbers:	Yes
Random Includes Symbols:	Yes
Confirm Delete:	Yes
Password Attempts:	10
Allow Clipboard Copy:	Yes
Show Password:	Yes
Number of Entries:	1

Figure 9–16. *The settings that determine the nature of Password Keeper*

Saved Messages

Messages that you choose to save are collected and stored in this folder for quick perusal.

Games Galore

All those bored moments at the airport or while waiting at the doctors can be turned to one of two things—one, productivity while using your BlackBerry's fabulous business and professional features; and two, fun by playing any one of BlackBerry's preset games. More than any other, it is the BrickBreaker (as shown in Figure 9–17) that stays closest to every BlackBerry owner's heart. As a disclaimer, we'd like to warn you of the serious health hazards this addictive game can cause, due to the joy it offers. If you find yourself playing this with increasing frequency, don't say we didn't warn you.

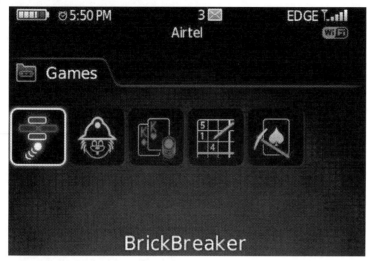

Figure 9–17. *A BlackBerry favorite—the BrickBreaker game*

Compare scores with friends and other BlackBerry users worldwide too. Post your high scores by pressing the Menu key and selecting Send High Score. You could check the high scores by going to High Score from the Menu options.

Look No More

You may think that you are unique to this phenomenon, but trust me most people face the same dilemma—what they are looking for *always* turns up in the last place they look. From the last drawer that you open, to the last file you check, your search object eludes you as much as it can. But with your BlackBerry, you need not spend innumerable hours searching.

Search for any interaction with a particular person or base your search on a keyword or phrase using the search feature. Once you launch it, you can type a name or any text that your want searched for. Along with that, you can also specify whether you want the app to look for it in your Messages, Calendar, Contacts, MemoPad, BlackBerry Messenger, or Tasks. You could also choose to select them all and then run the search (as shown in Figure 9–18).

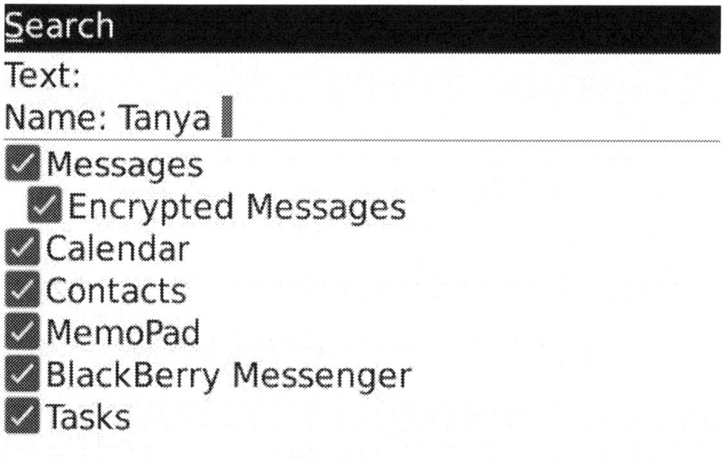

Search

Text:
Name: Tanya |

☑ Messages
  ☑ Encrypted Messages
☑ Calendar
☑ Contacts
☑ MemoPad
☑ BlackBerry Messenger
☑ Tasks

Figure 9–18. *An example of selected fields that determine the Search criteria*

Once you do so, the app will throw out the possible places where the name or key phrase (or both) has been used, as you see in Figure 9–19. You can expand and collapse each of the categories by selecting the plus (+) and minus (–) symbols next to the category. For instance, in the figure, the searched item had appeared 34 times in the Messages app, once in the Contacts and BlackBerry Messenger and none in the Calendar, MemoPad, and Tasks.

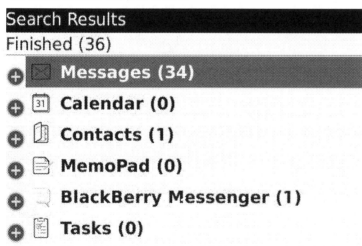

Figure 9–19. *The consecutive search results*

An additional list of Options that is offered to you from the Menu list of the Search App includes: Spell Check, Select All, Deselect All, Show Symbols, and Switch Input Language; other than the regular Help, Switch Application, Switch Input Language, and Close options.

What's Next?

Little or no Internet connectivity can cause serious setbacks in the work space. The ability to network and access information at all times is vital for any professional today. The BlackBerry As a Modem feature ensures you never have to compromise on your work by allowing your handset to double up as a modem which then can connect your computer/laptop to the Internet with commendable speed! Read on for more…

Chapter 10

BlackBerry as a Modem

The World at Your Fingertips...

All of us have at some point come across the word "modem." For some, it might just be a gadget that in some way helps to connect to the Internet. Though partly true, this definition is far too sketchy as compared to its capabilities. So, what is a modem? A modem—short for modulator-demodulator—is an electronic device that provides a communication interface, connecting your home network to the Internet through an Internet service provider. It encodes and decodes digital information that is sent and received, thus reproducing the original data.

Now, you can use your BlackBerry smartphone as a modem to connect your laptop or computer to the Internet. This process of using your cell phone as a modem to connect your laptop or PDA to the Internet (using cables or wirelessly) is called tethering. Though your BlackBerry handset is very capable of taking care of many tasks, the utility of the laptop cannot be ignored. So no matter where you are travelling to, or how many hours the layover is, whether your data card isn't working or your laptop Wi-Fi is down, the Internet connection stays right in your pocket.

However, you must make sure your data plan allows and supports this function. The user agreement of your cell phone service illustrates this for you. If your plan prohibits the use of your phone as a tethered medium, then using it for this purpose might violate the agreement, causing you to lose your service or worse, land yourself in legal problems. If your plan supports this, make sure you pay close attention to the charges involved, because you do not want to receive a shocking bill.

Setting Up Your BlackBerry as a Modem

You could set up your BlackBerry as an external modem so as to connect to the Internet. For this, you would require:

- BlackBerry Desktop Software, version 4.1 or higher
- BlackBerry Handheld smartphone that supports this feature
- BlackBerry smartphone Device Software 4.2 or higher

■   A Wireless Service Provider with a data plan that includes this function

The BlackBerry Desktop Software should be installed on your laptop and the software comes in a CD along with the phone. If you do not have it, you could download it from BlackBerry's official web site. The BlackBerry smartphones that support this feature are:

■   BlackBerry Tour 9630 smartphone

■   BlackBerry Storm2 9550 smartphone

■   BlackBerry Storm 9530 smartphone

■   BlackBerry Bold 9700 smartphone

■   BlackBerry Bold 9000 smartphone

■   BlackBerry 8830 World Edition smartphone

■   BlackBerry8820 smartphone

■   BlackBerry 8800 smartphone

■   BlackBerry 8707g smartphone

■   BlackBerry 8705g smartphone

■   BlackBerry 8703e smartphone

■   BlackBerry Curve 8900 smartphone

■   BlackBerry Curve 8330 smartphone

■   BlackBerry Curve 8320 smartphone

■   BlackBerry Curve 8310 smartphone

■   BlackBerry Curve 8300 smartphone

■   BlackBerry 7250 smartphone

■   BlackBerry 7130e smartphone

■   BlackBerry 7130c smartphone

Please contact your service provider to find out if this feature is available to you.

The step-by-step instructions differ between PC and Mac users as well as GSM and CDMA clients. I will run you through the processes involved to avoid any ambiguity.

Setting up for Windows (For GSM/GPRS/EDGE)

Setting up your handset as a modem can be carried out either by using the USB cable or through Bluetooth technology. If both your laptop and your BlackBerry are Bluetooth enabled, then you do not need to physically connect your smartphone to the computer. Setting it up for GSM/GPRS/EDGE mobile customers comprises of five main steps. They are the following:

1. Installing the BlackBerry Desktop Software.

2. Verifying the modem is installed and functioning.

3. Setting up the Access Point Name (APN).

4. Configuring dial-up networking.

5. Connecting to the internet using the dial-up network.

Installing the BlackBerry Desktop Software

When you install the BlackBerry Desktop Software v 4.1 or higher, it automatically should install the standard modem that is used by dial-up networking and the drivers that are used by the handset to communicate through the USB and visual communications port. However, this can be disturbed if you at some point upgrade your desktop software. Upon doing this, the visual communications port and the standard modem are removed. This can be troubleshot easily by rerunning the installation process of the BlackBerry Desktop Software v 4.1 and choosing Repair.

After completing this process, connect your handset to the PC, either through the USB cable or through Bluetooth. Launch Desktop Manager and let it run while you go through the rest of the set-up procedure.

> **NOTE:** To confirm whether the handheld is connected, check the bottom left corner of the Desktop Manager window. If you see your BlackBerry PIN displayed there, it is connected (see Figure 10–1).

Figure 10–1. *Screen displaying the BlackBerry PIN as an indicator of being connected*

Verifying the Modem Is Installed and Functioning

A quick double-check never hurt anyone, did it? Though this isn't a mandatory step, setting aside ten minutes to follow this through can save you a lot of troubleshooting time in the future.

First, you need to check whether your modem has been installed. To do this, go to Phone and Modem Options from your Control Panel and click on the Modems tab. Here, you will see your various modem drivers listed. Among these, you should see a new one called Standard Modem and the attached port (like COM4, COM11) next to it (see Figure 10–2). Depending on your operating system and computer, this port might vary. This means that the phone as a modem has been identified and installed properly.

Figure 10–2. *Confirming modem installation*

Next you need to cross-check whether it is functioning well. To do so, select the Standard Modem and click on Properties. Here, choose the Diagnostics tab and click on Query Modem. In the list, you should get a Success response, thus identifying it as a modem (see Figure 10–3). If you get this, you can be assured that the modem has been installed and is functioning correctly.

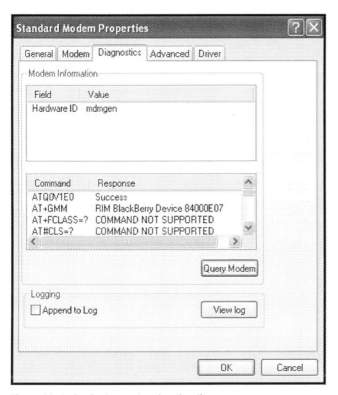

Figure 10–3. *Confirming modem functionality*

Setting Up the Access Point Name (APN)

This step requires you to have details from your service provider regarding their unique Access Point Names (APNs). An APN is a means of identifying the routing information between the data network and the mobile data user. This consists of two parts, the Operator Identifier and the Network Identifier. Simply put, the APN is like a web address of an access point that is given to the end user by the service provider for their data connection. Some of them have been listed for you a little later in this section.

To go through with this set-up, again go to your Control Panel and select Phone and Modem Options. After hitting the Modem tab, highlight Standard Modem and click on Properties. Select Change Settings. The Standard Modem Properties window will reappear, then click on the Advanced tab.

After you do this, it will ask you to fill in the APN details of your service provider under the Extra Initialization Commands field (see Figure 10–4). Here, you need to fill in the following:

```
+cgdcont=1,"IP","<the Internet APN>"
```

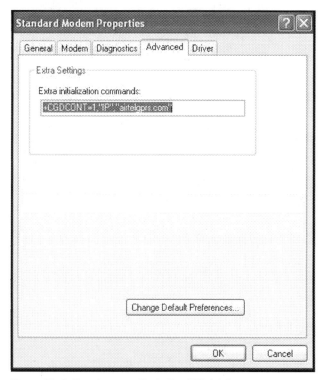

Figure 10–4. *Sample screen illustrating APN details*

Here are some of the service providers' APN details:

- Rogers Users: `+cgdcont=1,"IP","internet.com"`
- Cingular Blue/AT&T Users: `+cgdcont=1,"IP","proxy"`
- Cingular Orange Users: `+cgdcont=1,"IP","ISP.CINGULAR"`
- AT&T Users: `AT+cgdcont=1,"IP","WAP.CINGULAR"`
- UK Vodafone Users: `+cgdcont=1,"IP","internet"`
- SwissCom Users:`+cgdcont=1,"IP","gprs.swisscom.ch"`
- T-Mobile Users: `+cgdcont=1,"IP","wap.voicestream.com"`

If your service provider has not been listed here, please contact them directly for details.

After this, click on OK here as well as in the Phone and Modem Options window.

Configuring Dial-Up Networking

The processes involved in this step differ according to the operating systems, namely: Windows 7, Vista, XP, and 2000. I will illustrate them for you individually.

Windows 7

Here are the steps for Windows 7:

1. Select Network and Sharing Center from your Control Panel.

2. Next select Set up a new connection or network from Change your networking settings.

3. Select Set up a dial-up connection and click on Next.

4. From the list of modem options, select the modem that you just set up.

5. Type in the information from your Internet Service Provider including dial-up phone number (*99#), username, password, and connection name.

6. Select Connect.

Windows Vista

Here are the steps for Windows Vista:

1. Select Connect to from your Start options.

2. Here, click on Set up a connection or network and then choose Set up a dial-up connection.

3. Type in *99# in the Dial-up Phone Number field.

4. Now type in the username and password provided by your service provider.

5. Type BlackBerry in the Connection Name field.

6. Select Dialing Rules and with the created profile highlighted, click on OK.

7. Select Connect to be able to connect to the Internet.

Windows XP

Here are the steps for Windows XP:

1. Go to Network Connections, click on New Connection Wizard, and select Next.

2. Choose the Connect to the Internet option and click Next.

3. After selecting Set up my connection manually, go to Next.

4. Here choose Connect using a dial-up modem and then Next.

5. Select Standard Modem if the Select a Device screen appears and choose Next.

6. Give your connection a name in the ISP Name field (the name by which it will appear in your Network Connections) and select Next.

7. Type *99# in the Phone Number field and choose Next.

8. Here, you will need to specify which users of the system should have access to the connection. Once this is done, select Next.

9. Now type in the username and password provided by your service provider and then go to Next.

10. Select Finish.

11. Select Properties from the Connect Window.

12. Here, confirm that the Standard Modem appears under Connect Using field.

13. Now choose Configure.

14. Clear all fields including the Enable Hardware Flow Control.

15. Select OK.

Windows 2000

Here are the steps for Windows 2000:

1. From your Control Panel, select Network and Dial-up Connections/Network Connections.

2. Here, select Make New Connection/Create a New Connection and click on Next.

3. After selecting Dial-up to Private Network, click on Next.

4. Type in *99# in the Phone Number field and choose Next.

5. Here, you will need to specify which users of the system should have access to the connection. Once this is done, select Next.

6. Give your connection a name (the name by which it will appear in your Network Connections) and select Finish.

7. Select Properties from the Connect window.

8. With the Standard Modem highlighted under Modems, click on Configure.

9. Clear all fields including the Enable Hardware Flow Control.

10. Select OK.

> **NOTE:** If you are a T-Mobile customer, under the Networking tab in the Properties window for the dial-up connection, please clear the Enable LCP Extensions check box, along with all other check boxes that come under the PPP Settings window.

Connecting to the Internet Using the Dial-up Network

And now, folks, this is the part you've all been working toward—getting connected. So without any delay, let's jump right in.

1. Connect your BlackBerry handset to the laptop/PC either through the USB cable or Bluetooth.

2. Launch Desktop Manager. Remember, you need to have Desktop Manager running in the background.

3. If you have created a shortcut icon on your desktop, simply click on that, type in the username and password along with the dial code *99#.

4. If you did not do so, it's OK. Go to your Control Panel/Settings and choose Network Connections. Here, select the connection you created while Configuring the Dial-up Networking and fill in your username and password details as well as the dial code *99#.

5. Select Dial.

Now use your handset as a modem to surf the Internet to your heart's content.

Setting Up for Windows (CDMA/EVDO)

The process involved to set up the BlackBerry as a modem differs slightly between GSM and CDMA phones. Thus, if you use a phone that is of the CDMA/EVDO technology, read through this section. Most of the processes are very similar. The phones that support this are:

- BlackBerry 7100 Series
- BlackBerry 7200 Series
- BlackBerry 8700 Series
- BlackBerry 8800 Series
- BlackBerry Curve 8300 Series
- BlackBerry Desktop Software
- BlackBerry Pearl 8100 Series
- BlackBerry Tour 9630 smartphone

This process requires the following four steps.

1. Installing the BlackBerry Desktop Software.

2. Verifying the modem is installed and functioning.

3. Configuring dial-up networking.

4. Connecting to the internet using the dial-up network.

For GPRS/EDGE users, Steps 1 and 2 are the same as in the previous list. Therefore, I will only elaborate on the steps that differ.

Configuring Dial-Up Networking

As before, I will describe the various steps involved for different Windows Operating Systems.

Windows 7

The following are the steps for Windows 7:

1. Select Network and Sharing Center from your Control Panel.

2. Then select Set up a new connection or network from Change your networking settings.

3. Select Set up a dial-up connection and click on Next.

4. From the list of modem options, select the modem that you just set up.

5. Type in the information from your Internet Service Provider including dial-up phone number (#777), username, password and connection name.

6. Select Connect.

Windows Vista

The following are the steps for Windows Vista:

1. Select Connect to from your Start options.

2. Here, click on Set up a connection or network and then choose Set up a dial-up connection.

3. Type in #777 in the Dial-up Phone Number field.

4. Now type in the username and password provided by your service provider.

5. Type BlackBerry in the Connection Name field.

6. Select Dialing Rules and with the created profile highlighted, click on OK.

7. Select Connect to be able to connect to the Internet.

8. Select OK.

Windows XP

The following are the steps for Windows XP:

1. Go to Network Connections, click on New Connection Wizard and select Next.

2. Choose Connect to the Internet option and click Next.

3. After selecting Set up my connection manually, go to Next.

4. Here choose Connect using a dial-up modem and then Next.

5. Select Standard Modem if the Select a Device screen appears and choose Next.

6. Give your connection a name in the ISP Name field (the name by which it will appear in your Network Connections) and select Next.

7. Type #777 in the Phone Number field and choose Next.

8. Here, you will need to specify which users of the system should have access to the connection. Once this is done, select Next.

9. Now type in the username and password provided by your service provider and then go to Next.

10. Select Finish.

11. Select Properties from the Connect Window.

12. Here, confirm that the Standard Modem appears under Connect Using field.

13. Now choose Configure.

14. Clear all fields including the Enable Hardware Flow Control.

15. Select OK.

Windows 2000

The following are the steps for Windows 2000:

1. From your Control Panel, select Network and Dial-up Connections/Network Connections.

2. Here, select Make New Connection/Create a New Connection and click on Next.

3. After selecting Dial-up to Private Network, click on Next.

4. Type in #777 in the Phone Number field and choose Next.

5. Here, you will need to specify which users of the system should have access to the connection. Once this is done, select Next.

6. Give your connection a name (the name by which it will appear in your Network Connections) and select Finish.

7. Select Properties from the Connect window.

8. With the Standard Modem highlighted under Modems, click on Configure.

9. Clear all fields including the Enable Hardware Flow Control.

Connecting to the Internet Using the Dial-Up Network

In order to connect, follow these steps:

1. Connect your BlackBerry handset to the laptop/PC either through the USB cable or Bluetooth.

2. Launch Desktop Manager.

3. Go to your Control Panel/Settings and choose Network Connections. Here, select the connection you created while Configuring the Dial-up Networking and fill in your username and password details (if any) as well as the dial code #777.

4. Select Dial.

For Better Speed

If the Internet speed seems slow to you, you could try the IP Header Compression (IPHC) which is a scheme to compress UDP, TCP, and IP headers so as to increase bandwidth and speed. Please refer to Figure 10–5 for more information. To set this up, follow these steps:

1. Go to your Control Panel and select Network Connections. Here, select the desired network, right-click and go to Properties.

2. In Properties, select the Networking tab and with the Internet Protocol Version highlighted, click on Properties.

3. In the General tab, click on Advanced.

4. Here under the General tab and the PPP link, check the box to Compress the IP Header.

5. Select OK.

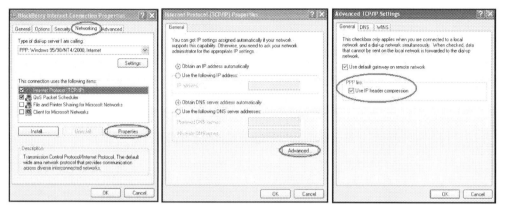

Figure 10–5. *Screens illustrating the process involved in IP Header Compression*

Setting Up for Mac Users

Believe it or not but setting up your BlackBerry to connect your Macintosh to the Internet is probably a simpler process than doing so with Windows! Before we get into that, however, the few standard requirements are:

■ BlackBerry Desktop Manager Software, version 1.0

■ BlackBerry Handheld smartphone that supports this feature

■ A Mac operating system

■ A wireless service provider with a data plan that includes this function

Once you have the above under control, the steps that follow are very simple.

1. Install the BlackBerry Desktop Manager Software v1.0 on your Mac computer.

2. Connect your BlackBerry to your Mac computer either using the USB cable or through Bluetooth.

3. Click on the Apple icon that is on the Menu bar.

4. Select System Preferences and choose Network for the list.

5. You will see a dialog box Indicating that a New Interface has been Detected.

6. Select OK.

7. Type in the information that you have gathered from your service provider regarding Telephone Number, Account Name, and Password.

8. Click on Connect.

SOME IMPORTANT NOTES

If you are a BES user on BES v 4.0, your Administrator must enable the "BlackBerry IPModem" setting on the BES. This is a new setting in the Version 4.0 of BES.

While using your handset as a modem, do not try to browse or use any third-party applications simultaneously as it might interfere with the connection.

If you use an older BlackBerry model that is not equipped with advanced modem functionality, you can utilize third-party applications such as MobiShark. So whether you use an older model or your service provider doesn't support tethering, you can connect to the Internet using your phone.

What's Next?

A company started as a research project in 1996 by two Ph.D. students today stands as one of the biggest, most widely recognized and respected companies of all time. The transition from the original 'Googol' to Google might have had its own trials and tribulations, but today Google holds its own as a world leader in technology. As obvious as it might be, your BlackBerry comes together with such inspiring set-ups to provide you the best. Read on to find out more about Google Apps on your BlackBerry.

Chapter 11

Google Apps on Your BlackBerry

Growth with Excitement Abundant...

This experimental venture started by two students has grown beyond a mere search engine and continues to take the world by storm. "Just 'Google' it, will you?" has become a common part of world lingo. The word "google" might have become synonymous with search but that has not stopped the company from venturing into other avenues to provide a bundle of applications and software solutions, meeting personal and professional needs with equal ease. BlackBerry's integration with Google Mobile Application suite comes as a reminder of its commitment to provide its users with the best available.

The Google Advantage

Small businesses across the world are turning to Google Apps for a complete solution. Educational institutions find the Google solution cost-effective and user friendly, appealing to both students and faculty alike. Entrepreneurs belonging to various industries like design and animation, media, culinary, shipment, and business have discovered the Google advantage. Some of the most obvious benefits are the following:

- *Universal*: Google is a universal brand today and that cannot be argued against. Work cultures around the globe use it, either in professional or personal capacity. Thus its technology isn't alien to anybody, irrespective of culture or geographical location.

- *Cost-effective*: The solutions offered by Google are far more cost-effective than most others available in the market, hence making it an instant hit with small businesses and other management.

- *Centralized*: Google minimizes issues that arise from incompatibility of versions and copy as everyone connects to the same server, thus reducing differences between regional offices in various parts of the world.

- *User satisfaction*: Once a Google user, always a Google user holds true, because the user satisfaction and convenience it offers remain unparalleled.

- *Flexibility*: The cloud computing technology adopted by Google gives its users the flexibility to work on their documents and files from anywhere. Content can be accessed from home and office alike. This advantage is of great value to the travelling professional, for obvious enough reasons.

- *Internet standards*: Google maintains and uses internet standards, thus allowing world-wide compatibility.

- *Sizeable storage*: Google's great capacity has and will be one of its biggest USPs. Not only is it beneficial to the corporate user, but is also very attractive to the student and aspiring professional.

- *Collaborate*: Collaboration with other users working on the same document simultaneously can be a very valuable feature. Real time changes are accessible along with histories so that changes in documents and calendars are clear and comprehensible.

- *Constant upgrades*: With numerous teams working on development, constant upgrades and newer solutions offered by Google make sure its users can access the latest in technology in a simple and easy-to-use manner.

- *Quality control*: Google maintains strict quality control checks to ensure that they offer nothing substandard, of which its user satisfaction is proof enough.

Overall, its entire plethora of advantages is the Google Mobile Applications suite on your BlackBerry.

About Google Mobile Applications

The Google Mobile App suite for BlackBerry was launched in the second week of September 2009 and came as a free download to all BlackBerry users across the globe. This application accumulates and brings together many of Google's key features and functions into one comprehensive app. You can download the mobile application by following this URL from your BlackBerry browser: http://m.google.com (see Figure 11–1).

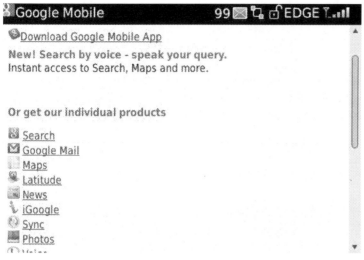

Figure 11–1. *The Google Mobile App download page*

NOTE: Though most applications are available across the world, there might be a few that are not yet accessible from certain countries and regions. If you do not live in the United States, please specify your country before downloading the app.

Here, highlight and select the Download option, as shown in Figure 11–2.

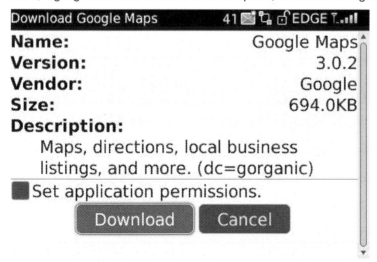

Figure 11–2. *A screen displaying the specifics of the app along with the download link*

This will just take a few minutes. You can choose to download the Google Mobile Application as a package or can opt to download individual applications of your choice by selecting them separately. Whichever you choose, once it is downloaded, you will be able to access it from your Applications or Downloads folders, as illustrated in Figure 11–3.

Figure 11–3. *Google Mobile application in the Downloads folder*

What are the benefits?

Why should you download and use Google Apps and how will it prove beneficial to you?

- Instant search on inquiries and questions without waiting for the browser to upload.

- Quickly search previous queries through the history option.

- Direct links to your Google Apps calendar are made possible by specifying your domain name.

- Access to web-based services such as Maps, News, and so on, along with other Google products with just a click.

- Upgrading and updating software and apps is now simple through alerts that are sent periodically.

NOTE: Though essentially free, additional charges may be applicable depending on individual service providers and plans. Please contact your carrier for further details on the same.

The Bundle of Joy

The applications that Google Mobile offers are nothing less than a bundle of joy. The following are some of the special Google Mobile App features that are sure to impress.

Google Maps

How often has it been said that men refuse to ask for directions? As true as that might be, it is only half the truth. Yes, men won't admit to other men that they are lost, but they will to their beloved gadgets. To all the women out there: make sure your men have Google Maps so that you don't have to suffer to feed their egos. To all the men: get Google Maps so that you never have to ask a soul. Some of the attractive features of this application are the following:

- See your location on the map, whether or not your device is GPS enabled. This also helps in getting driving directions without having to specify a start point.

- Search for any particular category through the business listings feature. This can also prove as a great advertising feature for business owners. To list your business, you need to go to the Google Local Business Center and create an account. You will also need to fill in details like the name, address, phone numbers, and business description. Make sure you use targeted key phrases in this so as to get the most out of business searches.

- Receive detailed routes through the Transit, Driving, and Walking directions options.

- The option Latitude allows you to share your current location with your friends and vice versa.

- Get real-time traffic updates so that you never find yourself stuck in a jam again.

- Make use of the street-level imagery option of venues and directions.

- Use the convenient turn-by-turn voice navigation, so that you hear the directions as you go.

Google Maps in Your Pocket

Google Maps comes as part of the package if you opt for the Google Mobile App suite. However, you can also download it separately by going to http://m.google.com/maps from your BlackBerry browser. Once it is downloaded, you can locate it from either your Downloads folder or Application folder, depending on your OS. You can also open it from your Google Mobile Apps.

After you launch it, the application will take a few minutes to find your location. Once this is done, the map loads itself and is ready to use. The following discusses some of the key features that Google Maps offers.

Search Map

If you need to know the way to the closest bank or the most suitable eatery location, a quick Search Map option is best for you. This application is a real life saver, especially while traveling to new cities. The search results yielded are concise and easy to understand, while prioritizing the search to areas around your present location. After you highlight them, they give the complete address along with a rating. If you select a particular result, it gives you the Address and contact numbers, as well as other details such as descriptions based on applicable keywords, e-mail addresses, parking specifics, and reviews from other Google Application users along with ratings.

Get Directions

Directions while you go are the main attraction of this feature. You will find options such as Driving, Transit, and Walking. Choose your mode of travel and specify the start and end point of your journey. You could do this by feeding in the postal address as well as locating it on the map. Once you have established these basics, the application throws out details to you including:

- The estimated distance in terms of km/miles as well as time taken.
- It also spells out the route to you specifying each turn and direction.
- You can also choose to view the route on the map.
- Choose to see the Reverse directions if you would like to interchange between the start and end points.
- You can save the route as a favorite to avoid the establishing procedure.

My Location

This shows you your present position based on GPS location in the form of a blue dot. If for any reason you do not have GPS enabled on your phone or your GPS is down, the service uses the information provided by the mobile towers around you to give an approximate positioning. If this is the case, then the application indicates the uncertainty in the form of a light blue circle that surrounds the blue dot (see Figure 11–4).

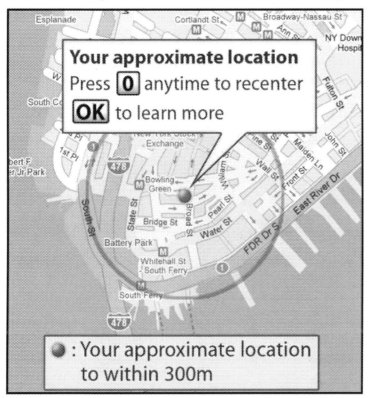

Figure 11–4. *An example screenshot showing the current location of the user*

Join Latitude

Latitude is a feature that allows you to share your current location with friends and colleagues who have it activated as well (see Figure 11–5). To join it, choose this option from the list. After doing so, you will have to sign in using your Google account details such as e-mail id and password. Then, choose the friends you would like to share your location with. The friends you send the request to shall get the invite through e-mail. You can control how much information you would like to share with all your added contacts or individual associates through your Privacy Settings.

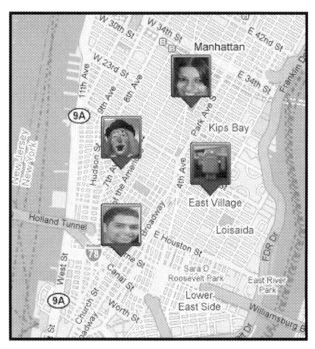

Figure 11–5. *The Latitude feature which is part of the Google Maps Application*

Show Traffic

This is particularly helpful when you are in a hurry and need to avoid traffic jams and holdups. If the service is available in your area, the traffic is indicated in the form of colored lines.

- Gray indicates the lack of information available.

- Red indicates the traffic speed to be less than 25 mph.

- Yellow indicates the traffic movement to be between 25 mph and 50 mph.

- Green indicates the traffic flow as more than 50 mph.

Satellite View/Map View

You can choose whether you would like to view the map in the Satellite mode or as a regular map.

Clear Map

If you want to clear the map of recent searches, markers, and directions; choose this option.

Favorites

You can save locations and routes as favorites for easy future referencing. To choose a location directly from the map, move the cursor to the desired point and press the enter key. The location is then marked with a cross. From the list of options, choose Save as Favorite.

Street View

This is a feature that might or might not be available to you, depending on your service area. It gives you directions not from a bird's-eye view but at the street level itself, guiding you through courses and turns. If it is unavailable at any location, the Street View option will not appear in the list. Once this street level imagery is opened, you can rotate the view just as you would pan on the map, using your trackball or clickwheel.

Zoom

Zoom in and out of a map, either in satellite or map views using this feature. This may take a couple of seconds to download and adjust to the chosen level of zoom.

> **NOTE:** If you have any further queries, you can also choose the Help button which is part of this options list.

Tips and Shortcuts

- Press # to see the directions and routes established on the map.
- Press 0 on the map to move the cursor to your current location.
- Press 7 to get traffic information on the map.
- Press 2 to switch between satellite and map views.
- Press * to view your saved favorite locations and routes
- Press 3 or i to zoom into a map.
- Press 1 or o to zoom out of a map.
- Press U to pan up on a map.
- Press J to pan down on a map.
- Press H to pan left on a map.
- Press K to pan right on a map.

Gmail

Gmail is Google's e-mail application that ensures you never have to use the delete button. With its large storage capacity, you find your e-mails as well as chat histories intact, for perusal at your will. Not uncommon are instances where businesses have adopted Gmail as their corporate e-mail platform. Excellent spam filtering, ability to store e-mails in comprehensive labels (folders) using filters, free POP3 (Post Office Protocol—version 3) and IMAP (Internet Message Access Protocol) accesses, commendable speeds in receiving and sending e-mails, the ability to have multiple Gmail accounts (five to be precise) accessed together without having to open each individually (even while replying to them, the Send As option allows you to send the reply from the valid e-mail address only), automatic addition of contact details from e-mails and suggestions while typing addresses are just a few examples of the numerous benefits Gmail provides.

Now you can get your Gmail on your handset, not only through the BlackBerry's push e-mail technology but also as a Google Mobile App. The Gmail App from Google is different as it retains Gmail's look and feel, thus enabling a more authentic experience. Some of the key features are the following:

- Experience the dependable Gmail familiarity with labeling, starring e-mails, and filtering.

- Easily switch between multiple Gmail accounts so that you never confuse between your work and personal e-mail.

- Use Gmail in the offline mode so that creating new messages and reading already opened ones can be done without an active connection—even on flight mode.

- Delete and refresh easily with the shortcut keys saving you much precious time and energy.

- Perform all regular Gmail activities such as undo, archive, and scroll at ease.

- Take advantage of having all your Gmail contacts with you on your device along with special lists of Most Contacted.

- Search through chat and conversation histories like you normally would.

Gmail in Your Pocket

The first time you launch Gmail from your Google Mobile Apps landing page, it might take a few moments to initiate. Once it is loaded, you will be able to perform and use the application as easily as you use the online version. After loading, it will ask you to sign into your account, using your existing e-mail address (your-id@gmail.com) and password. If you do not have a Google account, you can easily create one.

After logging in, you will see the recent e-mails in your mailbox. Like the online version, this too highlights the number of unread messages in brackets alongside Inbox (as illustrated in Figure 11–6).

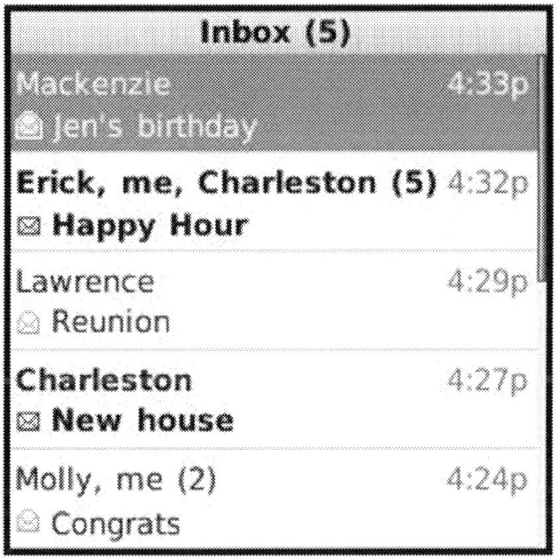

Inbox (5)	
Mackenzie	4:33p
✉ Jen's birthday	
Erick, me, Charleston (5)	4:32p
✉ **Happy Hour**	
Lawrence	4:29p
✉ Reunion	
Charleston	4:27p
✉ **New house**	
Molly, me (2)	4:24p
✉ Congrats	

Figure 11–6. *An example of the Gmail Inbox with read and unread messages*

While in the Inbox page, if you press the Menu button, you will be given a number of options, which essentially encompass all features you would need from the application. These are the following:

Inbox

This is where your received e-mail is stored and displayed. The e-mails that have not been read appear in the bold font. Along with the sender and subject, you also have displayed the date and time of receipt. The e-mails are stored in chronological order, with the most recent ones at the top.

Outbox

If you have typed out certain e-mails that couldn't be sent for any reason, such as low network coverage, then they are stored in your Outbox. This means that the outgoing messages that are held back are sent from this section, as soon as you receive coverage.

Mobile Drafts

Messages that are typed but aborted halfway get saved as mobile drafts. This great feature acts like your backup, so that no matter what mishap, you will never lose your important outgoing e-mails once you have fed them in.

Contacts

It's a boon to have Gmail on your mobile, especially because it makes available to you all your contacts. When you select this option, the application automatically lists for you your Most Contacted friends and associates. If you want a list of all your contacts, press the Menu button while on this page. Here, select the All Contacts option. The application might take a few moments to download all your contacts for the first time. You could also use the Search feature at the top of the screen to locate any of the contacts listed.

Search Mail

This does as it claims. It searches through your mailbox using any key word that you may have typed. This could be the name of the sender, a key phrase in the subject line, or in the body of the e-mail.

Compose Mail

Select this option to type out an e-mail. Once completed, press the Menu button. After doing so, you will see listed a number of options. Choose the appropriate one to proceed. The following list describes some of them for you.

Send

Choose this option to send the e-mail to the established recipient.

Finish Later

If you want to complete the e-mail later, select this option. When you do so, it will get saved as a Mobile Draft, which you can work on any time.

Discard

Choosing this option will delete the message, once it has been confirmed by you.

Add Cc/Bcc

If you want to send a copy of it to someone, you can add their address in the Carbon copy (Cc) field. Add Bcc (Blind carbon copy) if you do not want the other recipients to see the person marked on the e-mail.

Check Spelling

A spell check never hurt anyone. It is always worth using this option before you send out important official e-mails.

Clear Field

This option clears the highlighted field of the message, i.e., Subject, To, or even the message box.

Show Symbols

Selecting this feature will display various signs for you to use. These could be punctuation marks, numbers, and even arithmetic symbols.

Switch Input Language

This option allows you to switch between the chosen language and the others available. However, do not mistake this for a translation feature.

Open

This option opens the highlighted e-mail from the Inbox.

Refresh

When you select this, the mailbox refreshes itself, thus updating any recently received e-mails.

Archive

This feature has made the word "delete" redundant. Now, you can archive your unused and old messages, so that they stay out of your hair, but are not deleted and thus available to you at all times.

Mark As Unread

Using this option is advisable if you want a particular message to stand out, or if you want to reread it or work on it at a later time. Choosing this marks the e-mail in bold, making it appear as a new message.

Add Star

You can append this Add Star option to as many e-mails as you please. Again, it is a way to differentiate between important e-mails that you wish to stand out.

Report Spam

Use this feature to get rid of those annoying bulk messages that are sent to you that you do not wish to receive. Report it as spam and you will not have to deal with similar messages again.

Delete

The highlighted message will be deleted when you select this option. The application asks you to confirm your action. Once you do so, the message is deleted.

Other Options

You will notice that there is another option that is available as well. This is the More... option. When you choose this feature, it will list out for you various factors/categories that will retrieve your correspondence particular to that grouping. This initially shows you your records starting with the recent transactions only. If you scroll lower, then the earlier ones start downloading. Your e-mail is sorted in the following categories:

- *Starred*: Opens up your star-marked e-mails.
- *Chats*: Opens your chat sessions with various associates.
- *Sent Mail*: Opens your sent e-mails.
- *All Mail*: Opens up all of your e-mails.
- *Spam*: Opens your listed spam e-mails.
- *Trash*: Opens your deleted e-mails.
- *Labels*: Opens your labeled e-mail that you segregated.

Accounts and Settings

Maintaining multiple e-mail accounts so as to bifurcate work from personal e-mails is common practice today. And because Gmail satisfies both professional and casual expectations, it is natural for people to have more than one Google account. It is for such customers, that the Accounts option has been incorporated. By selecting this, one can easily add another Google app account as well as switch between the two easily.

The Settings option allows you to decide on secured networks, font size, notifications on new e-mails, confirmations before deleting, and signoff messages.

Tips and Shortcuts

- Press i to go to your Inbox.

- Press c to compose an e-mail.

- Press Shift + i to mark an e-mail as read.

- Press Shift + u to mark an e-mail as unread.

- Press k to go to a newer conversation.

- Press j to go to an older conversation.

- Press d to delete an e-mail.

- Press s to star mark an e-mail.

- Press e to archive an e-mail.

- Press ! to report an e-mail as spam.

- Press / to go to the search e-mail feature.

- Press z to undo.

- Press Shift + j to go to the next account.

- Press Shift + k to go to the previous account.

- Press o to open a conversation from a list of conversations.

- Press t to open the first conversation from a list of conversations.

- Press b to open the last conversation from a list of conversations.

- Press n to go to the next message while viewing a particular conversation.

- Press p to go to the previous message while viewing a particular conversation.

- Press o to go to the collapse or expand a message while viewing a particular conversation.

- Press r to reply to the message while viewing a particular conversation.

- Press a to reply to all recipients while viewing a particular conversation.

- Press f to forward the message while viewing a particular conversation.

Calendar

A missed appointment, a meeting unattended, a forgotten birthday or a date stood up—each of these are blunders that can spell doom, where a simple "It slipped my mind," won't really do. If you find yourself groping for excuses often enough, it's time you worked out a better plan of action. What you need is Google Calendar. This simple enough tool could be your personalized assistant, making sure you never forget again.

The Google Calendar (online version) offers features like integration with your Gmail account, while interpreting information in your message and offering subsequent addition options in the calendar directly. You can also create multiple calendars—personal and shared. When you create an appointment, an option of choosing the appropriate calendar is made available and events from different calendars are marked in different colors. Syncing and sharing of calendars with colleagues makes scheduling appointments a breeze. Another feature available is the ability to sync your calendar with other industry specific ones, which are updated real time, so that events saved on your calendar are always up to date.

Bringing all these features to your phone is the Google Mobile Applications suite. You can also download it separately by visiting http://m.google.com/calendar from your BlackBerry browser. Its key features are the following:

- Sync your Google calendar with your BlackBerry calendar to stay on top of your schedule and agenda.

- You can set up phone notifications so that you never miss that appointment.

- Calendar gets updated whether the entry is made from the phone or the computer.

Calendar in Your Pocket

Additions made from the computer or the mobile are synced, making sure both calendars tally completely. You also receive notifications in your mailbox, reminding you of entries and commitments in advance. If you want to download the calendar application individually, you can do so by visiting http://m.google.com/calendar.

The first time you launch the app, it will ask you for certain verifications such as name, location, and time zone, as illustrated in Figure 11-7. Confirm the details once and then the Calendar Application is good to go.

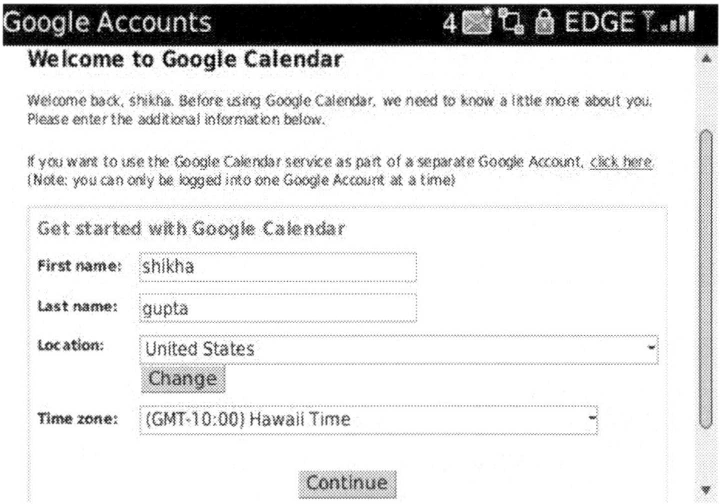

Figure 11–7. *The welcome page upon first launching the Google Calendar app*

Quick Add

This is made available to you on your mobile app. Make an entry by feeding in all the necessary information at once, and the system will translate it to create a new event on your calendar. For example, if you add "Meet Jason at office 5pm Thursday," the application will make the entry appropriately for you. Once you add an event while specifying the location, you also have an option of locating the address on the map along with driving directions to the place. For instance, in Figure 11–8, the calendar entry Thursday, Dec 17th has a Map option next to it.

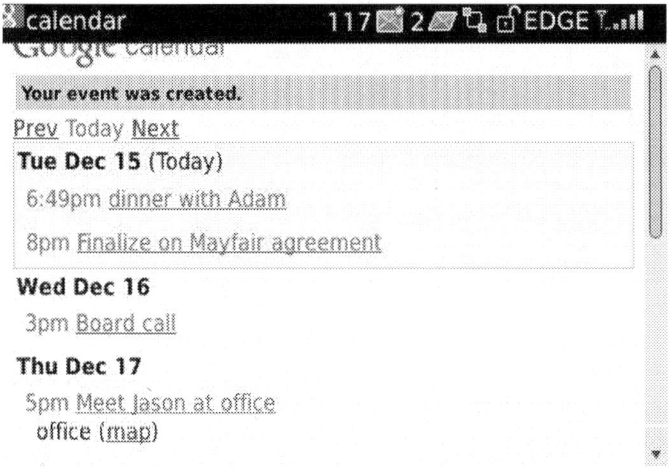

Figure 11–8. *Calendar entries shown on the mobile app along with a link to a map*

After you select this, the application takes you to a map (see Figure 11–9) and from there you can identify the location of the office and get driving directions to it, as shown in Figure 11–10.

Figure 11–9. *The map establishing the Office location*

Figure 11–10. *A quick search to establish a particular location*

Do Remember

- Holidays are marked in red.

- Only days with an entry are displayed on the mobile calendar.

- Limited settings can be altered through the Calendar Settings option.

- E-mail notifications of events and entries are sent to you as reminders.

NOTE: Google Calendar is available in various languages. However, a switch in language requires alterations in the Settings of the main Google Calendar on the computer. To do so, log onto http://www.google.com/calendar from your computer using your user id and password and change the language from the Settings section.

News

Information on the move is the most sought after benefit by most professionals today. Thus the solution to providing you with world events consistently is met by the application—Google News. Its key features being:

- Keep abreast with the times through the News search application.
- Latest news can be checked topic wise.
- News is accumulated from various sources across the world so that you get the complete story and not just one particular skewed/partial version.
- You can establish your order of preference so that the most relevant topics are tackled first.
- Customize your searches to get location specific news from anywhere.

Google News in Your Pocket

If you would like to download this application separately, you can do so by visiting http://m.google.com/news from your mobile phones browser. When you launch the News application, your phone takes you to the news home page through your browser. Here you can search based on key words and phrases as well as surf the news in general. The news pieces are displayed by headline and a two line beginning to the story (see Figure 11–11). Select a particular news item (headline) to get the full article. You also have listed the number of related articles to that particular story. Thus all major information associated with an event is now at your disposal.

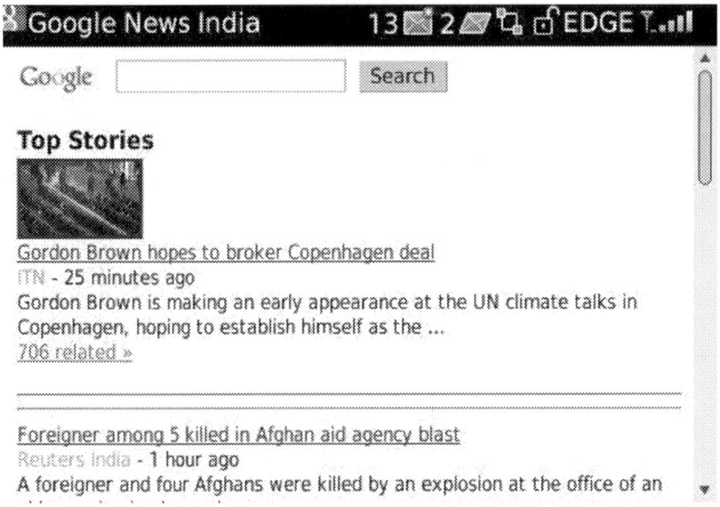

Figure 11-11. *The Google News page listing the top stories of the day as well as the Search option*

The Cherry on the Sundae

- The Select Edition option gives you the flexibility to choose which location-specific event information you would like to receive, i.e., UK, USA, India, or China.

- The Sections feature gives you the power to choose your topics of interest and displays news, as shown in Figure 11-12.

Figure 11-12. *The chosen sections in their designated order of preference*

- Add Section gives you the option to add as many customized sections as you would want, based on key words decided by you.

- Organize Sections helps you to prioritize between these chosen sections where you can delete as well as rearrange the order of the fragments, as illustrated in Figure 11–13.

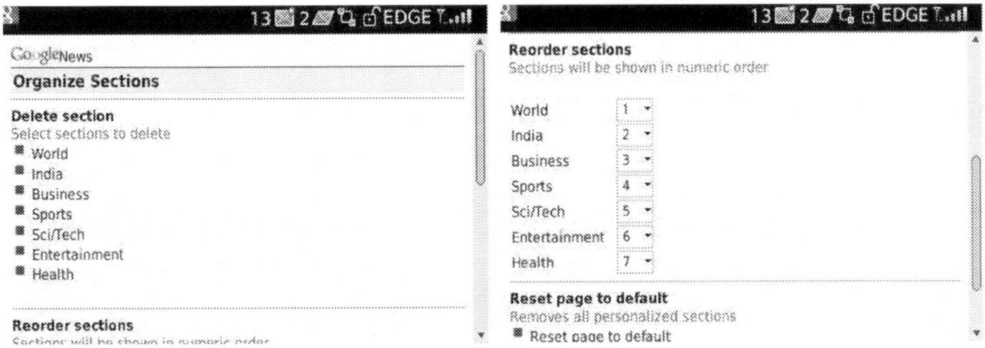

Figure 11–13. *Screenshots illustrating organization of the Sections based on priority*

Reader

Google Reader is a delightful application that helps you subscribe to your favorite sites, blogs, and web pages thus ensuring that you never miss a new post or article. You can use this app to check out your favorite web sites as well as share content with your associates and contacts. Some of the key features of this app are as follows:

- Stay connected through its checks on your subscribed sites and blogs.

- Simple and interesting reading comes as the added advantage to the concise and structured display of chosen material.

- Find new content of interest easily using the search feed option which lists results systematically and in a comprehensible manner.

- Share and recommend your preferred content with colleagues with just one click.

- Add the Google Reader gadget to your iGoogle application so that you get the info-at-a-glance advantage.

Google Reader in Your pocket

Get all the above and much more on your mobile by going to Reader from your Google Application. After you do so, it will ask you to sign in (see Figure 11–14). If you already do not have a Google account, you can create it from here too.

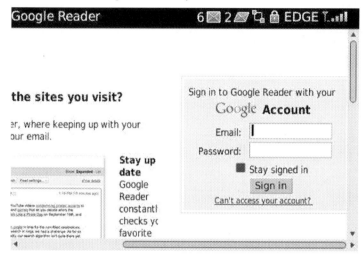

Figure 11–14. *After initiating the Reader, you need to sign in using your Google account details.*

NOTE: Java Script needs to be enabled for you to access your Reader from the mobile. Make sure it is so by checking your Browser Configuration which is part of your Browser Options.

Once signed in, your home page will open listing details like number of new articles and which web sites have these updates. The web pages that have new posts that you haven't read so far appear in bold along with the number of new articles. The total number of new stories/posts that are unread are also highlighted. As you go through the articles, the number of unread articles keep changing and readjusting to the changed status as long as it is in the Expanded form. You can also view the material in a List format. These adjustments can be made by altering it in the top right-hand corner of the screen.

From here, you can also Subscribe to more pages with key word searches as well as URLs, as illustrated in Figure 11–15.

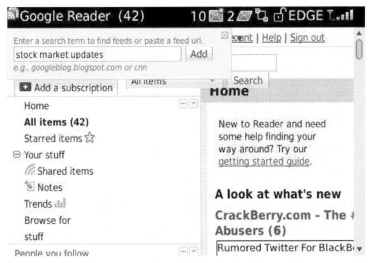

Figure 11–15. *The home page of the Reader application, showing the number of new stories highlighted as well as a search criteria*

Once you feed in the requirement, based on your search, the application throws up various relevant sites and options for you to choose from, along with the number of subscribers each of the sites have. If you still remain unconvinced, you can click/tap on the name of the site for further details on the same. After you have been convinced, choose the Subscribe button and it will be added to your Subscriptions list. It actually is that simple.

The Cherry on the Sundae

- *Star*: Mark your favorites with a star so that you never have to hunt your most trusted business blog down.

- *Share*: Just click/tap on this feature and share your articles or favored articles with associates.

- *Blog*: If you have your own blog, you can display the items you chose to share as a clip in it.

- *Notes*: Make notes on anything and share them with anyone you wish to.

Google Search

- Gives you quick access to the universal search engine and provides accurate results without having to navigate to the Google page at all.

- Speak your queries in English and the search engine responds to your voice.

- Eliminate the need to type your present location while searching for nearby options.

- The application suggests businesses and probable phrases as you type to maximize on time constraints (as shown in Figure 11–16).

- The search history feature allows for quick revisits of recent activity.

Figure 11–16. *An example of the suggestive Google search feature*

Google SMS

- You can SMS an inquiry to Google and you will receive an answer to your question in the form of an SMS.

- All businesses are listed so whether you are looking for the latest stock quotes or flight details, an SMS to "466453" (which spells out "GOOGLE") will lead you to the answer.

- It also provides with source links to certain queries so cross-referencing is possible too.

YouTube

- You can access YouTube videos from your phone, which have been optimized to suit your phones browser capabilities.

- You can upload videos to the site directly from your device.

- Specific searches and listings such as most viewed and top rated are made available for you.

- If you have a YouTube account, you could log into it and access your individual playlists and favorites.

- Search for any video you need with the help of the comprehensive search tool.

- You can communicate with other YouTube users from your mobile through commenting, rating, and so on.

- And you can find related video listings based on your searches, instantly.

GOOG-411 (1800-4664-411)

- A voice-activated search that helps you locate businesses with a simple call for no additional cost at all.

- You can ask by specifying your current zip code or city and state details after which GOOG-411 will connect your call to the desired address.

- You can ask for the information to be sent to you via a text message as well.

- The mapping option sends your phone the map of the locality around the business or query site.

Orkut

- Stay connected with your friends, family, and associates through the social networking site Orkut while on the move.

- You can view profiles and scrap friends from your handheld device.

Blogger

- Send in your blogs from wherever you are using this feature.

- You could post it either through a text message or through an e-mail using a unique e-mail address.

- If your mobile blog is set up, you can directly update your posts through your associated mobile phone.

Docs

- This allows you to view documents, spreadsheets, and presentations directly on your phone at any time.

- Just sign into your Google docs using your domain name.

Picasa

- View and share your photographs with your friends and family through this photo application using the software Picasa.

- Comment on others pictures and have them leave you notes.

- You can also connect with people sharing common interests by searching the Picasa Web Community.

Google Apps Connector

The ability to use built-in BlackBerry Applications by the BES user, to access their Google Apps—e-mail, calendar, and contacts—is made possible by the installation of the Google Apps Connector (GAC). What GAC does is integrate the Google Apps Messaging suite with the BlackBerry Enterprise Server so as to provide wireless synchronization of e-mail, calendar events, and contacts from Google Apps to BlackBerry devices. GAC works with Google Apps Premier and Google Apps Educational editions.

To download Google Apps Connector for BlackBerry Enterprise Server, please go to the following URL and follow instructions:
https://tools.google.com/dlpage/appsconnector.

The use of the Google Apps Connector provides the following advantages to the employee as well as the organization:

- It keeps the BlackBerry devices synchronized with the Google Apps that are applicable to your domain and need.

- It synchronizes the e-mail with less than a minute latency.

- It synchronizes Global Addresses allowing you to search through your domain GAL on your device.

- It synchronizes deleting, reading, and archiving between your BlackBerry devices and the Google Apps.

- It synchronizes between folders on your BlackBerry device and the labels in your Gmail inbox.

- It supports two-way synchronization of personal contacts with a slight delay of five minutes.

- It supports one-way synchronization of calendar entries from the Google Apps to your BlackBerry device.

Essentially, the Google Apps Connector stores a copy of the user's mailbox on the BES server in the form of Personal Store files. It also downloads approximately 1,000 e-mails along with contacts and calendar entries by default. That's the reason it is advisable to allocate at least 500 MB of disk space per user. An addition in the number of users may call for installation of extra database servers.

What's Next?

A compass in hand, a faded map tucked under the arm, a pair of binoculars and a hat to keep the away the sun—sounds like a stereotypical character out of a period film lost in the desert or on a voyage. Though the familiarity of these typical characteristics may make us smile, the bottom line remains—the gentleman is lost! If only he had with him BlackBerry Maps instead. No wonder we don't see compasses any more…

Chapter 12

Maps

Lost on the highway? Well, we're not talking about Lee Rocker's song here; if you really are lost on the highway, more than jamming it up, it is BlackBerry Maps that will come to your rescue. So sit back and read through this chapter so that you never find yourself begging for directions again. All the men out there, are your ears perked up?

BlackBerry Maps is a great application that comes with your BlackBerry handheld. Some of its key features include:

- *Tracking your position on the map*: If you have gone too far on that drive or find yourself on the lost highway, you can instantly find your location using this feature.

- *Tracking your movement on the map*: This helps you see where you are going and whether you are going in the right direction or not.

- *Finding a particular location on the map*: By typing in the postal address of the place, the application then establishes the location for you.

- *Finding a contact from the BlackBerry address book on the map*: This highlights the location of the fed-in address on the map.

- *Sending a link of the map to a contact*: Share your maps and directions with people who need the help via e-mail.

- *Saving a location through bookmarks*: This not only reduces typing time at a later date but also keeps all your favorites handy.

- *Receiving the route in text format*: Giving you all the directions from start to finish, in a written out comprehensive manner.

- *Viewing the route on the map, complete with turns and directions*: Seeing is believing.

- *Receiving information about points of interest through a comprehensive search*: You will always know where the closest hotel, shopping mall, hospital, or food joint really is.

However, this application does have a few requirements of its own. They include the following:

- A wireless data service plan from your service provider. Please contact them for further details.

- A running device software v4.1 or later. You can upgrade your present version from www.blackberry.com/upgrade.

- Available network connections to be able to download the map data.

> **NOTE:** AT&T does not support the Maps Application. If this is your service provider, please check with them for further updates.

Downloading BlackBerry Maps Application[1]

If you find yourself staring at a blank screen instead of the maps application, it could be that the application needs to be downloaded. This is a very simple procedure and requires just a couple of minutes.

BlackBerry Maps application has many advantages over other applications. For starters, the BlackBerry Maps can map an address from your Contacts directly without having to retype or copy and paste. It also allows you to set the direction in which you're heading as Up. This is not allowed in other applications (such as Google Maps). Plus, if you have a weak data plan or Internet connection, the speed of accessing the other maps through the browser might be a cause of concern.

To download the BlackBerry Maps application, log onto http://na.blackberry.com/eng/devices/features/blackberry_maps.jsp and download it for absolutely free. You could choose to download it directly from your phone's browser or through your computer. Both options are available to you here. Select the one most suited to you to proceed.

---

[1] BlackBerry Maps Application only works in the following countries: USA, Canada, UK, Austria, Belgium, Luxembourg, Czech Republic, Denmark, Finland, France (including Monaco), Germany, Greece, Hungary, Ireland, Italy (including Vatican City and San Marino), Liechtenstein, The Netherlands, Norway, Poland, Portugal, Slovakia, Spain (including Andorra), Russia, Sweden, Switzerland, Turkey, Lithuania, Estonia, Latvia, Slovenia, Croatia, Albania, Bulgaria, Moldova, Romania, Belarus, Bosnia Herzegovina, (Former Yugoslav Republic of) Macedonia, Serbia, Montenegro, Ukraine, Hong Kong, Singapore, Malaysia, and United Arab Emirates.

If your country is not listed here, you might need to download another map application, such as Google Maps, Gmaps, Spot for BlackBerry, Wayfinder Navigator, and so on, most of which are free and can be downloaded from the Internet or directly through your BlackBerry Browser Application.

Download Through the Computer

If you choose to download the application through the computer, make sure your BlackBerry device is connected to it using the USB cable. Once that is done, open the above-mentioned site through your Microsoft Internet Explorer. This is because the web page that follows uses ActiveX Controls that are available only in Internet Explorer. If you do not have Internet Explorer, you should opt for the feature that allows for downloading directly through your smartphone.

Assuming you have Internet Explorer and choose to download it with the computer, select your preferred language and click on Download (see Figure 12–1).

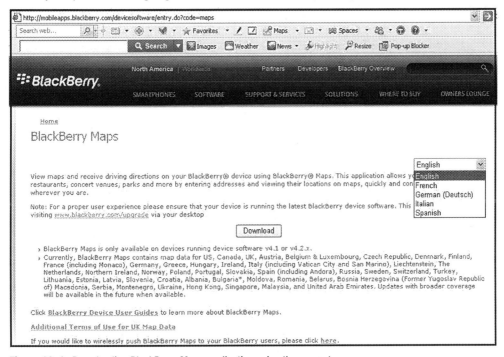

Figure 12–1. *Downloading BlackBerry Maps application using the computer*

Reconfirm your language options and click on Next. After this, the software will take you to the Terms and Conditions page. If you accept the terms, choose I Accept and click on Next. Follow the instructions to proceed.

Download Through the BlackBerry Browser

After choosing this option, you will be taken to a page that asks for the e-mail address associated with your BlackBerry handheld. Type it in and click on Submit (see Figure 12–2).

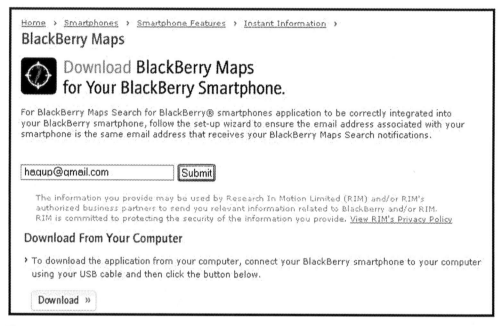

Figure 12–2. *Dowloading BlackBerry Maps Application using the BlackBerry Browser*

Shortly after, you will receive a mail from BlackBerry in your inbox with a link that takes you through the download process (see Figure 12–3). Click on that link and follow the instructions to proceed.

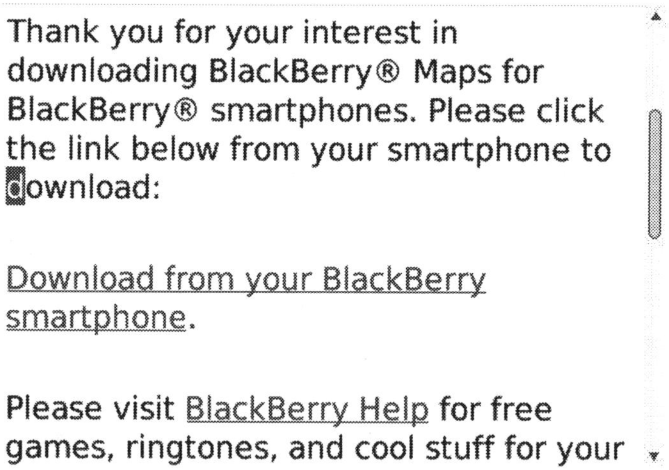

Thank you for your interest in downloading BlackBerry® Maps for BlackBerry® smartphones. Please click the link below from your smartphone to download:

Download from your BlackBerry smartphone.

Please visit BlackBerry Help for free games, ringtones, and cool stuff for your

Figure 12–3. *Screen illustrating the message and download link received through e-mail*

BlackBerry Maps

From finding the location of a meeting scheduled in a foreign land to satisfying your sudden craving for ice cream, BlackBerry maps will show you the way. To use BlackBerry Maps, your GPS needs to be turned on. If you use a model that is not GPS enabled or your wireless provider doesn't support location-based services, you can use Bluetooth-enabled GPS receivers that can be paired with your BlackBerry easily. Your location-based software uses the GPS in your device to help you get around, give you directions, illustrate your present position, as well as help you find the closest search solutions.

Turn on your GPS by going to the Options application and selecting Advanced Options from the menu. From the list, select GPS. Turn the GPS Services field to Location ON. Now press the Menu button and select Save. You can always turn off the GPS technology by selecting Location OFF from the same page.

Navigational Aid

Once you have the application downloaded, you are ready to start using it. Without wasting any further time, let's get to the basics.

Go to the Maps application to activate it. Some of the navigation techniques are as follows:

- Pan a map by rolling the trackball in the direction you would like to go. Just slide your fingers in any direction on the screen if you are a BlackBerry Storm user and on the trackpad if you use the BlackBerry Curve, instead of the trackball.

▓ Zoom a map by pressing the trackball once. Here, along with the map, you will see a scale on the left corner of the screen. Zoom in by rolling the trackball up and zoom out by rolling the trackball down. Select a particular level of zoom by pressing the trackball again (see Figure 12–4). If you use a device that does not have a trackball, then press the Menu button and click on Zoom. Use your finger on the scale to zoom in or out in case of touchscreen and slide your fingers up or down on the trackpad as need be.

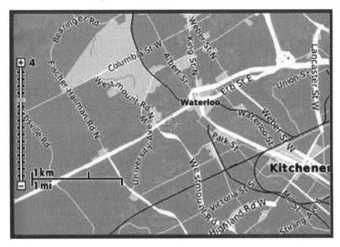

Figure 12–4. *Zooming in and out of the Maps*

▓ To zoom in on a location, highlight the location marker and press on the Menu key. Select Zoom To Point from the options, as illustrated in Figure 12–5.

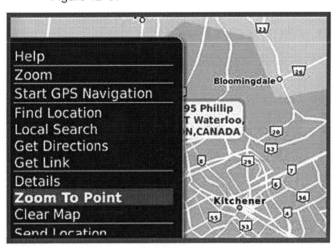

Figure 12–5. *Zooming to a particular point on the map*

Locating All

Have an important meeting with a partner and do not know the way? Such situations would normally call for measures involving frantic calls and stress. Now relieve yourself of such strain and anxiety by using the location feature. It helps you find out where you are, the location of an address, as well as the location of a contact on the map.

On a map, press the Menu button and select Find Location, as shown in Figure 12–6.

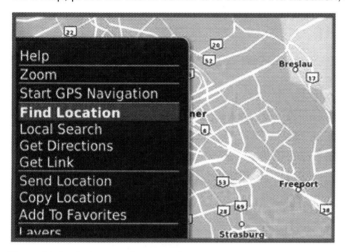

Figure 12–6. *Finding a particular location on the map*

After selecting it, you will find yourself with three options:

- *Where Am I*: This will tell you your present location.

- *Enter Address*: This will illustrate for you the typed-out address position on the map. Either type the address out directly or check the Advanced option if you wish to feed in the information in specific address fields.

- *From Contacts*: This allows you to choose a contact directly from your address book (one whose address has been established already, i.e., colleagues, family, and friends), and illustrates their position on the map. You can save two addresses per contact, under Work and Home titles, respectively.

You could also follow one of these options:

- *Favorites*: This option allows you to access already established favorites directly.

- *Recent*: This option is a real saver and helps you revisit certain locations, without having to establish them all over again.

Search the Market

Local Search is a very valuable feature, especially when one is hard-pressed for time and is a boon to the weary traveler; a tool that identifies the closest businesses is priceless. Just select the Local Search feature from the Menu options. Upon doing this, you will be asked to type out the category or requirement in the form of key words, such as café, pharmacy, courier, travel agency, printing press, theatre, and then choose Enter. The map will throw out nearby probable options for you to choose from. You can also get directions to the one you select.

Favorites and More

You can bookmark certain addresses so that you do not have to retype their specifics time and again. This gets saved to your favorites section and allows for quick reference. To bookmark an address, go to Add To Favorites from the Menu options. The address will be highlighted for you. If it is correct, click on OK (see Figure 12–7).

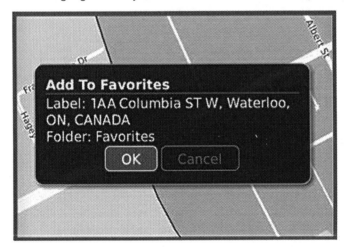

Figure 12–7. *Adding an address to the Favorites foldertips*

- ▓ You can rename the bookmark in the Label field and change the location of the bookmark by altering the Folder field.

- ▓ Change the location of a bookmark by highlighting it in your Favorites section and selecting Edit from the Menu options. Change it accordingly and Save.

- ▓ Add another folder by selecting Add Subfolder from the Menu options of the Favorites section.

- ▓ Delete a bookmark by highlighting it and selecting Delete from the Menu options.

Directions from Start to End

If you want the exact direction from one place to another, either through the shortest route, the fastest route, or avoiding highways or avoiding tolls, this is your section. Select Get Directions while the Map application is on from the Menu options. Specify a start point either by clicking on it in the map or by giving the coordinates/address. Once the start point is established, repeat the steps to fix an end location. The application will highlight your search requirement along with giving you route options (see Figure 12–8). Once this is established, select Search.

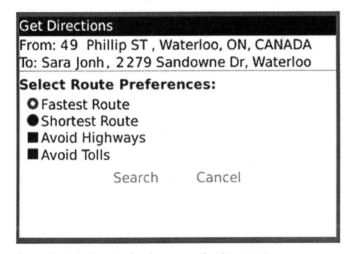

Figure 12–8. *Getting the directions as per the chosen route*

After getting the directions, by pressing on the Menu key, you could:

- *View it on the Map*: This will show you the route on the map along with specific instructions vis-à-vis turning points and road curves.

- *Get Reverse Directions*: You could get the directions from end to start point by choosing this option. It will show you the best route back.

Forwarding Directions and Routes

If you want to send the route to a colleague, choose the Send Directions option from the Menu list while in the Map application. Next, the application will ask you how you would prefer to do so, i.e., via e-mail, MMS, or PIN. Choose the appropriate format to send (see Figure 12–9).

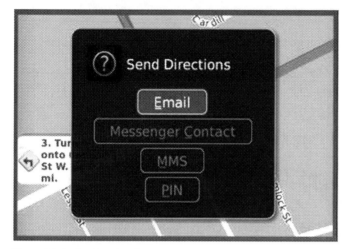

Figure 12–9. *Sending directions to a contact*

NOTE: You could also forward it by choosing E-mail Location from the Menu Options.

Tracking Yourself Moving

To track your movement, on the map, click the trackwheel and select Start GPS. You will notice that as you move from one place to another, the map changes while your position remains centered to the screen at all times. The only problem is that the back light goes off shortly, resulting in distraction while driving (if you are) to illuminate. Therefore, in order to set your backlight on while tracking your movement on a map, select Options from the Menu list and set the Backlight Timeout When: (Battery Power field) accordingly between 100% and 20%. Press the Menu button and select Save.

What's Next?

Music today has moved on from being just a means of entertainment. Most people have grown to love it so much that it becomes a part of their identity. How often have you caught yourself asking a new acquaintance their choice in music? I am sure, plenty. While at work or in the subway, while at the gym or relaxing at home, music has come to mean a great deal to many of us. Obviously, BlackBerry would not overlook such an important facet of our existence. Realize the relationship between the BlackBerry and the iPod in the next chapter.

Chapter 13

BlackBerry as an iPod

The Musical Touch

Even though the music feature might not have too much to offer to the professional users in the direct sense of the word, its positive effects can't be ignored. If stress is the biggest killer, then music is one of the most therapeutic ways of dealing with it. Nervousness, anxiety, temper, tension—these emotions find common place in business and professional setups. Listening to a few minutes of preferred music can help calm agitated nerves to a great extent—thus making it a facilitator to your professional needs. So tell me then, if something contributes towards your improved performance (reducing blunders and fumbles due to nervousness or cracking up due to pressure), doesn't it become an important enough tool in your workspace?

What does "BlackBerry as an iPod" mean? As funny as that may sound, it basically is a means for you to sync your music files with your smartphone using playlists from iTunes or Windows Media Player. You also have an option of syncing individual songs from the source files directly. This song transfer and playlist management is made available to you either by using the BlackBerry Media Sync software or by using Roxio Media Manager for BlackBerry. BlackBerry Media sync works with music files alone, whereas Roxio Media Manager can be used to manage your videos, music, and pictures together.

To get started, the only installations required are an external memory card and the Desktop Manager Software. You could also include third party applications to that. However, that remains optional. The Desktop Manager Software is available for Mac as well as PC users. It usually comes along with your phone package but can also be downloaded from BlackBerry's official site. The links to downloading them are:

- For Mac users:
  http://na.blackberry.com/eng/services/desktop/desktop_mac.jsp

- For PC users:
  http://na.blackberry.com/eng/services/desktop/desktop_pc.jsp

Roxio Media Manager

This is the media player that comes as a preset along with your Desktop Manager software. On launching the desktop manager, and selecting Media Manager, you will find yourself in the media library where you can control pictures, music, and video media file transfers all in one place. Its drag and drop feature makes transferring data a quick and simple task.

It also automatically offers to convert the format as per your choice, be it for optimal playback or as per advanced conversion options (see Figure 13–1).

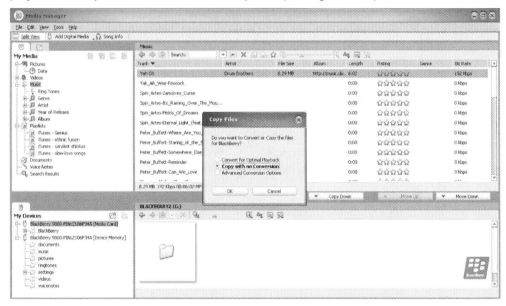

Figure 13–1. *Screenshot illustrating the various conversion options that are available through the application*

Roxio also maintains the information associated with the media files and transfers it to the smartphone library. For further details on managing music through this software, you could look at the online help available at Roxio Media Manager.

> **NOTE:** Media Manager for BlackBerry is only available for models that have a trackball including the Pearl 8100 series, the Curve 8300 series, and the 8800 series.

BlackBerry Media Sync

This is free software by RIM that helps you to transfer playlists and music files from your Mac as well as PC to your smartphone through iTunes and Windows Media Player alike.

BlackBerry Media Sync also has a unique feature that permits you to decide how much or how little memory space should be used by the downloaded music, hence guaranteeing free space at all times. By setting this, the software automatically stops syncing more music once the limit is reached.

The process involved for this is as follows:

1. First connect your BlackBerry handheld to your computer using the USB cable.

2. From the task bar, click on Start and choose Programs.

3. In Programs, Select BlackBerry Media Sync. On doing so, a welcome screen should open.

4. Once that is done, type a personalized name for your BlackBerry device in the name field.

5. In the Keep __%Free From Music field, denote the memory card/on board memory (in case of mass storage facility) space that should be kept free from music files and click on OK.

Simple as that.

Media Sync is only compatible with devices featuring software v4.2 or higher. If your OS is of a lower version, you might want to upgrade it beforehand. Also, devices that do not have mass storage capacities should make sure external memory cards such as MicroSD are properly inserted before syncing.

The BlackBerry Media Sync Software can be downloaded from the official web site. The direct URL is http://na.blackberry.com/eng/services/media/mediasync.jsp.

> **NOTE:** As Media Sync allows you to maintain both Windows Media Player as well as iTunes playlists simultaneously, there would be a possibility of duplication of music files on your smartphone, especially if both playlists draw music from the same source files.

Transferring Music Files

This as a process is fairly simple and does not require more than two or three simple steps. Transferring music files can be done in one of the following ways:

- Using Roxio Media Manager
- Using a mass storage device
- Using Bluetooth

Using Roxio Media Manager

To transfer music files this way, first connect your handset to your computer using the USB cable. After that, launch the Desktop Manager and double click on Media Manager. Once that's done select Music Files to drag and drop the music accordingly (see Figure 13-2).

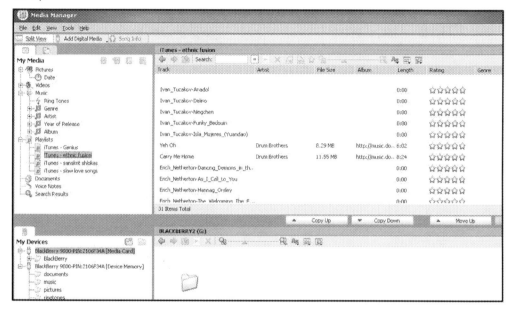

Figure 13-2. *A screen representing an example list of songs made available through Media Manager that have been taken from the iTunes playlists*

Using a Mass Storage Facility

To utilize this feature, make sure your mass storage mode is turned on. On connecting your handheld to your computer, you'll get a prompt asking you about the connection. Select Yes to proceed. Then, from Devices with Removable Storage in My Computer, select Removable Disk. Again, drag and drop the music files according to your requirement.

Using Bluetooth

Using Bluetooth allows for wire elimination. This can be done directly from your handheld without having to connect to a device physically. However, you need to make sure that your Bluetooth is enabled and is paired with the Bluetooth enabled device. Once this is done, select the media type (ringtones, music files, and so on) from your Media Application and press the Menu key. Here choose Receive Using Bluetooth and select Save.

Media Application

The Media Application of your BlackBerry is easy to understand and operate. Here, you will find options such as Music, Videos, Ringtones, Pictures, and Voice Notes (see Figure 13–3).

> **NOTE:** We touched on the Media application in Chapter 9. Here we cover the specifics of using music on your BlackBerry, as it's a more natural place for this discussion.

Figure 13–3. *Screenshot highlighting Music as part of the Media options*

On choosing the Music option, you shall see a screen with a whole set of options that arrange your music files based on Artists, Albums, Genres, Playlists, and All Songs. It also gives you an option to shuffle the songs randomly playing them back-to-back (see Figure 13–4).

Figure 13–4. *The list of preset options available for optimal music organizing*

While Playing a Music File

When a song is playing, you can stop it, pause it, or play the next and the previous directly (see Figure 13–5). You can also forward or rewind a particular song by dragging along the progress bar.

Figure 13–5. *A sample song paused while playing in the Media Application*

Along with that, view songs and videos while playing any music file by pressing the Menu button and choosing Music Home. From this menu, you can select Repeat, Replay, Shuffle, and Show Playlist. Select any as per your need and enjoy your music.

Playlist Management

A playlist is a programmed list of music files that can be created from any audio content to play songs that are grouped together in the desired order. For instance, you could have a playlist based on genre, artist, tempo, occasion, and so on. The BlackBerry facilitates for you to make standard as well as automatic playlists, as described in the upcoming sections.

Standard Playlist

The standard playlist is created by selecting individual songs from your music files and manually adding them. To do so, select the Playlist option from Music in your Media application. Here, select New Playlist and further narrow it to Standard Playlist. Give it a name and then press on the Menu key. Here select Add Song and then choose a song from your media files. Repeat this process to add songs individually. Once your playlist is completed, press the Menu button and select Save.

You could, at any given point, alter this playlist by adding, moving, or deleting songs from the playlist. To do that, once the playlist is highlighted, press the Menu button and select View. From here, you can Add Song by pressing the Menu key as well as Delete and Move the highlighted song as your heart desires. Don't forget to Save once you have completed your edits.

Automatic Playlist

The automatic playlist can be created routinely without constant manual intervention. This can be done by specifying the criteria on which the playlist is based. This could either be by artist, genre, song, or album. Even when you add new songs to your device that meet these criteria, the application automatically adds it to the playlist along with demonstrating to you that it has done so, in the form of an indicator next to the playlist.

This can be created by going through Media application➤Music➤Playlist➤New Playlist. Here, press the Menu button and select Automatic Playlist. After giving it a name, select the (+) symbol next to either: Artist, Genre, or Album (see Figure 13–6).

Figure 13–6. *Creating Automatic Playlists in the Media Application*

Specify the details to which the playlist should be applicable. You can have multiple criteria that are applicable to the same playlist too. After completing your settings, press the Menu button again and then Save.

Quick Tips

- To find out how much free space you have left on your device memory or media card, go to Memory that is either part of your Options application or Device options, depending on your BlackBerry model.

- Press the Mute key to pause a song or video. Press it again to resume.

- Press N to play the next song in the same category.

- Press P to play the previous song in the same category.

- Press and hold the Volume key down to play the next song in a playlist.

- Press and hold the Volume key up to play the previous song in a playlist.

PLEASE NOTE

- Some of the songs that you download from the iTunes library might be DRM (digital rights management) protected or in the .m4p format that only allows for playback using Apple products such as iTunes media player, iPod, or an iPhone. However, there is software such as TuneClone available in the market that converts the protected .m4p to an easily usable mp3 or WAV format legally. Thus, by using this software, you will be able to play all your iTunes songs on your BlackBerry with ease.

- Software that can be used for the same purpose while specializing in ringtones is the BlackBerry Ringtone Maker. It enables you to convert different audio files such as WMA, WAV, RA, M4A, AAC, AC3, OGG, and so on to MP3 format that can be saved as BlackBerry ringtone directly. It also helps you to extract audio in the MP3 format from video files which can be converted into ringtones easily.

What's Next?

Ice cream comes with nuts, toppings, and cream; watches offer the day, month, year, or even temperature; houses come fully loaded, appliances and all—and our appreciation of the product with multiple add-ons ascends. Third-party applications, added downloading privileges, a couple of free apps thrown in and heightened browsing experiences provide a glimpse into the BlackBerry App World (BAW). Well, let's just say, it's the cherry on the top!

Chapter 14

Understanding App World

My Berry, My World...

In this chapter, you will be introduced to BlackBerry App World (BAW) which is a storehouse of applications ranging from weather forecasts to games to music and even to news updates. Chapter 15 will take you through a wide range of business applications that will help you with expense tracking, travelling, database management, and so forth. All the applications that are covered in the next chapter can be found at BAW, thus it becomes essential for you to know how to download and use it. BAW is a sleek, user-friendly platform; the applications range through an extensive list of categories. They are the following:

- Business
- Entertainment
- Finance
- Games
- Health & Wellness
- IM & Social Networking
- Maps & Navigation
- Music & Audio
- News
- Photo & Video
- Productivity
- Reference & eBooks
- Shopping
- Sports & Recreation
- Themes
- Travel
- Utilities
- Weather

BAW is a RIM application distribution service that allows BlackBerry consumers to update and download third-party applications. It makes available apps that are both free of cost as well as paid for. The user can download these applications directly from their handset as well as through an online transaction. The only requirement being that your handset should have an OS of v4.2 or higher. The payment (for paid-for applications) is powered by PayPal. Therefore, you should have a PayPal account so that these transactions can be made. If you do not have one yet, visit www.paypal.com and create an account. In fact, there also is a PayPal mobile application available at BAW. For more details on downloading and using it, please refer to Chapter 15.

Because of its recent development, BlackBerry App World is only available in certain countries.

- In some countries, both free as well as paid-for applications are available. They are: US, Canada, UK, Ireland, Austria, Germany, Spain, France, Portugal, Luxembourg, Belgium, Netherlands, and Italy.

- However, there is a whole inventory of free applications that is offered by RIM in the following nations: Brazil, Venezuela, Argentina, Chile, Mexico, Colombia, Ecuador, Peru, Panama, Costa Rica, Jamaica, Aruba, Bahamas, Cayman Islands, Barbados, Trinidad and Tobago, Dominican Republic, Hong Kong, Singapore, Indonesia, and India. Users from the preceding countries are eligible to use the free applications but cannot use the third-party applications that require payment.

BlackBerry App World by some is considered to be RIM's version of Apple's App Store.

Basic System Requirements

BlackBerry App World provides BlackBerry users with an environment to explore, update, and download applications. However, to utilize this feature, there are some basic system requirements that need to be met. They are the following:

- A BlackBerry Device Software of version 4.2 or higher. You can find out your device's OS by selecting About from the Options menu. Here, your phone will display all your software details including the operating system, model details, networks, etc.

- BlackBerry Smartphone with a SurePress touch screen or a trackball.

- A service plan that allows you to access the BlackBerry Browser.

NOTE: You can update your BlackBerry Device Software by following this URL: http://in.blackberry.com/services/devices/.

Downloading Made Simple

You could download BlackBerry App World directly from your mobile as well as your desktop computer. The process is simple and shouldn't take more than a couple of minutes.

- To download it directly from your mobile just follow one of the following links: www.blackberry.com/appworld/download or www.mobile.blackberry.com (see Figure 14–1).

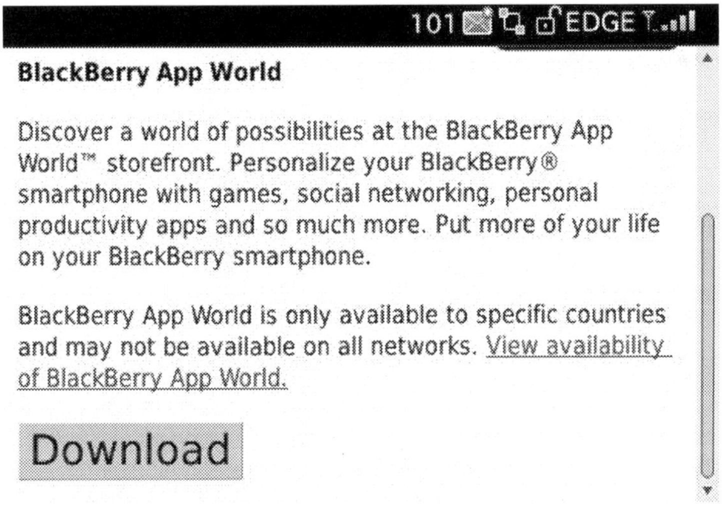

BlackBerry App World

Discover a world of possibilities at the BlackBerry App World™ storefront. Personalize your BlackBerry® smartphone with games, social networking, personal productivity apps and so much more. Put more of your life on your BlackBerry smartphone.

BlackBerry App World is only available to specific countries and may not be available on all networks. View availability of BlackBerry App World.

Download

Figure 14–1. *The screen that allows for direct download through the handset*

- To download from your computer, go to http://in.blackberry.com/services/appworld/ and click on Download BlackBerry App World. This will take you to a page where you need to type in your e-mail address (the one that is associated with your smartphone) and select Submit. You will then receive a mail in your inbox. Follow the instructions given to proceed.

- To download from your desktop computer directly to your phone, again visit http://in.blackberry.com/services/appworld/ and connect your handset to your computer through the USB port. Once that's done, click on Download (see Figure 14–2).

Download BlackBerry App World

BlackBerry App World™ is available for free. If you have a PayPal® account, and if your BlackBerry® smartphone meets the system requirements, then you're ready to download BlackBerry App World from your smartphone or from your desktop computer.

From your BlackBerry smartphone

Simply visit www.blackberry.com/appworld/download from your smartphone to download. Or, enter an email address that's integrated with your BlackBerry smartphone below and click submit to have a download link sent to you.

> The information you provide may be used by Research In Motion Limited (RIM) and/or RIM's authorized business partners to send you relevant information related to BlackBerry and/or RIM. RIM is committed to protecting the security of the information you provide. View RIM's Privacy Policy.

Email Address :

☐ YES, I'd like to stay informed about updates to BlackBerry App World

Submit

Figure 14–2. *The online version for downloading BAW*

> ▓ Downloading through Virtual Preload is also a possibility. Some carriers provide the BlackBerry smartphone with a built-in BlackBerry App World shortcut icon in the applications list. All you have to do is click on the icon which will start the downloading process. For details on whether your handset is eligible for this, please contact your service provider.

On initiating the download through any of the above processes, you will be shown a License Agreement. Once you have confirmed your consent, the download process begins. Once downloaded, the BAW icon appears on the Home screen or part of the Applications screen as an individual icon in BlackBerry Devices with an operating system of 4.5 or earlier. If you are a v4.6 or later user, then you will find the BAW icon in your Downloads folder.

Let's Explore BAW

Now comes the exciting part, the discovery of this world of possibilities. Once you have completed the download process, this world opens itself to you with just a simple tap/click. To enter, all you need to do is select the BlackBerry App World icon (see Figure 14–3).

Figure 14–3. *The BlackBerry App World Icon in the Downloads folder of v4.6 software*

Upon doing so, you will find yourself looking at a screen with certain applications that are selected by RIM and listed for you to check out, complete with user ratings, price, and a brief explanation. Figure 14–4 is one such example.

Figure 14–4. *An example of one of the specially listed applications by RIM*

You can scroll left or right, so as to go through the other applications that were shortllsted by RIM. If you would like to examine any one in particular, just click/tap on it to proceed.

Information at Your Doorstep

The look and feel of an application plays a pivotal role in our perception of it. This is why the BAW environment provides you with every option so that you can make a well-informed choice with no scope for ambiguity or doubt.

Upon clicking on the application, you will be directed to a screen that offers you information such as the vendor, the version, and the size of the application. It also gives you complete details of the price. While scrolling down, you are given a brief outline on what the application entails along with special features and innovations. You can also follow a link that enables you to contact support, to direct any queries to the developer's support team.

Apart from that, it also lists the following options for you:

- Download: When you click on this, the download process starts.

- Reviews: This option takes you to an entire discussion forum where you can read reviews submitted by users of the application. This not only gives you a clearer understanding of the general opinion, but also helps you identify areas that could be a cause of concern. With all this information at your disposal, you can decide whether your purchase will deliver what it promises.

- Recommend: You could choose to recommend it to a contact too. For instance, if you come across a great business application, you could recommend it to your colleague immediately through this option. When you select this, the software asks you for your mode of communication, i.e., through PIN, E-mail, SMS, MMS, or Messenger. Choose the appropriate option.

- Screenshots: This is where the look and layout can be gauged by you. Clicking on this option will take you to a series of primary screenshots of the application. This option is particularly valuable when choosing themes. You've got to know what the theme looks like before you download it now, don't you?

Figures 14–5a, 14–5b, and 14–5c illustrate the preceding discussion.

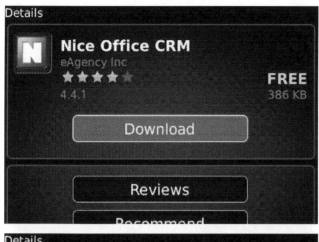

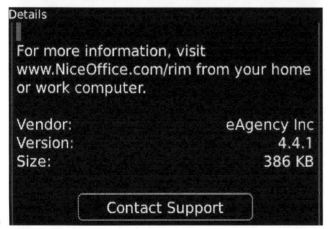

Figures 14–5a, 14–5b, and 14–5c. *These figures illustrate the details provided by the application before downloading.*

And the Applications Are...

Clear and concise categorization can save valuable time, effort, and energy. While it all sounds very sensible, having to make this segregation can be quite cumbersome. Well, BAW does this for you; it lists all the applications in various sections. This means you can browse the available applications by any of the following:

- Categories: Surf through the applications based on the categories listed at the beginning of this chapter. Under each category, you will find a further break down of applications based on their exact nature. For instance, under Business, you'll find options such as Business Tools, Data Collection, Real Estate, Sales, and Services, Time Tracking, and so on.

- Top Free: This lists the most regularly downloaded applications that are available free of charge. However, this will not be broken down by category and is more like an amalgamation of popular apps.

- Top Paid: If yours is a country that can use the paid applications option, then this link takes you to the most used paid for applications available on BAW. Similar to Top Free, this too will not catalog the apps by function.

- Search: You could also run a direct search on the basis of a search term or key word.

- My World: Like the name suggests, this is your domain. The applications chosen by you appear here with their current status (installed / uninstalled etc).

The following icons will help you identify these options better:

The Category Icon lists the applications based on category.

The Top Free Icon lists applications based on the most popular free applications.

The Top Paid Icon lists the applications based on the most popular paid-for applications.

The Search Icon searches based on keywords.

The My World Icon lists all your selected and downloaded applications together.

Pass the Money, Honey

As mentioned earlier, there is a list of applications that are paid for. Most of the apps are very affordable and reasonably priced; however, the range varies between $2.99 and $999.99. The payment mode is directed through PayPal and purchasing a paid app requires an account.

Upon clicking the Purchase option, you will be asked to clarify whether you have a PayPal account or not. If you do not have one, it will recommend you create one on the web before proceeding. If you do have an account, log in using the e-mail id and password that is associated with your PayPal account. This need not necessarily be the one associated with your BlackBerry handset.

The final check screen illustrating all the details such as price along with tax and source of funding (like your bank account) will appear for you to confirm. When you are happy with the details shown, select the Buy Now option. After you do this, the download process should initiate immediately.

> **NOTE:** If, during the downloading, there is a break in the signal or internet connection, BAW resumes the download as soon as connectivity is reestablished.

Rated

Once you download the application, you are entitled to one more feature—rating it. To do this, go to the application and click on it. When it opens, it will list options such as Run, Reviews, Recommend, and Screenshots. Upon selecting the Reviews option, you will be given an option of Add Review. You can add your review of your experience as well as rate the application ranging from none to five stars, with five stars being the best. It is through these ratings that other consumers and RIM get their most authentic feedback, so do take a few moments to complete this.

What's Next?

Business travelers and expense trackers, social networkers and mind-mappers, file managers and text editors—professional roles and responsibilities range through a wide spectrum, each complete with its own set of tasks and duties. It is only fair that they get all the tools they need to be able to meet these requirements optimally. No wonder BlackBerry has a whole array of business applications directed toward these high achievers.

Chapter 15

General Business Apps

It's All About Business

BlackBerry's booming land office *business* doesn't come as a shocker to anyone. Its popularity is high and growing. You can be assured I mean *business* when I reiterate the practicality in adopting this gadget. I am convinced that the BlackBerry has made it its *business* to simplify your life, just like I have made it mine to prove this very fact to you. So dropping the monkey *business* for a while, let's get down to some serious business applications.

This chapter will introduce and discuss various third-party applications that can be downloaded onto your device. These will assist you in handling and running your business more efficiently. The applications covered in this chapter are a mere example of the multiple apps that are available in the market. In this vast ocean of information, all I do is provide you with an introduction to them. How you optimize on this is up to you.

The following categories are covered, providing you with apps within each group:

- Apps for business travelers
- Financial and expense trackers
- Apps that help you get things done
- Mind-mapping and brainstorming tools
- Apps that let you remote connect to and control your computer
- Jobs searching apps
- Note taking and text editing
- File management apps
- Databases and information managers
- Shipment and package tracking apps
- Social networking and messaging apps
- Miscellaneous apps that help in further optimization

Apps for Business Travelers

Today, traveling from one part of the globe to the other isn't as big a deal as it was a couple of decades ago. Flights connect the remotest of places to the busiest cities. To "Travel the world and the seven seas," (from the song "Sweet Dreams") has become common business. If you are a jet-setting professional, you can expect to spend a great deal of your time at airports or on the move. In times like this, a 24x7 assistant that organizes and plans your travel schedule, helps you with translations, or manages your hotel bookings might seem like a godsend. The travel apps offered for your BlackBerry do just this, while helping you sort out your currency conversions and locale-specific searches.

Organizer Apps

There a number of apps offered which help you structure and organize your trips better, offering convenience and synchronization alike. One such application is WorldMate.

WorldMate Live: Travel Like a Pro

WorldMate Live—Travel Like a Pro is brought to you by WorldMate and is a free app available at BlackBerry App World. Download it from here and find essential travel assistance at your disposal immediately. It supports most devices and carriers while being available in all countries.

You will need a WorldMate account to use this application. You can create it from their web site (www.worldmate.com) with a user ID and password of your choice. After downloading the app, you will be required to give your consent to the license agreement. If you do accept the terms, select Next to proceed. After that, you need to specify your country and city of stay. Once this is done, use your user ID and password from the live web account. If you do not have one, you can create it directly from this point as well. Log in using this ID and password to start using the app.

WorldMate Live: Travel Like a Pro is a free application. The advantages of using it are as follows:

- Make hotel bookings and get the best deals in a few simple steps. You can also fill in details of your preferences, so that the application narrows down searches.
- The items that are listed in your itinerary come complete with navigational details using the maps application of your choice.
- Weather forecasts and details from across the globe.
- Calendar synchronization with your schedule.
- Local searches and reviews at your disposal through solutions like Yelp.
- Currency conversions.
- For your convenience, the World Clocks feature is offered as well.

There is an advanced version of the app called WorldMate Live Gold. Though this is a subscription-based model, you are offered a seven-day trial period so that you can be sure before you opt for it. However, if you are a frequent flier then this is a wise investment, as it gives you access to a few extra features that are well worth it. They are the following:

- A flight status tracker that will give you real time updates on flight schedules and delays.

- Alerts pushed to your BlackBerry keeping you updated at all times. That means less time wasted at the airport and more time spent productively.

- A travel directory that gives you contact information for airlines, hotels, and so on, as illustrated in Figure 15–1.

- Alternate flight options.

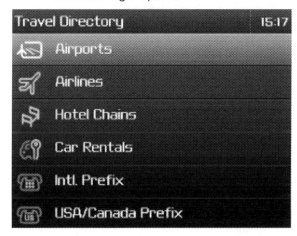

Figure 15–1. *Sample screen of Travel Dictionary*

Some of the features offered by WorldMate Live (see Figure 15–2) are as follows:

- *My Trips*: You can create a new trip in one of three ways: first, by forwarding all your travel e-mail confirmations to trips@worldmate.com; second, by logging into worldmate.com directly; and, third, by selecting the Add New Trip option from the Menu list.

- *Clocks*: World clock giving you time and day details.

- *Flight schedules*: This is a Gold membership service that gives you lists of various flight timetables.

- *Flight status*: Another Gold service that keeps you informed about your departure position.

- *Connections*: You can connect with your colleagues on the move by adding them as your connections. For this, you will simply need to send them an invite and get an acceptance from them to be able to exchange travel information.

- *Day/Night Map*: A map displaying the time of day, by time zone.

- *Travel directory*: A listing of critical travel information and contact details.

- *World weather*: Access to city specific weather details around the world.

- *Hotel booking*: Book hotels through this service. Other than that, it also makes available the option to set your preferences like price, star rating, brands and amenities desired and their importance.

- *Currency converter*: Helps you figure out various currency rates with regular updates.

- *Local search*: Find out the best restaurant, shopping, nightlife, and so on, through the local search offered by Yelp, complete with user reviews and recommendations.

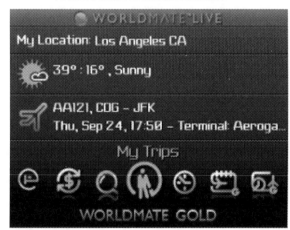

Figure 15–2. *WorldMate Live landing page*

You can synchronize your trips, create itineraries, change your location, check on promotional offers, and invite friends by pressing the Menu button and choosing the option accordingly. From this point, you can also alter your settings like trip reminder, flight reminder, temperature format, calendar sync settings, mapping application (BlackBerry Maps or Google Maps, depending on the applications found on your device), date format, and so forth.

Guide Apps

Applications that help and direct you in a new city or destination are guide apps. Where to eat, which sites to visit, how to understand and use public transport like the tubes in London or the subway in New York are some of the questions and solutions that these apps cover. Detailed maps of Walt Disney World Florida like WDW Maps brought to you by UPinPoint.com, or the closest restroom through SitOrSquat can be found in the Guide Apps section of BAW, giving you all the solutions you need of a place. I shall give you a broad introduction to some of them.

WCities London

A guide that is brought to you by M2MOBI BV covers current events, nightlife and tourist attractions for both locals as well as travelers. Find out which of your friends are located close to you as well as post picture updates. Figure out the hippest nightclubs to visit and understand the local flavor. There are WCities applications available for many locations including Amsterdam, Berlin and Athens.

Local Eats

This application is a foodie's delight bringing you the best restaurants and eating joints across US cities and parts of Canada (see Figure 15–3).

Figure 15–3. *The Local Eats branding*

The app is brought to you by Magellan Press, Inc.—the creators of WhereTheLocalsEat.com. It uses GPS location software to offer the best options. Restaurants are listed by category, neighborhood, the best search results, and in alphabetical order. Some of the other features include the following:

- Detailed driving directions to the chosen location
- User reviews and recommendations included

■ Pictures of the eateries along with the option of uploading your own pictures to the gallery

■ Ability to mark restaurants as favorites and share the same with friends and colleagues

■ Special offers and dining coupons made available occasionally

NYC Subway Trip Planner

An amazing app brought to you by railbandit.com, NYC Subway Trip Planner also works offline. That means this application continues to give you information even when connectivity isn't available. The subway maps and schedules are preloaded and thus do not require constant connectivity. All you need to do is choose two New York subway stations either on the map or through the pick list and you will be given direction details along with train timings, trip maps, and stop lines, as illustrated in Figures 15–4 and 15–5.

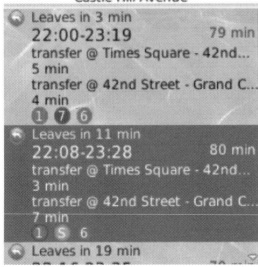

Figure 15–4. *NYC Subway Trip Planner illustrates route*

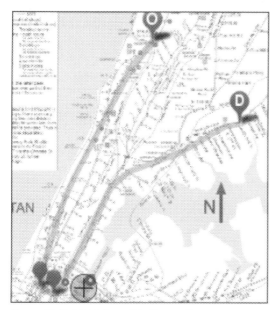

Figure 15–5. *NYC Subway Trip Planner illustrates route on map*

This is a paid-for application, but is sure to simplify your life—whether you are new to the city and struggling to find your way around or are a local and need a simpler solution to getting around. The app is supported by all BlackBerry devices and carriers.

Translators

One of the biggest hurdles faced by all travelers is the language barrier. Technology has truly reduced this obstacle through intuitive apps on your smartphone. Forget the little translation books. You will have all the terms and phrases right in your pocket. A great translation application is the Interlecta Translator.

Interlecta Translator

This translation app is one of the most user friendly apps available. It does not require you to learn anything new. It seamlessly integrates with the operating system. This application is brought to you by Interlecta OOD and is offered free of cost for a limited period. It is supported by most BlackBerry devices and by all carriers. It also is available in all countries except the United Kingdom.

With this app, you can translate any text on your screen, be it an SMS message, an e-mail, or a document. You can also share this translation with your colleagues and friends (see Figure 15–6).

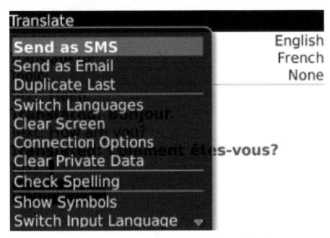

Figure 15–6. *Share translations with Interlecta Translator App*

NOTE: For our UK friends, other applications such as Navita Translator are also available which are free of cost.

Financial and Expense Trackers

Money, money, money—when it comes to taking care of it, it doesn't seem funny any more; neither in the poor man's world, nor in the aristocrat's paradise. And, if you have decided to make a career out of managing funds, you will need all the help you can get, and more. Good old dependable BlackBerry comes to the rescue, bringing with it some solutions, for both personal and professional aid.

Expense Tracking

You can now track your expenses and forward them to your company directly using some third party solutions. No more swimming in bills and accounts. A simple app will do the trick. There are a number of solutions that are available, which can be downloaded from BAW. Apart from Expense Log Pro 2 (which I have covered for you), another great application worth a try is HandyLogs Money.

Expense Log Pro 2

This application is a product of Motek Americas Inc. and is a complete expense management system for the professional and business user. The application is linked to their web site so you will need to have an account with them beforehand. It supports most devices, all countries, and carriers. Some of the features that come bundled with the application are as follows:

- Access to your accounts through the mobile app, meaning you can use them whenever you like.

- Access to many more features like printing and archiving offered through the web site.

- Ability to mail reports from your mobile app directly.

- Colleagues can view your expenses at your discretion as you can sync the material at any given point from the menu options.

- Reports can be saved as Excel sheets and PDF documents before submissions.

- Automatic currency conversion as well as mileage calculations depending on your settings beforehand.

- You can e-mail the expense log directly from the application too, as illustrated in Figure 15–7.

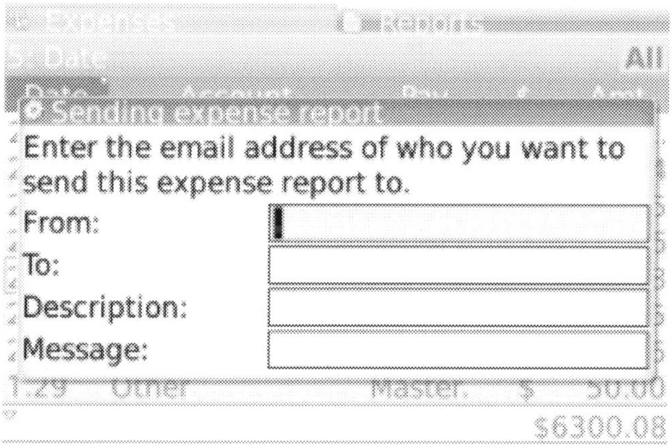

Figure 15–7. *Expense reports can be e-mailed directly using Expense Log Pro 2*

Once you log onto Expense Log Pro, you will see a welcome screen which will ask you to specify your currency, preferred date, and conversion formats as well as reimbursement rates before proceeding. First select the date/month formatting and then your chosen mileage unit (miles or kilometers). After that, you will need to indicate which currency it is that you use, for your total expense tally. Next, you need to confirm your mileage rate as in your payment per km/mile.

After that, you will need to configure your expenselog.net account details with that on your mobile application using the same user id and password. Once you fill in this data, the syncing process commences. After that, select Next if you agree to their terms and conditions. Once that is done, you are ready to use the application.

Getting started is very easy. All you need to do is select Add from menu list to add a new expense (see Figure 15–8). After you do this, the application will ask you details such as the following:

- *Date*: When the expenditure happened.

- *Category*: Whether the expense pertained to business, personal, or other reasons. You also have an option to create a new category here.

- *Account details*: This is where you can confirm the reason for the expenditure with categories ranging from entertainment, logging, meals, phone, supplies, travel, trips, etc.

- *Payment*: The mode of payment—cash or other.

- *Currency*: The currency used.

- *Vendor*: To whom the payment was made.

- *Attendees*: The people who attended it/were part of it.

- *Notes*: Any special notes that you would like to add.

- *Subtotal*: The amount paid.

- *Taxes*: The taxes applied.

- *Total*: The total expenditure.

- And lastly, whether it is reimbursable or not.

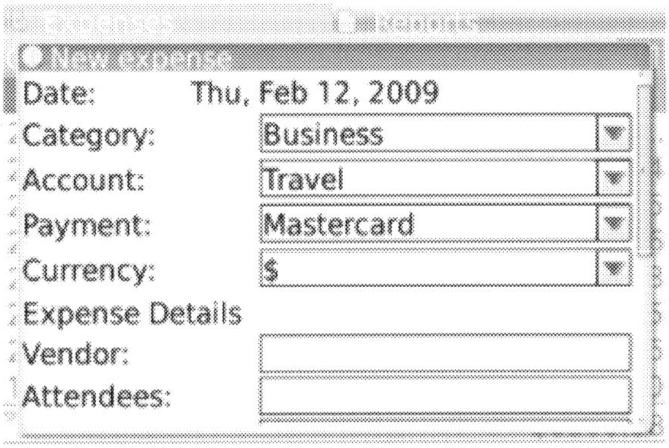

Figure 15–8. *Sample Screen of expenditure log*

After filling in the required fields, just select Save from the Menu options. There, your entry has been recorded.

With any entry highlighted, if you press on the Menu button, options such as Edit, Sort, Add, Delete, Sync now (which syncs the expenses to www.expenselog.net), User set up (leading to your e-mail id and password details), Preferences (such as Mileage Rates,

Default Settings, Network Options as well as Edit options), E-mail report, Reports, and so on, can be controlled from here.

Stocks

Watching out for your own company isn't enough. It's also important to know what's going on in the market and the position of your competitors. If you are an investor, then this vigilance becomes even more valuable. Luckily for you, there are solutions that will help you keep abreast with real-time developments; one such app is the Blue Mobile. Other than that, an app that is worth a mention is the iStockManager—TD AMITRADE by iStock Manager. This "Provider of Brokerage Services" is a free application available at BAW.

Blue Mobile

This product gives you access to local, regional, and global markets while offering real time information on stocks, commodities, and currencies. Brought to you by Blue System ME Ltd. this free application gives you comprehensive graphs and charts as shown in Figures 15–9 and 15–10.

blue mobile* NYSE				
Symbol	Last	Net	Net%	Open
Bank of USA	12.72	0.74	6.19%	12.20
Blue Square	9.49	0.33	3.60%	9.38
Citigroup	3.51	0.03	0.86%	3.50
Exxon	73.87	0.03	0.04%	74.00
Ford	6.16	-0.03	-0.47%	6.15
Gen Electric	13.54	0.15	1.08%	13.43
Intertape	1.17	0.00	0.00%	1.17
JPMorgan	34.84	0.00	0.00%	35.07
Morgan Stan	29.58	0.32	1.09%	29.58

Figure 15–9. *An example of the World Indices screen from the Blue Mobile app*

Figure 15–10. *Blue Mobile graphs help you understand company stocks.*

Though it supports all devices, it isn't available in all countries[1].

Advantages and key features of this product are illustrated in Figure 15–11, and also include the following:

- Stocks, financial futures, currencies, bonds, commodities, metals, energy, and mutual funds in real time unless prefixed with an "!".

- Use preloaded watch lists along with provision to make your own.

- Watch lists can be set as the Home screen for quick access too.

- Breaking news and business related bulletins are available.

- Switch between streaming mode and snapshot mode easily. In streaming mode, the quotes are updated continuously whereas in snapshot mode, the quotes are updated only on refreshing, which can be chosen from the menu options.

- You can receive preset alerts through the instant messenger.

- Instant messenger facilitates secure conversations with colleagues through the application directly.

---

[1] The countries that it doesn't support are: Anguilla, Antigua and Barbuda, Aruba, The Bahamas, Barbados, Bermuda, Cayman Islands, Dominica, El Salvador, Fiji Islands, Grenada, Guadeloupe, Guyana Haiti, Honduras, Hong Kong SAR, Jamaica, Martinique, Panama, Papua New Guinea, Saint Kitts and Nevis, Saint Lucia, Saint Vincent and the Grenadine, Samoa, Suriname, Tonga, Trinidad and Tobago, Turks and Caicos Islands, Vanuatu, and the British Virgin Islands.

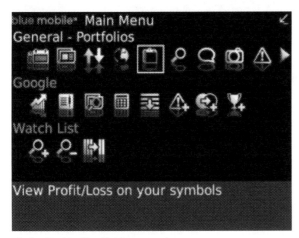

Figure 15-11. *Blue Mobile app main menu*

When you run the application for the first time after downloading, it will ask you to register. On the basis of this registration, you are provided with login details. You can skip this step if you're already a registered user. It will ask you for your mobile number, e-mail id, and a chosen password. After that, you will be asked if you agree to the Blue System Services and Interactive Data's Terms and Conditions. To check these out, press the menu button and select the individual agreements from the options listed. Next specify your connection (BIS, BES, Wi-Fi, and so on). Once that is done, select Receive Login from the Menu options.

Blue Mobile will provide you with a login based on the information you provided them. Make sure you note this down, because you will need it for your further interactions. Data charges might be applicable while using the market data. Once you have completed the registration, select Connect Streaming from the Menu. You will be given a few tips that will be very helpful in your usage of the application; go through them carefully. These tips can be referred to at a later date through the help (?) option from the Menu list too.

> **NOTE:** Get access to over 100 markets worldwide by going to http://bluesystems.info and subscribing to desired exchange data from My Account.

Shortcuts that will help are as follows:

- Press S to contact the customer support team.
- Press N to open news headlines.
- Press H to go to help.
- Press Z to open Quick Quote.
- Press C to open charts.

Personal Banking

All services regarding individual banking and facilities such as personal loans, current and saving accounts, home loans, mortgage loans, credit card services, and so forth come under the personal banking umbrella. Check out the various services it provides through the Personal Assistant application.

Personal Assistant

An app that comes highly recommended by CNN, Fox News, TechCrunch, and CNET, as is mentioned at BAW[2], is the Personal Assistant application. A Pageonce Inc product, it is a free application that supports all devices, countries, and carriers.

It boasts of delivering various life management applications that cover essential aspects of social and financial demands. They include investment portfolios, frequent flier miles, credit card supervision, real-time bank account status updates, mobile minute tracker, bill organization, travel itineraries, and shopping management to name a few.

All of the preceding are accessible on the same page (as illustrated in Figure 15–12) so that you do not have to navigate from one to the other in order to view your details. You can also control your account through the online version of the application at http://www.pageonce.com.

Figure 15–12. *Find all your accounts listed in one page with Personal Assistant*

NOTE: RIM has developed an application called Wallet. This is available at BAW and stores your personal information which can be used to fill in forms, thus reducing effort while making online purchases.

---

[2] http://appworld.blackberry.com/webstore/content/814

Apps That Help You Get Things Done

Apps that keep track of your tasks and follow-ups, help in making notes, store brainstorming ideas, list contacts, and watch out for your sales force—complete business tools that help you set targets and achieve them—now *those* are apps that will help you get your jobs done.

Upvise

Upvise is a complete business tool from Unyverse Pte Ltd that will help you look into most aspects of running your business as well as personal life. It has solutions for the individual and the small business executive. And what's more, this application is offered free of cost and supports all devices, carriers, and countries.

You will need an Upvise web account (that can be created by visiting www.upvise.com) to use this application optimally. It is on-demand collaboration software that provides mobile solutions to small business owners by providing a mobile computing platform, thereby reducing the stress and effort involved with servers and backups. Sharing data with your team on the computer as well as on the mobile is now an easy task.

Upvise has a business as well as a personal solution for its users. You can choose whichever is applicable to you. The solutions and features that it provides for the personal user are as follows:

- *Contacts*: Here you can import and export contacts (from and to your BlackBerry address book) along with maintain details of individual as well as company groups and region specific information separately.

- *Notebooks*: Fill in details and notes in this section.

- *Quote of the Day*: Get profound quotes delivered to you on your handset.

- *RSS News*: Get access to your favorite sites and news items.

- *Shopping lists*: Maintain shopping lists by category so that you never miss a thing.

- *Wikipedia*: Search the web and maintain saved searches for later reference.

Some of the business functions that this application fulfills are as follows:

- *Managing contacts*: Individual business contacts can be stored here along with company specific details. In the company details, you also have the provision to fill out details like addresses, number of employees, notes for new activities, tasks, and probable opportunities to name a few. The addresses also can be linked to Google Maps so that you can get directions to reaching them. Provision to assign tasks for yourself and co-workers is also available.

- *Jotting down ideas and brainstorming results*: Through the Ideas feature, catalog the ideas into custom-made categories and share them with colleagues.

- *Notebook*: This is like your note pad. It is flexible and can accommodate a great number of notes that could cover various topics ranging from customer suggestions to minutes of a meeting, as is obvious from Figure 15–13. Any information that you might want to refer to later can be stored here.

- *Projects*: Keep an eye on projects and their development, jot down tasks pertaining to a project, mark them as completed once they have been, make specific notes, identify milestones as well as hurdles right here.

- *Sales*: This feature allows you to keep a track on any leads you might get that could be converted to business opportunities, various quotes, and products (see Figure 15–14). Along with that a means to channelize sales forecast by month or owner.

- *Keeping track of tasks and responsibilities*: Use the Tasks feature for this. Maintain lists of overdue, eventual, as well as everyday task lists and mark them as competed as you go along. You can also categorize them on priority, by owner, date, contact, company, and so on.

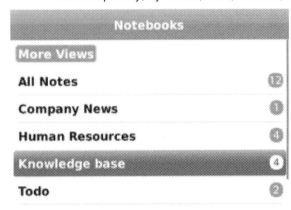

Figure 15–13. *The Notebook service by Upvise*

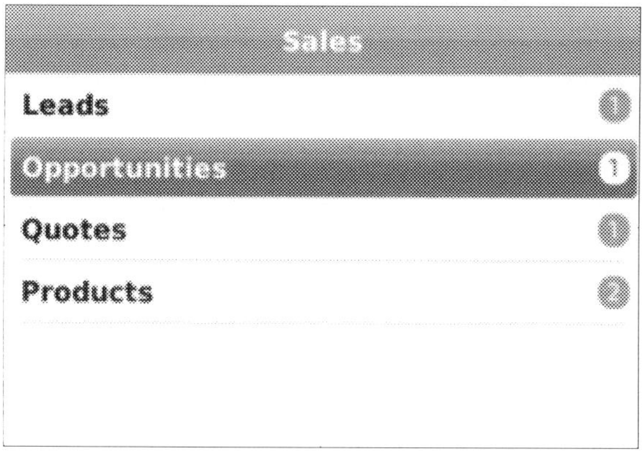

Figure 15–14. *The Sales Solution Upvise offers*

All in all, a great app that truly helps you get things done.

Mind-Mapping and Brain Storming Apps

Brainstorming as we all know is a very crucial part of any organization. From advertising to IT, from corporate settings to public relations, brainstorming has and always will be a fundamental process. Any innovation is born out of an idea which in turn brings about progress. And development is something every industry craves.

bMind

This solution is brought to you by Glam Software. Though it comes with a price tag, it delivers benefits and handiness. An application that supports all devices, countries, and carriers, bMind also supports one other factor: creative thinking.

The worst fate a great idea can have is getting lost in translation. How many times have we all thought of brilliant solutions and deep concepts which have slipped away because we could not execute them? Or disappeared simply because that moment of clarity evaded us when we did have the means to jot it down. Never find yourself in a sorry situation like that again, for bMind gives you the following opportunities:

- Make task lists and organize your chores systematically.

- Jot down ideas immediately, without having to lose out on any important facts.

- Maximize on extra time by note making wherever you may be.

- Create to-do lists and have them e-mailed to you and colleagues instantly, as shown in Figure 15–15.

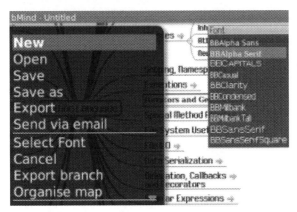

Figure 15–15. *An illustration of the various functions of the bMInd App*

You can create links to your various nodes as well as attach notes to the mind map, as Figure 15–16 illustrates. Drag and drop options are made available too. You can add various icons, colors, and styles so that they stand out.

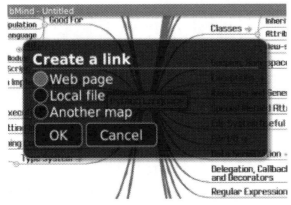

Figure 15–16. *Example of the bMind link attachment*

Apps That Help You Remote Connect To and Control Your Computer

Who can remember a time when remote controls were not invented and each time you needed to switch a channel, you would need to get up and go to the television? Ouch, just the thought of it is painful. What the remote did was bring us convenience, but the apps that help you to remote connect to and control your computer do not come merely as handy tools, but ones that can prove to be greatly beneficial and valuable.

RDM plus Remote Desktop for Mobiles

A complete application that helps you connect to your computer and control it using your BlackBerry. A feature like that had got to get your attention. So if I have it, read on...

RDM plus Remote Desktop for Mobiles is a product by SHAPE services and supports all devices, carriers, and countries. It is available at the BlackBerry App Store and is a charged for application. A December 2009 release, it is a considerably light application in comparison to the services it offers. Whether you want to copy files, move, edit, or delete them completely, the RDM plus Remote Desktop for Mobiles software will take care of it for you, without your needing to be at your Mac or Windows computer.

- It allows you to access multiple computers remotely for no additional charge at all.

- It safeguards your material though strong encryption.

- It works even through firewall settings.

- It offers a command history feature that helps you quickly locate commonly used commands effortlessly.

- Supports all connections like BIS, BES, Wi-Fi, and so on, with equal ease.

- It has sophisticated file management features, thus simplifying core processes.

- Quick shut down and reboot commands help save precious time and energy.

- Manage your e-mails—send and receive messages remotely too.

- Edit documents and manage folders easily.

Apart from the above, it is compatible with both Mac and Windows.

To get started, you would need to download the RDM+ Desktop software and install it in the computer(s) that you would want to access from your handset. You could download this software for no charge from http://rdmplus.com.

There are two factors involved in downloading and installing this application. They are the following:

- RDM+ Desktop should be installed on your computer. This is a free download.

- RDM+ Client should be installed on your device. This can be downloaded from www.bb.rdmplus.com through your BlackBerry's Browser.

After the setup and installation, you will see a screen that lists out various functions (see Figure 15–17). This is your RDM+ dashboard. This is the main and basic screen of the application that helps you carry out various functions.

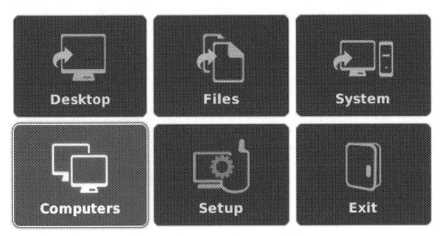

Figure 15–17. *Example of the RDM Plus Remote Desktop main menu*

- The Desktop icon takes you to your computer's desktop, from where you can control it directly.

- The Computers icon lists the number and details of all the systems associated to and connected with your device.

- The Files icon starts the file management. Here you can exchange and create files which then get updated in your PC too.

- The Setup icon launches the screen set features.

- The System icon launches the system functions like drives and settings, which can be controlled from your handset.

- The Exit icon closes the application.

> **NOTE:** RDM+ offers a seven-day free trial period to test out the application which is available at the rdmplus web site. Also remember that RDM+ Clients are supported for BlackBerry handsets with a running OS version of 4.2 or higher only.

Remote Print

This is a simpler application that allows for printing of documents, PDF files, and Excel sheets directly from your handset. The application uses the printers that are installed on your computer to print the files from the smartphone. This simple yet constructive solution comes from Chocolate Chunk Apps. Though it supports all countries and carriers, it only works with certain devices: BlackBerry 8520, 8530, 8900, 9000, 9500, 9520, 9530, 9550, 9630, and 9700 to be precise. It also requires a PC and Wi-Fi network or a BES environment. Though BlackBerry 9630 and Storm 1 do not have Wi-Fi facility, the application will support them if they use a BES connection.

Like RDM+, even this is comprised of the following two main components:

- Print Server—a PC application
- A BlackBerry (mobile) application

After installing the two and setting a connection between them, any file from the BlackBerry will be printable through printers associated with the desktop. You can connect your handset to multiple PCs by installing the Print Server app on them. If you want to change the printer that is in use, you will need to do so by changing it in the Print Server settings.

Once installed, you can print pictures, files, documents, excel sheets, entire folders, PDFs, contact details, and addresses—basically any doc you would like. This application also allows you to transfer files from your handset to your PC through the Wi-Fi connection or through the BES network as Figure 15–18 illustrates.

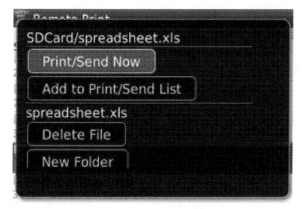

Figure 15–18. *File transfer through Remote Print*

Job Searching Apps

The ways of the world leave me baffled sometimes. We go through school and college, get ourselves varied educational qualifications and fancy degrees. But at the end of the day, for most people, it all boils down to the job one manages to bag... almost making one wonder whether the knowledge gained was merely to earn riches or expand one's mind? Anyway, let's save that for another time. For now, getting a job that gives us satisfaction and fulfillment should be our primary goal (at least idealistically).

On the other hand, most of us overlook another function of Job Searching programs that is widely used today—as a research tool. That's right; companies use these to keep an eye on their competitors' hires, market standing, and new trends (lots of jobs in one area means lots of interest in that area), which can then be translated into business models and opportunities. So if you do not fit into the above "job searching" category, this aspect of the sites and applications might interest you.

Search Jobs Beyond com

This is a simple and neat application from BEYOND.COM INC that does not require setup processes or signing in. It is a light application—16 KB to be precise—and will not affect your handset in the least. It supports all carriers, devices, and countries. All you need to do is download it from BlackBerry App World. Once that's done, run the app. On doing so, it will take you to a page that will ask you to fill out certain fields like Job Keywords, Job Location, preferred Industry, and E-mail address. After filling in these details, select Search Jobs (see Figure 15–19). That's it; the application will direct you to the appropriate industry web sites and local career sites based on your location specification.

Figure 15–19. *Search Jobs Beyond com search fields*

Apart from doing this, you can also save your favorite searches/jobs which can later be shared with anyone you please.

My opinion: A basic application that delivers what's promised.

Note Taking and Text Editing Apps

Doodles and scribble pads, diaries and journals, post-its, paperbacks, hardbacks, and spiral bound books… The documentation of personal thoughts has found various expressions and mediums over the years. Here is another—and this one is here to stay. These electronic booklets and notepads do come with their own set of advantages. They are less susceptible to loss of content and they do not deplete the environment of trees and greenery; apart from being downright convenient. If you agree, read on…

Documents To Go Premium Edition

Documents To Go Premium is an all-round application that facilitates creating new documents as well as editing existing ones. You can view and work on Word documents, excel sheets, power point presentations as well as check out PDF files, all on your handset. A DataViz product, this app is a professionals dream. The price tag attached to it stands nowhere in comparison to the umpteen benefits that it brings to the table.

Some of the key features and advantages include the following:

- It is the only application (as is claimed by DataViz) that retains original file formats once an edited file is forwarded from the smartphone.

- This complete application brings with it advanced viewing and editing functions.

- It retains the BlackBerry's look and feel, making it a user friendly and easy to understand application.

- Documents received by various means—e-mail, attachments, Bluetooth, and so on, can be opened and edited with ease.

- Documents To Go Premium Edition 2.0 also comes with the added benefit of Desktop Application that allows for file synchronization. That means that once the handset and the PC application are synced and connected using a USB cable, all changes and edits made in one will get updated in the other too.

- The ability to open password protected word documents that were created in Word 2007.

- Spell checks made available.

- Advanced formatting also incorporated.

- A 30-day free trial included, after which the application can be bought directly.

- Maintains original formatting of documents.

- It integrates with the e-mail application for opening word documents which can be edited immediately.

After launching the application, you can either open an existing document or create a new one, as shown in Figure 15–20.

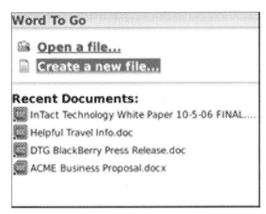

Figure 15–20. *Documents To Go Premium Edition with create new file option*

After opening an existing document, you will need to choose Edit Mode from the menu options to be able to make any changes to it. Once in the edit mode or with a new document opened, when you press the Menu button, the following options are made available to you:

- *Find*: You can search the document using a key word. There also is a provision for you to replace this word with another one of your choice. It also asks you to specify whether the search should be case specific or pertain to the word alone. Options like Find, Replace, or Replace all complete this search feature.

- *Check Spelling*: This scans the document for any spelling error and also suggests probable alternate spellings that you can choose from.

- *Select*: By choosing Select, the specified lines/content pieces get picked which then can be cut, copied or formatted.

- *Select All*: This just highlights the entire document to be edited.

- *New*: Start a new word document by choosing this function.

- *Open*: Choose this to open an existing file from the application or any one from the phone's memory.

- *Save As*: This allows you to rename the document and save it differently. As soon as you do so, the file is renamed.

- *Send via E-mail*: The document can be mailed directly from this point by selecting this option. However, do make sure not to make further changes in the content or document before the sending process is completed for that might cause the sending of the e-mail to fail.

- *View Mode*: If you have opened an existing document and chosen the Edit Mode, then this option appears allowing you to switch back to just viewing the document.

■ *Format*: This is an integral part of this edition. After selecting this option, you will be given a list of choices to choose from. Namely: Bold; Italic; Underlined; Font (which lists parameters such as Font Name, Font Size, Superscript, Subscript, Strike through, Double Strike through, Small Caps, All Caps, Text Color and Highlight Color); Paragraph (on opting for this you can alter the Alignment, the Left and Right Indent, Spacing etc); Bullets and Numbering, Hyperlink; Bookmark, Increase Indent (of the selected paragraph) and Decease Indent (see Figure 15–21).

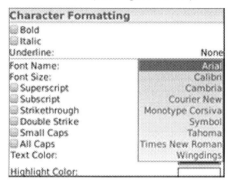

Figure 15–21. *Documents To Go Premium Edition—file formatting*

■ *Insert*: You can choose to do a Page Break, add a Bookmark, add a Hyperlink, Table, or Comment through this feature.

■ *Table*: Insert a table by specifying where to insert rows and columns and how many of them.

■ *View*: This helps you to view Comments, Footnotes, and Endnotes along with Table of Contents.

■ *Zoom*: Choose a zoom ranging from 25 % to 200 % from here.

■ *Go To Top*: Takes you to the top of the document.

■ *Go To Bottom*: Takes you to the bottom of the document.

■ *Go To Bookmark*: Takes you to the bookmark.

■ *File Properties*: This spells out details like the name of the document, its type (e.g., MS Word 2007), its location (where it is saved), size, and when it was last modified.

■ *Word Count*: The number of paragraphs, words, characters, and characters including spaces are illustrated here.

■ *Preferences*: This spells out the author preferences including track change options.

■ *Check for Updates*: To check for updates, you will need to connect to the DataViz web site through the handsets web browser.

- *Activate Premium Edition*: If you are on the trial period, only then will this option show in your menu list.

- *Word To Go*: Gives you the basic details of your edition including version, registration number, and so on.

- *Show Symbols*: Shows you the punctuation symbols for you to select.

- *Close*: This just exits from the currently opened document.

Additional Apps

Apart from the above, there are some amazing note taking and managing applications that deserve a special mention. Some of them are listed here for you:

- *Voice To Text by MyCaption.com*: This is a speech-to-text application for your memos, tasks, SMS, e-mails, and calendar appointments.

- *Location Notes by Tworoads Software*: An application that allows you to save details regarding your GPS coordinates which can be shared using e-mail and messaging is also an interesting solution.

However, one application that stood out for me was the Bug Me!—Notes and Alarms. Here it is.

Bug Me!—Notes and Alarms

This application does exactly as it says—it bugs the life out of you. Don't get me wrong, because I mean it in good spirit. It is an easy application to use and is like combining your alarm clock and note pad. Jot down notes on the go and set alarms and reminders for them. When the time comes, you can be sure that the application will remind you of it.

This fun application is brought to you by Electric Pocket Ltd and supports all devices, carriers, and countries. Available for a minimal charge at the BlackBerry App World, its popularity is quite evident. Some of the special features that deserve a mention are the following:

- It allows you to mark notes as urgent so that the important ones are never missed.

- You can also mark the completed ones to avoid confusion.

- Setting alarms for certain notes turns the note into a reminder.

- Search through your notes with key words and tags.

- The application recognizes phone numbers and web addresses so that you can access them directly from the note itself.

- Send your notes to colleagues and friends through e-mail and SMS, as Figure 15–22 illustrates.

- Create notes from received messages directly.

- Notes can be stored in your calendar and tasks for later reviewing.

- You can customize your alarm along with the repeat timings.

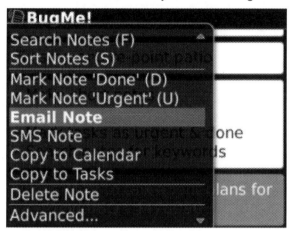

Figure 15–22. *The option to e-mail note offered by Bug Me!—Notes and Alarms*

File Management Apps

There is no point in creating and not being able to organize it properly. Thus the need for file management applications that aid in transferring files as well as storing and arranging them systematically.

File Manager Pro—Zip and File Utility

File management has been simplified and stylized by this application. You can zip and extract files, sort them out, search through folders, and edit at your will. This application is a Terra Mobility product and is available at the BlackBerry App Store for a basic cost. As is the case with most of the apps that you have looked at so far, this too supports all devices, countries, and carriers. Just download it from BAW and it is good to use.

Some features that deserve a mention are the following:

- The ability to extract files from zipped folders that are received through e-mail.

- Features enabling folder compression, either before they are sent or archived like those shown in Figure 15–23.

- Search functions along with Spell checks.

- Edit features offering functions like move, rename, create new folder, copy, and delete.

- Sorting files by their size, category, name, and date.

- Save files in the favorites section, thus enabling quick location.

- Files can be searched on the basis of case sensitive as well as word only criteria. The search is carried out through multiple folders and sections.

- Viewing of file and folder properties is made available.

- One of the fastest applications, it carries out folder navigation with speed and accuracy.

- Customized file display that provides various options regarding labels, sizes, and formats.

- Simplified procedure to open documents which can be edited through built-in applications like Doc To Go.

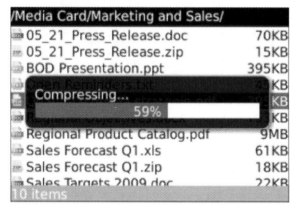

Figure 15–23. *Compression option by File Manager Pro—Zip and File Utility*

The options menu also highlights certain parameters which help customize the settings. They are the following:

- *Display Columns*: Specify what you would like to have displayed such as names, size, date, etc.

- *Sort By*: How you would like the folders to be sorted, e.g., name, category, etc.

- *Sort Direction*: Whether you would want the files to be sorted in ascending or descending order.

- *Show Hidden*: If you would want to show the hidden files or not.

- *Compression Level*: The level of compression you would want to apply.

- *Open To*: On reopening, whether you would want it to open to its last location, main page, etc.

- *Thumbnail Size*: If the display format is set to use thumbnails, then you can specify the desired size of thumbnails here.

▨   *Thumbnail Label*: How you would want the thumbnail label to appear (name, name, and size, etc).

File management can be a wearisome task, but with options like File Manager Pro available in the market this can easily be changed.

Wi-Fi File Transfer

Forget about having to connect your handset to your computer with a USB cable, forget about buying expensive Bluetooth receivers… Just this one app from Chocolate Chunk Apps and you can transfer pictures, music files, or videos from your device to your PC or Mac at Wi-Fi speeds.

Though this application only supported the Bold originally, today it is available to all devices that are Wi-Fi enabled with an Operating System of version 4.5 or more. That means that this solution is for BlackBerry 8320, 8800, 8820, 8830, 8900, 9000, and 9700 devices only. However, it does support all countries and carriers. All that you need is for your handset and computer to be on the same Wi-Fi network—and the presence of the application on the device (obviously).

Some key features include the following:

▨   Transfer any file from the device memory or the micro SD card to your computer and vice versa (see Figure 15–24).

▨   Take advantage of file transfer through Wi-Fi speeds.

▨   No need to connect the device using the USB cable. No need to launch Desktop Manager or Roxio.

▨   File transfer is carried out through the Browser directly.

▨   You can create new folders as well as edit existing ones from the browser.

▨   It supports most browsers including Safari, Firefox, and Internet Explorer.

▨   A trial version is also available so that you can purchase it after complete satisfaction.

▨   A Lite version of the application is also available that allows you to carry out all functions except file edits and uploading of files to your BlackBerry.

▨   As it uses the Wi-Fi network, you do not use up your data plan.

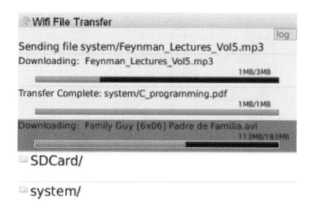

Figure 15–24. *Sample screen of file transferring through the Wifi File Transfer App*

The setup process is fairly simple and its usage, even more so. Download the application on your device. Along with that, make sure your device and computer are on the same Wi-Fi network. Then launch the application and select Wi-Fi Info. Copy the Berry IP Address from here and paste it in your Browser Application. That's it! You can now start transferring file and data at will.

Databases and Information Managers

Think of a requirement and you can be assured that BlackBerry has a solution to offer, especially if you are a business user. We all know how important database viewing and management can be. Check out the apps in this section to help you view and organize your database from your handset remotely.

Wireless Database Viewer Plus

Whether the changes are made to your database using your handset or your computer, you can be sure that the latest information will be available to you through the wireless synchronization that this application offers. Cellica Corporation brings to you the solution—Wireless Database Viewer Plus, which supports all devices, countries, and carriers.

Be it SQL Server, Microsoft Access, Microsoft Excel, Foxpro, or any other ODBC-enabled database, you will be able to access it from your device. The Wireless Database Viewer Plus version 2.7 syncs desktop database with your 3G, Wi-Fi, or EDGE devices, offering a complete solution to all. The key factors that go in this application's favor are the following:

- You can create a new database from your handset and have it reflect on your database records.

- Categorization of information helps to organize it better.

- Features like Find, Edit, Cut, Copy, and Paste take it beyond a mere viewing solution, as Figure 15–25 illustrates.

- Various Fonts and Color settings also made available.

- Shortcut keys make navigation through records and grids quick and simple.

- Operations like Sum, Maximum, Minimum, and Average also feasible.

- You can also filter and sort out the information.

- Options of viewing of multiple tables as well as individual ones also provided.

- Data can be sent to the phones micro SD card for storage as well.

- It also supports Unicode language database like Chinese, Russian, Japanese, etc.

Figure 15–25. *Some of the features offered by Wireless Database Viewer Plus*

Installation of this application is done in the following two parts:

- Downloading the mobile app

- Downloading the PC app

The mobile app can be downloaded from BlackBerry App World. The PC component needs to be downloaded from http://www.cellica.com. Installation instructions and details will also be available here.

> **NOTE:** When it comes to security, one can never be too careful. That's why we highly recommend a thorough and comprehensive research effort to make sure this solution works for you.

HanDBase Enterprise Database Manager

HanDBase Enterprise Database Manager version 4.1.2 is a solution brought to you by DDH Software, Inc. It is another user friendly application that supports most devices and all carriers in all countries. This is a paid for application and can be downloaded from the Internet.

It offers its customers the use of free predesigned mobile databases that are available on their web site. The solution can be used to check, track, and log information remotely through the BlackBerry device. It is also used to download company data. It allows for synchronization between the handheld and computer so that both are kept up to date with latest developments. Like Wireless Database Viewer Plus, this too supports any ODBC enabled database.

A trial version of the application is available at http://www.ddhsoftware.com.

Shipment and Package Tracking Apps

Someone once said that the sign of a good application is one that you use regularly which in turn simplifies your life for you to an extent. The truth in that statement is brought out by the comfort and conveniences brought to all by the shipment and packing tracking apps. From small business owners or individuals, apps like these are applicable to all. Read on to get more details on one such solution.

UPS Mobile

I am sure you are already aware of the advantages of using a consistent shipping company to deliver your packages. You are more familiar with the processes involved and have a better grip on the timelines and schedules. In that spirit, UPS has launched its mobile initiative, which helps you to track your shipment, right from your BlackBerry (see Figure 15–26).

Figure 15–26. *Sample screen of UPS Mobile's Shipment Tracking service*

Some of the advantages of doing do are as follows:

- You can access your account status and other information anytime and anywhere using your smartphone.

- It helps you to predict probable shipping charges and deliveries.

- UPS service locations are shared with you, for your perusal.

- You can create shipping labels from the app directly along with nicknaming the shipments.

- You have access to your address book (if you have it uploaded on the UPS web site) which allows storage of up to 2000 addresses.

- You can cross-check and go through your recent tracks as well.

- If you are an account holder, then you can save shipping and payment preferences and apply those to your transactions.

Social Networking and Messaging Apps

This category of applications does not require too much explanation. The wide spread use of networking and messaging applications is common practice in most countries today. Though they might be brushed off as teeny-bopper fascinations, they do come with their own advantages. The expediency of their user friendly interface and maneuver has led them to become instant hits with all age groups. Let's face it, networking with appropriate people in any form, business or personal, can never hurt. To the business user as well, a strong network will always be looked upon as an asset.

Apart from that, these sites are a great place to tap current trends and potential markets. They reflect on popular culture so beautifully, that they have become an invaluable tool to the researcher. Reaching out to target groups and audiences is another advantage. Their demographic and specific-age focus give them the added advantage of becoming one of the strongest marketing platforms. Though very casual in their appearance, their business advantages remain unshakeable.

So let's delve into this seemingly lighter yet imperative faction of apps.

Social Networking Apps

There are a number of social networking apps available. From networking sites high on popularity such as Facebook and Twitter to the less known ones as well, you will find a whole plethora of apps to choose from. Of course, most of the social networks today have a mobile app that can be downloaded from BlackBerry App World. That means if you are an Orkut, MySpace, or any other social network user, the probability of a mobile solution is high. Do check out BAW for the apps they cover.

Facebook

Clearly one of the most widely used applications today, Facebook's popularity has been unprecedented. That is why bringing this networking module as a BlackBerry app didn't take long. Though the application does not do complete justice to the vast online network, it is a means to keep you connected to your Facebook account and contacts. No matter where your work may take you, if you have this app downloaded, you can be assured of getting news and status updates, along with picture comments and uploads at all times.

After downloading Facebook, you will be asked to accept the License Agreement. Select I Accept, if you do so, to proceed. After that, just type in your existing e-mail id and password that is associated with your Facebook account and select Login. If you do not have one, you will need to first create one by visiting www.facebook.com from your computer or browser.

Now, you need to specify which (if any) applications should connect with your Facebook account. You can choose to allow your BlackBerry Messenger, Calendar, and Contacts applications to exchange data and information with your Facebook account (as illustrated in Figure 15–27).

- *BB Messenger*: Your Facebook notifications will appear on your BlackBerry Messenger application.

- *BB Calendar*: An event invitation will get added to your BlackBerry Calendar.

- *BB Contacts*: Your BlackBerry contacts get updated with latest profile pictures and other information. However, this requires usage of network data services which might be subject to additional charges.

Figure 15–27. *The sync feature offered by Facebook's mobile app*

Once you agree to the preceding, your Facebook contact e-mail gets linked to your specified BlackBerry e-mail. Next, select Save. You are now ready to use your Facebook app.

The features available to you are: News Feed, Status Updates, Photos, Links, Notifications, Uploading Photo options, Friends List, Adding Contacts, Writing on someone's Wall, and Messages. You can check out your friend's profiles and Poke them, write on their Wall, send them a Message, view their Albums, check their Photos, Request their phone contact, etc., as shown in Figure 15–28.

Figure 15–28. *Facebook's various available options*

After you press the Menu button, depending on which feature you have highlighted, other option lists are presented. They are the following:

- With any of the seven top row icons, i.e., News Feed, Notifications, Upload a Photo, Friends, Add a Friend, Write on a Wall, and Send a Message highlighted, if you press the Menu button, you will see options like: Refresh, More, View My Profile, View News Feed, View Status Updates, View Photos, and View Links.

- If your profile picture is selected then you press the Menu button, you will see: Send Myself a Message, Write On My Wall, View My Profile, View My Profile Photo, and Connect to BlackBerry Contact included along with the ones mentioned above.

- If you have your Status box selected, then an additional Share option is also seen.

Apart from the above, the regular features such as Help, Options, Show Symbol, Switch Input Language, Switch Application, and Close are also provided.

Some shortcuts for you are listed here:

- Press N to view notifications.
- Press J to add a friend.
- Press W to write on someone's wall.
- Press M to send a message.
- Press U to upload a picture.
- Press F to view a friend list.
- Press S to view the news feeds.

UberTwitter

Twitter is a no longer a mere social networking platform. To some, it has become a way of life. If you are a diehard Twitter buff, then this app is a must have. It supports all of Twitter's core functions, including the more complex ones like tweet shrinking, embedded video and picture uploads, and URL shortening. Brought to you by UberTwitter Inc, this app is supported by all devices, countries, and carriers, and as is mostly the case with the best things in life, is free of cost.

Once you install it from BlackBerry App World (either directly on your device or through your computer) you will need to log in using your Twitter user name and password. If you do not have a Twitter account, you will have to create it by visiting www.twitter.com from your computer.

After feeding in your details (user id and password) select Verify Account. Once verified, click on Next. You can update your Google Talk status with your last Twitter update. If you wish to do so, give your GTalk details like user id and password or simply skip the step by selecting Next. Then you will be asked to clarify certain Twitter options, such as whether you would want the app to add your location to every tweet and picture, or whether you would want to specify each time instead, and updating your Twitter profile location, which uses the cell towers around you to specify your present position. If you want your position to be determined, you will have to specify which method you would like them to adopt in doing so. However, it does warn you that the more accurate the means, the faster it drains your battery life.

Select the font size, font type, and style you would like to use for your timelines and proceed. Next, set the size of the images in your timeline and the interval for automatic timeline refreshes ranging from one minute to four hours or even Never. Set other Options next, like number of tweets in timeline, successful tweet confirmations, visual notifications on replies, visual notifications on new tweets, icon cache size, and so on. After that, you will need to specify your network options. Once you are done, select Save. The application will load as per your desired commands.

NOTE: You will need to set UberTwitter as a running application in the background if you wish to receive new tweet or reply notifications. That means once you close the application, it automatically goes into the background, but is functioning nevertheless.

Create New Tweets, look up My Friends, My Followers, Favorites and Timelines, Search Twitter, and go through Trending Topics along with options to Copy and E-mail Tweets—all by pressing the Menu button. You can alter any of your Twitter settings by selecting Options from the same menu. Of course, any queries can be sorted out by referring to the Help feature, also available there.

Some shortcuts that you will love to know for the Timeline screen are as follows:

- Press U for an update.
- Press T to go to the top of the page.
- Press B to go to the bottom of the page.
- Press Space for page down.
- Press Shift + Space for page up.
- Press R to reply.
- Press K to reply to all.
- Press F to follow.
- Press A to go to account screen.
- Press P to refresh.
- Press S for search.
- Press V for favorite.

Instant Messaging Apps

Instant Messaging is another crowd puller. The practicality and usage earns it great respect. Though it might not be the best means of formal communication, quick checks and updates within teams and professionals is always feasible. For informal use, this surely wins my vote. I will be covering some of them for you.

BlackBerry Messenger

Brought to you by Research In Motion Limited, BlackBerry Messenger is a free application; it allows for communication between any two BlackBerry devices from any part of the globe with the help of the BlackBerry PIN (Personal Identification Number). Every BlackBerry handset has its own unique PIN and this can be used to communicate with another BB user, as was also illustrated for you in Chapter 5.

All you need to do is download it from the BlackBerry App World if you do not have it already. Once that is done, go to the Menu options in the App and start by adding contacts. You will need your colleague's/friend's PINs to be able to add them. When you do so, a friend request is sent to them. Once they accept the invite, they become part of your Contacts list. The same is applicable to receiving an invite.

Just select the contact's name to start a conversation (as shown in Figure 15–29).

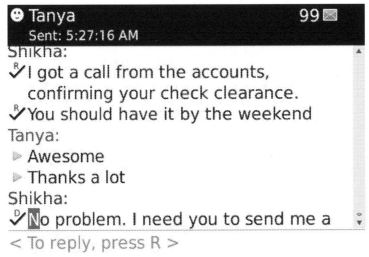

Figure 15–29. *A sample conversation between two BlackBerry Messenger users*

The conversations record history, so that you never lose track of the flow. While in a conversation with someone, if you press the Menu button, the following options are made available to you:

- *Check Spelling*: This is a spell check option. In the new version of the application 5.0.0.57, the Check Spelling As You Type feature has been restored for all devices.

- *View Calendar*: This option takes you to your Calendar Application.

- *Clear History*: You can clear the previous conversation by selecting this.

- *Copy History*: Copy your conversations, if you need to, using this.

- *Invite to a Conference*: You can invite contacts to participate in a conference through this feature. If there are multiple people participating in a conversation, the icon next to the conversation changes as well.

- *Send a File*: Send a file stored on your device, like documents, music, pictures, ringtones, or voice notes using this option.

- *Send a Voice Note*: Use this to record a voice note and send it immediately.

- *Send my Location*: Share your current location with a contact.

- *Forward Contact*: Forward your BlackBerry or Messenger contacts from here.

- *Contact Information*: This displays the recipients contact details.

- *Ping Contact*: It's a way to buzz a contact, with the intention of getting his/her attention, as illustrated in Figure 15–30.

- *Edit Auto Text*: An automatic correction of misspelled words.

- *Show Symbols*: Shows the emoticons and punctuations.

- *Switch Application*: Switches to other applications without quitting or closing the current.

- *End Conversation*: Ends the conversation in progress.

- *View Contact List*: Takes you back to your contact list.

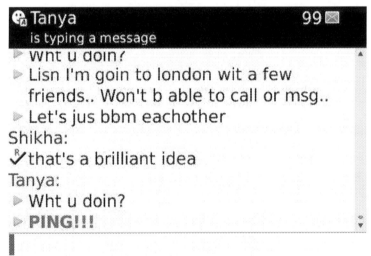

Figure 15–30. *A sample conversation with the "Ping" feature*

Google Talk

If you already are a Google Talk user on your computer, then you will love the BlackBerry app for it. It is very close to the web solution and offers most of the features made available to you on the Internet. Download Google Talk from the BlackBerry App World directly from your handset or by mailing yourself a link to it from the web site. Once you do so, you will need to log into your existing account (see Figure 15–31). If you do not have an account, you can create it by visiting http://google.com/accounts from your desktop.

Google Talk

Username:

Password:

Sign In

■ Remember password
■ Automatically sign me in

Need an account?

Figure 15–31. *The Google Talk login page*

Once logged in, you will find all your Google Talk contacts—friends, colleagues, and family—already uploaded. You can use this messaging suite immediately. Some of the features offered by it are the following:

- Update your status at any time by selecting your name or choosing My Details from the menu list. Here you can alter the picture/icon next to your user id, create custom status messages, and intimate contacts whether you are busy or free to chat.

- Select a contact to chat with them.

- Share files such as pictures, voice notes, contacts, and so on.

- Add new friends and people to your list.

- See friend details by selecting Friend Details from the menu list, while the contact is highlighted.

- View conversation histories of chats carried out from your handset.

- Use emoticons to express your feelings better.

- You can invite multiple contacts to participate in conversations like conferences.

- Use Google Talk as well as other applications simultaneously, with the Switch Application feature available to you in the menu list options.

- E-mail an entire chat with a friend by opening the menu options and selecting E-mail Chat.

- You can also block a contact from the same option list.

Use it as you would use your regular Google Talk messenger, with the added advantage that it goes with you wherever you want to take it. That's incentive enough, right?

Miscellaneous Apps That Help in Further Optimization

Apart from the above, there are a great number of additional apps that are available. These apps range from calculators to memory boosters. Though they might not be directly related to your business applications, their features and functions will surely enhance your BlackBerry usage and experience. Do glance at these specific apps.

PayPal

PayPal online is a means to simplify money transactions without the need to share financial information with anyone. It also record your expenditure history (transactions made through it), so that all your expenses are tracked.

This powerful and extremely useful tool is now available to you on your BlackBerry handset. It is brought to your by PayPal which is an eBay company and is accessible in all countries and carriers. You will need a PayPal account, so if you do not already have one, you can register from http://paypal.com. Once you are a registered user, just log onto your PayPal account with your registered e-mail id and password. No fee is charged for domestic personal payments when funding with a bank.

Figure 15–32. *Screen illustrating a transaction between two people using PayPal*

Once logged in, you can transfer funds (as shown in Figure 15–32), make online purchases, and receive money from others; all with the registered e-mail id or telephone number of the person.

Business Card Reader

Announced by SHAPE as their New Year gift to all BlackBerry users comes Business Card Reader. Some might recall that this kind of an app is not completely alien to the smartphone market. It has already been successful with the iPhone and now has made its way to the BlackBerry as well. It can be downloaded from various sites including the app store of the crackberry site (www.crackberry.com).

If you are a junior sales representative or the CEO, this app is a must have for all of you. One of the most tedious jobs of meeting new people and expanding your network is feeding in their personal data into your phone book. If you happen to be at an expo or exhibition, the Lord save you. Mobile numbers, e-mail ids, addresses, landline numbers, extensions… phew. Personal contact data can drive any sane person up the wall. Grieve no more; this application brings to you the advantage of storing all this information (and more) with a simple one step solution. It's as simple as taking a picture. Wait a second, it is just that…taking a picture.

The Business Card Reader is a scanning application that identifies the information from a business card and stores it in the appropriate fields in your address book. Smart, isn't it? The application uses ABBYY's text recognition technology. This application supports BlackBerry Bold 9700, BlackBerry Tour, BlackBerry Storm, BlackBerry Storm2, and the BlackBerry Curve 8900. This is the case because the application requires a high resolution camera with auto focus capabilities that these models offer. The solution is available in English, Spanish, French, German, and Italian as of now, but assures to widen this spectrum sooner than later.

Pocket 10B SE Business Calculator

A solution that comes as a boon to any finance executive, the Pocket 10B SE Business Calculator is suitable for anyone associated with the subject. The MBA student's dream, this application has been developed by Lygea Calculators and supports most devices and all carriers in all countries.

Some of the functions are as follows:

- Labeled output displays indicating interest rates
- Cash flow analysis
- Business percentages
- Calendar functions

Its utilities in the world of finance are innumerable. Its intuitive development gives it an edge through the function lists in the menu options. If you want to see more, do check out its seven-day trial version available at BlackBerry App World before purchasing it.

Where's My Phone Pro

Who hasn't lost their phone even once? I doubt anyone can claim such. Wait a minute, even if you lost and recovered it, you had lost it at some point. It's true when they say that the object one is searching for is always found at the last place one would look. Losing a phone can be very nerve racking, especially if it is your good old BlackBerry. Well, this app just simplifies this search for you. Now wherever your phone might be hiding, under the couch, in a hidden pocket of that humongous handbag or in your car glove compartment, you can be sure of finding it. All you need to do is send an e-mail to it.

The application supports all devices, countries, and carriers. It also offers a free trial before you purchase it. You will need to set your preferences and details in the beginning, as Figure 15–33 illustrates.

Figure 15–33. *Options page of the Where's My Phone Pro App*

The application requires you to share the e-mail address associated with your BlackBerry (BIS or BES), beforehand.

Some of the features include:

- Alert screen graphics.

- Alert tones of your choice.

- Your contact information is displayed on your screen, thus helping the finder reach you.

- Have your phone call you at another number so that you can hear where it is (from the ambient noise).

- Ability to auto-delete your e-mails.

- Your lost BlackBerry's location can be e-mailed to you on other GPS supported devices.

- Activate alarms loud enough to wake a neighborhood (just kidding— but loud for sure) even if your phone is on silent.

- Code word feature that protects the applications option screen.

- For instance, if you lose your phone, all you need to do is send an e-mail to it from the nearest computer. You can also send it using your own e-mail id. You need to set a code number beforehand, and the application uses the subject line to identify what you want it to do. The codeword is used to send the application the command. Simple commands like LOCATE (to get the location of the phone using GPS), CALLME (to get the phone to call you on the specified number), and START (to start the alarm) make it an easy process. The application keeps you updated through mails and also includes your battery status in every message.

When you misplace your phone, you are that much more likely to retrieve it.

MemoryUp Pro Mobile RAM Booster (Specially Designed for BlackBerry)

This little application is one big help. It recovers your wasted memory, thus increasing your available memory. Simple, isn't it? It is brought to you by EMOBISTUDIO and is designed specifically for BlackBerry users.

It supports all devices countries and carriers and offers its features for a minimal charge. Some of its main features include:

- Auto memory boost that goes on in the background, thus providing unused available memory.

- Manual memory boost with just one simple step like is shown in Figure 15–34.

- You can set performance goals, as best to your requirement.

- It warns you when the phone's memory reaches a critical point.

- A comprehensive memory status report illustrating used, free and total memory graphs.

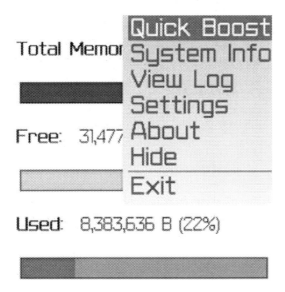

Figure 15–34. *Options offered by MemoryUp Pro Mobile RAM Booster (Specially Designed for BlackBerry)*

So all you BlackBerry buffs who find themselves at a loose end due to limited memory, check this app out for it may just be the answer to a few prayers.

Tether

Originally called TetherBerry, Tether is an application that simplifies the process of using your phone as a modem to connect the laptop/computer to the Internet, through the smartphone's data plan. Brought to you by Tether, this application supports all devices, all countries, and all carriers except Metro PCS US.

The application frees you from any kind of tether fees as it uses the data plan of your smartphone to give you the best results—with quick Internet connectivity being primary. According to BlackBerryInsight, a speed test was performed on the 9700 which showed a 147% faster download speed and 294% faster upload speeds than the IP Modem. That's a margin that you cannot ignore.

Tether is available at BlackBerry App World for a basic fee. However, discounts are offered (for a limited time period) on the Tether web site, which you can use.

NetworkAcc—Mobile Network Accelerator

An EMOBISTUDIO product, NetworkAcc—Mobile Network Accelerator is an application that helps you to boost your mobile network and coverage, thus ensuring better speeds and fewer holdups. This means that all your network-related activities, such as e-mailing, browsing, uploading, and so on, can be done much faster.

The app is available for a minimal charge at BlackBerry App World, and supports all devices, carriers, and countries. It does not require you to install or attach any extra hardware or device. It is a completely software-driven solution. You can notch up the network gear on a range of 1 to 5, depending on your need for speed. It also has an auto-pilot mode, where it automatically gauges the network and optimizes it when necessary (see Figure 15–35).

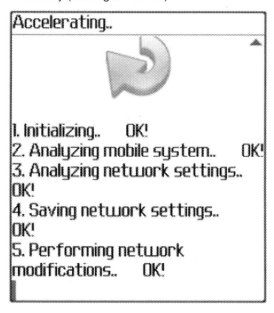

Figure 15–35. *Example of NetworkAcc's signal boost process*

BlackBook

The thought that comes to the mind on hearing "Black Book" is a bunch of numbers written in a little diary which is stashed away for none to see expect the person to whom it belongs. Well, this application is just that. You might argue that this has nothing to do with professional work, but you stand to be corrected. If you have made a career in PR or celebrity management, if you deal with secretive agencies or have an exclusive clientele; then you will understand that contact information is vital and needs to be protected. Even if you do not fit into any of the above vocations, a little app that safeguards your special contacts does sound exciting, doesn't it? For isn't that what we call privacy?

The BlackBook application is nothing but a hidden contact list (see Figure 15–36), that can only be opened with a specific customized code. The BlackBook app doesn't even have an icon. To launch the application, the user must feed in the code from the keypad.

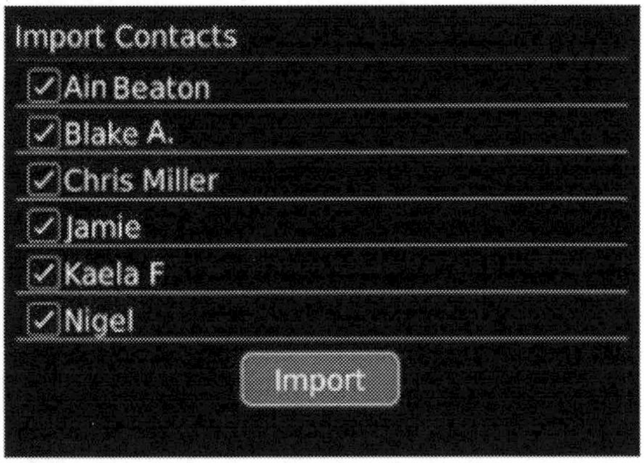

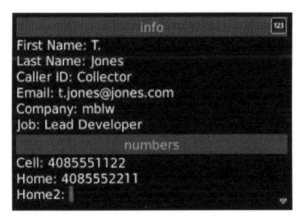

Figure 15–36. *Import Contacts feature offered by BlackBook*

All the contact fields are editable so that you can keep your secret contact list up to date at all times, as Figure 15–37 shows. It also allows filtering for incoming as well as outgoing calls, SMSs, and e-mails. It supports most devices/models and all countries and carriers.

Figure 15–37. *Contact information that can be edited*

Once you download it you will need to reboot your handset (take out the battery too). When you restart it, press the red end button five times to launch the application. This application is an instant hit with all users. Don't believe me? Just go through the comments on BlackBerry App World.

NOTE: When installing, make sure to set all the permissions to Allow.

A Special Mention

As you come to the end of this book, I find it difficult to refrain from pointing out one last aspect that has eluded most of us for a long time. Today's high expectations and pressures have caused many a ruin around us. That younger people are being diagnosed with diseases like cancer and instances of premature heart attacks does not surprise anymore. Such disastrous occurrences compel us to pay closer attention to our physical and mental well-being. It's time we made taking charge of our health a serious business. Isn't sound health our first responsibility to ourselves and the people around us? Without trying to sermonize, I would like to take the liberty of including a couple of health apps in this section.

Total Fitness

This application is an all-round solution to a general health, diet, and workout watch that you can carry out on a regular basis. MOBITEQ does a fine job of bringing this application to you which supports most devices, all carriers, and countries. Though it is a charged-for application, the price is minuscule compared to the benefits a health app can bring to you (see Figure 15–38).

Some of its features are as follows:

- Various workout routines and animations come preloaded.

- You can feed in details of individual workouts and log your cardio and weight training accurately.

- Goal specific routines are also available.

- You can check and keep a track on body structure pertaining to body fat percentages, weight, blood pressure, pulse, etc.

- Helps you to keep a track on your nutrient intake: specific and exact, so that you can calculate your carbohydrates, vitamins, fats, etc., intake, accurately.

- View graphical representations of your intake versus your target on a weekly as well as monthly basis, as Figure 15–39 illustrates.

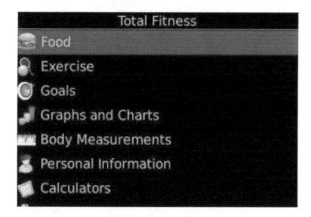

Figure 15–38. *An example of the various features offered by Fitness Pro*

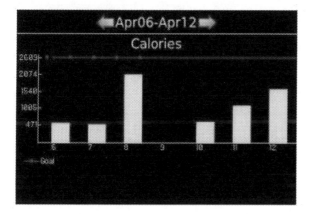

Figure 15–39. *A calorie intake graph by Fitness Pro*

HandyLogs Heart

HandyLogs LLC brings to you HandyLogs Heart, a solution that will help you keep tab on your cholesterol and blood pressure at all times (see Figure 15–40). The app supports all devices, countries, and carriers and is available at BlackBerry App World for a basic fee. It combines various factors that could affect your health, such as daily exercise, body weight, glucose levels, nutrition, and medication, to give you a comprehensive picture of your health status. It stores health data for multiple years so that you never lose out on critical information. It also allows your loved ones to track your health remotely; thus giving them the best gift of all—satisfaction.

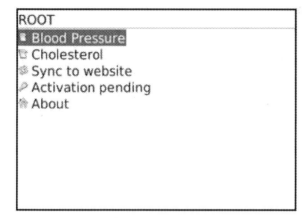

Figure 15–40. *The root menu from HandyLogs Heart*

Some of its features are as follows:

- It provides you with graphical representations of your health data on a daily to yearly basis.

- It takes a backup of your information on HandLogs.com when you synchronize the two, so that you never lose any material.

- It has the ability to e-mail and print health records from the HandyLogs web site also offers aid.

A New Beginning

As I sat down to write out a conclusion for this book, I realized that, no matter what I said, I wouldn't be able to summarize the contents of it in a paragraph or two. All that is to be said is that I hope you take from this what was intended—an introduction to an invaluable professional aid, and the desire to continue that process of discovery. Download applications, use and discuss them, and don't forget to leave your review, for it's your opinion that will help carve the future of newer solutions. Keep abreast of changing trends and newer updates so that you always stay on top of your game.

Just go ahead and have fun with the device. It's strong. It's durable and it's smart. It's the perfect professional assistant...

Index